THE UPSIDE OF TURBULENCE

ALSO BY DONALD SULL

Made in China

*Success Against the Odds:
What Brazilian Champions
Teach Us About Thriving in
Unpredictable Markets*
(With Martin Escobari)

*Why Good Companies Go Bad and
How Great Managers Remake Them*

THE UPSIDE OF TURBULENCE

SEIZING OPPORTUNITY IN AN UNCERTAIN WORLD

Donald Sull

HARPER
BUSINESS

An Imprint of HarperCollins*Publishers*

HarperCollins books may be purchased for educational, business, or sales promotional use. For information, please write: Special Markets Department, HarperCollins Publishers, 10 East 53rd Street, New York, NY 10022.

FIRST EDITION

Designed by Kris Tobiassen

Library of Congress Cataloging-in-Publication Data

Sull, Donald N. (Donald Norman)
 The upside of turbulence : seizing opportunity in an uncertain world / Donald Sull.—1st ed.
     p.   cm.
 Includes bibliographical references and index.
 ISBN 978-0-06-177115-6
 1. Strategic planning.   2. Business cycles.   3. Entrepreneurship.
 4. Management.   I. Title.
 HD30.28.S885 2009
 658.4'012—dc22
 2009013606

09 10 11 12 13   OV/RRD   10 9 8 7 6 5 4 3 2 1

To our children, Charles, Phillip, Elizabeth, and Genevieve, and all the young people making their way in a turbulent world. May they face an uncertain future with a sense of adventure, not fear.

CONTENTS

THE UPSIDE OF TURBULENCE

1.

THE STONE IN DAVID'S SLINGSHOT

I was six years old when my grandfather first took me to see the American Steel and Wire plant in Cleveland, Ohio, where he worked for forty-two years as an engineer and then as a supervisor. As a guest, I could only proceed as far as the guard house, but even from that distance the plant terrified me—it was enormous, loud, and smoky. My grandfather held my hand and reassured me that the plant was a safe place, like a fortress. When we went back to his house for lunch, I colored pictures of the mill as a giant castle with cauldrons of molten metal to pour on attackers, defended by an army of burly soldiers clad in steel armor.

In the 1960s, the United States Steel Corporation, which owned the plant where my grandfather worked, appeared an equally unassailable fortress. Founded in 1901 by business magnates, including J. P. Morgan and Andrew Carnegie, U.S. Steel was at its inception the largest industrial corporation in the world, accounting for two-thirds of American raw steel production and one-third of global output.[1] The corporation's size, market share, balance sheet, asset base, and technology constituted insurmountable barriers. Although its overall share slipped during the twentieth century, U.S. Steel remained one of the pistons driving America's economic progress. When employees joined U.S. Steel operations in Pittsburgh's Monongahela Valley in the 1960s, supervisors explained that should a war break out, the Mon Valley was one of three locations the Soviet Union would bomb to cripple the U.S. economy.[2]

The company was so strong, U.S. Steel executives openly challenged presidential power. Harry Truman tried, but failed, to appropriate the mills to ensure sufficient steel for the Korean War. When John F. Kennedy called for restraint in price increases, U.S. Steel executives initially ignored his request, and then raised prices anyway. The steelmaker only reversed the price hikes after Kennedy attacked U.S. Steel executives in a televised presidential press conference. In 1970, the company built a monument to its success—the U.S. Steel Tower—the highest skyscraper in Pittsburgh, encased in Cor-Ten, a steel alloy designed to weather the elements in perpetuity.

Turbulence roiled the steel industry in the decades that followed. The 1973 OPEC oil shock quadrupled the price of oil and sparked a deep recession, followed by years of stagflation, a brief recession in 1980, and a more severe downturn the following year. Other forces buffeted steelmakers' profits, including technological shifts, exchange rate volatility, government policy, raw material costs, prices, and changing customer preferences. Each variable was volatile on its own. Mini-mill technology disrupted established production methods; governments imposed and retracted tariffs, changed environmental liabilities, and privatized state-owned mills.[3] Customers in the automotive, appliance, and packaging industries substituted plastic and aluminum for steel, and sometimes switched back. Mergers and bankruptcies reconfigured the competitive landscape.

U.S. Steel struggled to adjust. By 1986, the company's share of domestic shipments had fallen below 15 percent, it had lost money in steel for five consecutive years, and its stock had fallen to its lowest price in over thirty years. Management eliminated one-third of production capacity, diversified into oil and gas, and changed the corporation's name to USX, but failed to halt the downward slide. Carl Icahn made a hostile takeover bid that triggered further restructuring and ultimately left U.S. Steel a shadow of its former mighty self. In 1979, the company's steel operations employed 171,654, but the number had fallen to 27,173 a decade later.[4]

As a member of the manufacturing practice with the consulting firm McKinsey & Company, I worked out of an office in the U.S. Steel Building in the mid-1980s. Successive rounds of layoffs left entire floors of the building empty, and many survivors looked exhausted and beaten. The Mon Valley lost nearly fifty thousand steel and related jobs in the 1980s, leaving little for the Soviets to bomb. The decline and fall of the U.S. Steel empire perplexed me. The gales of creative destruction gust through steel like every other industry, but if any company could withstand the storms, surely it was U.S. Steel.

A few years later, I moved to Akron to work at the Uniroyal Goodrich Tire Company. Akron fared no better than Pittsburgh. For nearly sixty years, five tire makers dominated the market, four of them based in Akron. In the span of eighteen months, four of the five tire makers disappeared as independent companies through mergers or acquisitions by foreign competitors. Our largest customers, the

Detroit automakers, continued their decades-long slide, like a car crash in slow motion. America's industrial heartland, once the engine of economic growth, had degenerated into the Rust Belt. In 1992, I entered the doctoral program at Harvard Business School to study why companies failed in turbulent markets. My interest was more personal than academic. I wanted to understand how the industrial heartland of my youth had come to resemble a rusting hulk.

My research uncovered an insidious dynamic. To succeed, managers must commit to a specific mental map of the world, and reinforce it with processes, resources, external relationships, and a culture that support their worldview. With time and success, these commitments harden. When markets shift—and in a turbulent world markets always shift—managers find themselves ensnared in a web of commitments that they themselves have woven. They respond to turbulence by accelerating activities that worked in the past, a dynamic I termed *active inertia*. Executives saw changes in the market and responded, but hardened commitments channeled their actions into familiar grooves. Active inertia devastated industries beyond manufacturing, contributing to the decline of minicomputer leaders, including Digital, Wang, and Data General, hindering traditional airlines' response to low-cost carriers and hastening the demise of regional banks.

Active inertia explained a lot, particularly why leading companies such as U.S. Steel or General Motors falter in turbulent markets. But it didn't explain everything. In particular, the theory did not account for companies such as Toyota or Carnival Cruise Lines, which not only survived but thrived in turbulence. Most of all, active inertia did not explain Mittal Steel. Lakshmi Mittal built his first steel mill in Indonesia in 1976, and within two decades he had created the fourth-largest steel company in the world by acquiring underperforming assets in Mexico, Canada, Trinidad, Germany, Ireland, Kazakhstan, and the United States.[5] Along the way, Mittal amassed a personal fortune worth $2 billion, securing him a place on *Forbes*'s list of global billionaires. Having watched market turbulence gut the mighty U.S. Steel, I was perplexed how anyone could parlay a single mill into a global empire in such an unforgiving industry.

Mittal did not owe his success to favorable industry conditions. During the 1990s, steel remained a byword for an unattractive sector trapped in a perpetual downturn. A study of the global steel industry in the 1990s conducted by Boston Consulting Group found that steel companies, on average, destroyed value for their investors and underperformed other basic-materials industries.[6] Thirteen U.S. producers, including LTV and Wheeling-Pittsburgh, went bankrupt in a single three year span. The BCG report concluded that "capitalism alone cannot solve this problem," and recommended government intervention to save the global steel industry. Their report did not once mention Mittal.

Mittal succeeded by embracing turbulence, not avoiding it. He made his largest bets in emerging markets characterized by extreme volatility. In 1995, Mittal heard that the government of Kazakhstan planned to sell its biggest steel mill. Many Westerners learned everything they know about this country from the mockumentary *Borat: Cultural Learnings of America for Make Benefit Glorious Nation of Kazakhstan*, an entertaining albeit unreliable guide to a country larger than Western Europe, which is wedged between Russia and China and sits on large deposits of natural resources. The plant, known as the Karaganda Metallurgical Complex (Karmet), is one of the largest single-site steel mills in the world. When the Soviet Union crumbled, Karmet fell into disrepair, and by 1995, it was operating at less than half capacity. Without paying customers, the factory relied on barter for 80 percent of its sales and printed its own currency to pay employees. With more than thirty thousand workers, the factory was the main employer in the city of Temirtau, whose fortunes fell with the mill's. Temirtau's population shrank by 40 percent, and the city suffered from widespread heroin abuse and AIDS. Kazakh prime minister Akezhan Kazhegeldin informed Mittal that any buyer would have to run the city's orphanage, hospital, trams, schools, and newspaper, as well as the mill.

Mittal did not disregard Kazakhstan's turbulence. The company's financial reports catalogued daunting uncertainties, including foreign exchange risk, price fluctuations, inflation, volatile interest rates, a range of possible taxes, an evolving legal system, environmental regulations, and the possibility of nationalization. To top it all off, the operation sat on a geological fault susceptible to earthquakes. Undaunted, Mittal bought the plant within a month of seeing it, also acquiring the local coal and iron mines to supply raw materials. When the power system later collapsed, Mittal bought that as well.

By 2008, Lakshmi Mittal had created the largest steel company in the world, ArcelorMittal, and emerged as the fifth wealthiest person in the world, far ahead of well-known billionaires such as Michael Dell, George Soros, and Michael Bloomberg. The rise of Mittal and the fall of U.S. Steel illustrate the question that motivates this book: how can companies endure and even prosper in turbulence?

For more than a decade, I have sought out the most turbulent markets in the world, and conducted research to isolate what separates winners from losers. My colleagues and I have analyzed matched pairs of more- and less-successful firms within volatile countries—including book-length studies of China and Brazil—and fast-moving industries, including telecommunications, enterprise software, and Europe's fast fashion industry (see figure 1.1).[7] These studies revealed a set of practices that characterized successful firms.

These initial findings marked the midpoint, rather than the end of the research.[8] To test their robustness, I submitted each finding to three additional screens. First, does an insight work in theory? Screening findings against established theory forced me to articulate *why* something worked, and helped me to separate insights with hard theoretical edges from fluffy notions. Second, does it generalize to other domains? People grapple with turbulence in many domains,

FIGURE 1.1 Selected Research Pairs

Emerging markets	Industry	More Successful	Less Successful
China	Beverages	Wahaha	Robust
China	Food	Ting Hsin	Uni-President
China	Appliances	Haier	Red Star
China	Personal computers	Lenovo	Great Wall
Brazil	Brewing	Brahma	Antarctica
Brazil/Europe	Aerospace	Embraer	Fairchild Dornier
Brazil	Conglomerate	Votorantim	Grupo João Santos
Brazil	Banking	Banco Itaú	Unibanco
Middle East	Banking	Garanti Bank	Demirbank

(cont.)

Developed markets	Industry	More Successful	Less Successful
United States	Cruising	Carnival	Norwegian Caribbean
United States	Enterprise software	BEA	Novell
United States	Tire and rubber	Goodyear	Firestone
United States/Asia	Automotive	Toyota	General Motors
United States/Europe	Telecom equipment	Nokia	Motorola
Europe	Fast fashion	Zara	Benetton
Europe	Telecommunications	Telefónica	Telecom Italia
Europe	Airlines	easyJet	Go
Europe	Banking	Banco Santander	Banco Popular
South Korea	Conglomerate	Samsung	Daewoo

including combat, improvisation, new product development, and scientific inquiry. If an analogous conclusion emerged independently in a nonbusiness setting, it increased my confidence that the insight was more general. Finally, do the recommendations work in practice? I tested my initial findings with consulting clients and executives in a one-week "boot-camp" on managing in turbulent markets that I teach at the London Business School. If executives found an idea useful in their own companies, I kept it. If a finding failed any of these three tests, I rejected it.

TURBULENCE RISING

Daily news reports and analyses hammer us with the message that we live in exceptionally turbulent times. Founded in 1850, Lehman Brothers successfully weathered the Civil War, multiple recessions, four financial panics, two world wars, depressions, oil shocks, and 9/11, but it could not survive the 2008 economic crisis. Systematic research supports the intuition that the world is growing more turbulent for firms. A comprehensive study of equities traded on all major U.S. stock markets found that the volatility in returns of individual stocks more than doubled between the early 1960s and the late 1990s, spiking when the economy entered recession and when stock markets crashed.[9] Greater volatility at the firm level has not increased aggregate market volatility, because the more violent upward and downward movements of individual shares cancel one another out.

In a series of studies, Professor Diego Comin and his colleagues have documented a sharp increase in firm-level turbulence.[10] The volatility of revenues, profitability, and employment of publicly traded firms in the United States has more than doubled between 1960 and 2000. The spread between corporate bonds and ten-year Treasury notes, another measure of firm-level risk, increased fourfold over the same period. Comin found that global stocks increased in volatility in the late 1990s. He also found that greater turbulence at the firm level translates into instability in wages, particularly since 1980.

Firms struggle to keep pace with shifting markets. The average life expectancy of a firm listed on the S&P Index decreased from ninety years during the 1930s to under twenty-five years by the late 1990s, while the probability that a public firm would disappear in any given ten-year period more than doubled from the 1960s to the 1990s.[11] The odds that a high-performing firm would be dethroned from industry leadership tripled between the 1970s and the 1990s.[12] The increase in turbulence is neither uniform across industries nor steady over time, but the broad trend of greater turbulence at the level of the individual firm is clear.[13]

We live in turbulent times, and it is worth pausing to recall how much has changed in a short period. Every year the accounting firm PricewaterhouseCoopers surveys global CEOs.[14] When they began the survey in 1996, fewer than one-third of CEOs regularly logged on to the Internet, and few saw China, Russia, or India as priority markets. The decade that followed, according to Pricewaterhouse-Coopers, was one of "high-speed change" and "unsettling twists and turns." It included Enron's implosion; the popping of the dot-com bubble; the 9/11 terrorist attacks; the Gulf War; a sharp jump in commodity prices; the rise of the so-called BRIC economies of Brazil, Russia, India, and China; and the growing salience of environmental concerns.

All of these changes preceded the 2008 credit crunch and global recession that followed. *Turbulence*, as I will use the term throughout the book, refers to rapid and unpredictable changes in the environment that influence a firm's ability to create value.[15] Many commentators equate turbulence with the current downturn, but this is shortsighted. Multiple measures, including stock returns, firm mortality, profitability, technology diffusion, and raw material prices, all point to the same conclusion—the global economy has grown more turbulent in the past few decades. The rise in turbulence may not be uniform over time or hit all industries or countries with equal force, but the general trend is clear. Moreover, the three factors that drive turbulence—dynamism, complexity, and competition—are likely to amplify volatility in the future. Turbulence did not begin with the current downturn, nor are we likely to return to a predictable world after the recession ends.

Dynamism describes the frequency and magnitude of change in an individual variable that influence a firm's ability to create value. *Complexity* refers to the number of and interactions among forces that influence value creation. *Competition* extends beyond product markets to include clashes over scarce resources such as capital, distribution partners, and talented employees. All three drivers of turbulence have increased in recent decades.

Dynamism is the change in individual variables. The range of relevant factors precludes an analysis of each, but some critical economic variables have grown more volatile in recent decades. Since the Bretton Woods system of fixed exchange rates collapsed in 1971, currencies have fluctuated more wildly against one another. The most extreme fluctuation is a currency crisis, defined as a large and abrupt depreciation in a country's currency often followed by economic upheaval and a drop in output. A few large currency crises—such as the "Asian contagion" that spread from Thailand in 1997 and the Russian "Ruble crisis" a year later—make the headlines, but smaller crises have become common in recent decades, with nearly 250 between 1978 and 2003.[16] Prices for a wide range of commodities have also displayed greater volatility in recent decades.[17]

People often assume that changes occur in a linear fashion. Indeed, some trends, such as aging populations in developed countries, follow a predictable straight line. Many variables, however, are prone to nonlinear shifts: home prices fall off a cliff, commodities spike, consumer acceptance hits a tipping point. The psychological effect of changes can magnify their influence out of proportion to their actual impact. Five years after the 9/11 terrorist attacks, one-third of Americans reported that they worried they might personally experience a terrorist attack.[18] Statistically, however, they were one thousand times more likely to die from complications related to obesity.[19]

Complexity, the second source of turbulence, describes the number of variables that influence a firm's ability to create value, as well as possible interactions among these factors. As firms become more interconnected with the global economy, they increase their exposure to unanticipated changes from multiple directions. Even a business as uncomplicated as microbrewing faces complexity. In 2007, the price of barley nearly doubled when U.S. farmers shifted to planting corn in response to government subsidies for corn-based ethanol. These regulations, in turn, were motivated by politicians' anxiety about increasing oil prices and supply disruptions.[20] The scarcity of barley coincided with poor weather in Europe that limited yields of hops, just as the dollar was falling against the euro. It's hard to imagine a simpler business, yet the profits of U.S. microbrewers were influenced by a wide range of global forces, ranging from European weather to oil prices, that were beyond their ability to predict or control.

Greater integration of the global economy intertwines the fates of companies with far-flung economies and exposes them to a much wider range of possible changes, many arising outside their line of sight. The integration of formerly communist countries into the global market economy is a dramatic example, but it is part of a bigger trend toward closer integration in markets for raw materials, finished goods and services, capital, and labor.[21] Capital markets have grown 60 percent more integrated, relative to the fragmentation into local stock and credit markets at the end of World War II. Integration broadens sources of funding but also spreads economic crises more widely, infecting economies around the world. When subprime borrowers in America sneezed, the world caught cold. New technologies also diffuse more quickly. Technological breakthroughs discovered between 1750 and 1900 took an average of 119 years to diffuse globally.[22] By the first half of the 1900s, they disseminated in half that time. Inventions discovered after 1975 required only sixteen years to spread globally. A retreat from globalization in the future, were such a retrenchment to take place, would not eliminate complexity; it would shift its sources from international markets to the vagaries of government policy. The free flow of information through the Internet would be nearly impossible to reverse.

Contextual variables, such as exchange rates or geopolitics, resemble forces of nature. They influence performance, defy prediction or control, and remain indifferent to the fate of individual firms. Competitors, in contrast, go out of their way to discover and exploit their rivals' weaknesses. The rise of emerging market champions such as Mittal has intensified competition in recent decades. Companies from emerging markets now lead a wide range of global industries, including brewing (Anheuser-Busch InBev, SABMiller), consumer electronics (Samsung), and information services (Infosys, Tata Consultancy Services, Wipro).

Many people dismiss emerging market competitors as a transient threat, like the rise of Japan Inc., which terrified Western managers throughout the 1980s, before receding into the background. The comparison to Japan Inc. is comforting but misleading. Japan's Ministry of International Trade and Industry coordinated the expansion, targeted a few sectors, and encouraged similar companies to expand globally. The Japanese competitors rose as a group, and largely fell as a group, with a few exceptions such as Toyota. The defining characteristic of emerging market competitors, in contrast, is their heterogeneity—in country of origin, business model, industry, and strategy. Some of their individual experiments are bound to fail, but the diversity of approach increases the odds that others will succeed.

The turbulence of China, India, and Brazil overwhelms most start-ups from these countries. Emerging market firms face low-cost domestic rivals and well-funded multinationals. They must satisfy discerning customers with limited disposable income, while coping with extreme levels of regulatory and macroeconomic turbulence. Emerging markets constitute a harsh selection environment that weeds out most start-ups. The hardy firms that survive, however, emerge as fierce competitors which excel in turbulent markets and look abroad for growth opportunities. Global expansion allows emerging market champions to tap new markets, diversify risk geographically, build economies of scale, and engage in multipoint competition with multinationals. A recent survey found that two-thirds of the CEOs of fast-growing companies, most from emerging markets, intended to expand globally rather than focus exclusively on their domestic market.[23]

The rise of venture capital has also increased competitive intensity. Venture capitalists make early investments that allow start-up firms to explore potential opportunities and scale quickly. Venture capitalists have funded firms such as Google, Microsoft, Intel, Genentech, Apple, Cisco, Starbucks, Home Depot, Staples, eBay, and Medtronix that have disrupted old industries and created new ones. These household names represent a tiny fraction of all companies that raised venture capital funding. Between 1980 and 2006, U.S. venture capitalists invested in more than twenty-three thousand start-ups. Not all have been home runs, but many have created value. Nearly one-third of venture-backed firms have gone public or been sold to a larger competitor.[24] The proliferation of venture-backed firms intensifies competition for incumbent players.

RISKY BUSINESS

Turbulence, for many, equals risk, and risk equals bad news. In 1999, the London Business School hosted a case competition in which students analyzed the Mittal case study. Lakshmi Mittal judged the entries. The students identified a long list of risks facing the company and unanimously advised Mittal to take chips off the table while he was ahead, diversifying into other industries or selling his steel business altogether. Their presentations echoed discussions I had with U.S. Steel executives, who viewed every change in the steel industry as a threat—globalization meant low-price imports, while technological innovation disrupted their established processes.

A focus on the downside of turbulence extends beyond steel. In 2007, the World Economic Forum ranked contingencies by their potential impact on the global economy.[25] These included man-made threats such as asset price collapse, retrenchment from globalization, civil wars, oil price shocks, a hard economic landing in China, instability in the Middle East, transnational crime, a fall in the U.S. dollar, failed and failing states, proliferation of weapons of mass destruction, and international terrorism, rounded off with natural disasters reminiscent of biblical plagues, including chronic disease, tropical storms, earthquakes, inland flooding, and loss of freshwater. Although the authors conceded that one man's risk may be another's opportunity, only a single item on their list—nanotechnology—lent itself to a positive spin. In 2007, the *Wall Street Journal* commissioned a survey of more than twenty-one thousand people from twenty countries and found respondents anxious about threats lurking in the future. The paper summarized its findings in the title: "The Age of Fear."[26]

Framing events as a threat helps to mobilize the resources required for an aggressive response. In an excellent study of newspapers' reaction to the Internet, Professor Clark Gilbert found that most newspaper executives ignored the Internet until the late 1990s.[27] When they finally took notice, they framed the new technology not as a way to engage in an ongoing discussion with their readers but as a threat to existing advertising and subscription revenues. Most newspapers then embarked on crash-course efforts to build an online presence to counter the threat. Despite mounting losses in their online businesses, print executives doubled investments annually, hurling money, people, and attention at the new business in an effort to protect their current profits.

Framing change in negative terms gives rise to a response known as "threat rigidity," that entails a contraction of authority, reduced experimentation, and focus on existing resources.[28] Gilbert's study documented all three dysfunctions of threat rigidity. In the newspapers he studied, top executives called the shots in the online businesses, in contrast to their bottom-up management in other units. Senior executives dictated templates for sales, business models, and product development that limited their subordinates' room to experiment. The rapid influx of resources, moreover, prevented newspapers from experimenting on a small scale before growing the business. They expanded the online businesses before working out the kinks. Finally, the newspapers replicated existing resources online. More than 85 percent of the newspapers' Web content rehashed articles from the paper, while ignoring features that were not part of their traditional print offering, including social networking, online auctions, or breaking news from third parties.

Turbulence produces not only risks but also opportunities, and fixating on threats obscures the upside of turbulence. A recent study found that nearly half of large companies surveyed had a chief risk officer, but how many employ a chief opportunity officer? If anyone could recognize the Karmet opportunity, it should have been U.S. Steel executives, with nearly a century of experience running large plants and dealing with local communities. Indeed, the Kazakh government invited a team from U.S. Steel to turn the plant around. Despite their expertise, the U.S. Steel team saw only risks, missed the opportunity, and passed on the acquisition. Mittal, in contrast, saw opportunities everywhere. "Emerged, emerging or submerging markets," he said, "they all represent opportunity to me."[29]

Of course, the world faces real challenges, but framing them as threats is not necessarily the best way to address them. In his 1968 book *The Population Bomb*, Stanford professor Paul Ehrlich analyzed the growing population, political unrest, and famine embroiling the Indian subcontinent and predicted that "the battle to feed all of humanity is over. In the 1970s the world will undergo famines— hundreds of millions of people are going to starve to death in spite of any crash programs embarked upon now."[30] Ehrlich dismissed as "fantasy" the possibility that India could avoid widespread starvation and conflict over food. Peering into turbulence, he saw only famine and war.

While Ehrlich foresaw doom, the plant geneticist Norman Borlaug glimpsed an opportunity to breed high-yield disease-resistant wheat. His strain helped India and Pakistan to double wheat production between 1965 and 1970, become self-sufficient in food, and avoid widespread starvation. Borlaug won the Nobel Peace

Prize, while Ehrlich removed his prediction from later editions of his book.

THE UPSIDE OF TURBULENCE

An uncertain future cloaks unseen risks but also holds unanticipated opportunities. Turbulent markets create opportunities in three distinct ways: turbulence introduces new resources into the economy, enables innovative combinations of existing resources, and stimulates novel consumer demand. Opportunities resemble the creation of a new dish in cooking, which arises from a new ingredient, an innovative recipe for combining familiar ingredients, or a shift in tastes.

Opportunities from new ingredients. In the sixteenth century, European explorers discovered unimagined ingredients in the New World, including the tomato. Italians initially thought tomatoes poisonous and used them only as decorative plants. Eventually, Neapolitan chefs experimented with the new fruit, which thereafter became a staple of Italian cuisine. This new resource enabled previously inconceivable sauces, including puttanesca, Bolognese, and marinara.[31]

The business analogue occurs when new resources enter the market. Resources include both hard assets (oil reserves or real estate, for example) and intangible assets (brand, technology, or expertise). Throughout the 1990s, politicians privatized money-losing mills, and the percentage of global steel production controlled by governments decreased from 70 percent to 30 percent, flooding the market with previously unavailable "ingredients." Mittal spotted the opportunity to build an empire from unwanted assets, and negotiated low prices for the steel mills. The government of Trinidad spent

$500 million to build a plant that it sold to Mittal seven years later for $70 million, while the Mexican government invested more than $2 billion on a plant that it offloaded for $220 million less than a decade later.

Newly privatized plants were not the only resource that created opportunity for Mittal. In Trinidad, the government was paying $20 million a year for a team of sixty German technicians to manage the factory. Mittal replaced the consultants with Indian managers and technical experts who earned one-tenth what the European advisors made. Mittal was among the first executives to tap emerging markets for labor. He recruited Indian managers frustrated by the dearth of opportunities at home and placed them in his newly acquired mills.

Opportunities from novel combinations of resources. A new dish can emerge by combining existing ingredients in an original way. Consider the humble sandwich, named after John Montagu, the fourth Earl of Sandwich.[32] An inveterate gambler, Montagu ordered salted beef placed between two pieces of toasted bread so he could dine without interrupting his gambling. Bread and meat had existed for millennia, as had gambling, but Montagu combined familiar ingredients in a new way to fulfill a long-standing desire for fast food.

Novel combinations of existing resources played a supporting role in the Mittal story. Mittal's first plant in Indonesia included a novel arrangement of two existing technologies. The first was an electric arc furnace, which produces steel by melting scrap metal rather than by smelting iron ore, coke, and limestone in a traditional furnace. Fearing a disruption to his supply of cheap scrap, Mittal adopted a second technology known as direct reduced iron, which transformed iron ore powder into metallic pellets—a substitute for scrap metal. In 1976, Mittal broke ground amidst rice paddies to build what he dubbed "an integrated mini-mill," combining the iron pellet technology with an electric arc furnace to produce low-cost steel bars for Indonesia's booming construction market. The constituent technologies had been around for decades, but Mittal pioneered their combination. Mittal later deviated from the integrated mini-mill and acquired plants employing traditional steel-making technologies.

Opportunities arising from novel combinations are linked to innovation, whose breathless fans have stretched the term so widely that it can cover anything new or good. A tight definition of innovation, however, consists of a novel combination of existing resources, in the spirit of the sandwich. Innovations come in many flavors— they can reconfigure a technology, process, supply chain or business model; sustain or disrupt an existing trajectory; extend existing practices; or break with the past. But all are examples of novelty from recombining existing resources. As the Mittal example illustrates, innovation is not the only, or even most important, way to create value in a turbulent world. Later in the book, I will argue that the singleminded focus on innovation so common in management over the past decade is not only misplaced but often dangerous to the extent that it distracts people from other ways to create value in turbulent markets.

Opportunities from shifting tastes. Opportunities also arise when consumer preferences shift, much as a change in diners' tastes creates demand for new dishes. In 1963, Robert Atkins, a New York cardiologist, read an article in the *Journal of the American Medical Association* describing a low-carbohydrate diet, and adopted a modified version of the weight-loss plan hoping to lose three pounds in a month.[33] After Atkins lost twenty pounds, he abandoned his cardiology practice and founded an obesity clinic. Within five years, Atkins's diet achieved wide publicity, earning him guest appearances on *The Tonight Show* and inclusion of his diet in *Vogue* magazine.[34] Although the low-carbohydrate diet is controversial (a 2003 issue of the *Harvard Health Letter* dubbed it "the bad boy of diets"), it attracted an estimated thirty million Americans to give it a try. The popularity of the Atkins diet created an opportunity for hundreds of new low-carbohydrate meals, including the oxymoronic low-carbohydrate pasta, which would have found a limited market had Atkins not shifted tastes.

Changing tastes also played a critical role in Mittal's success. He could have purchased the plants for a dime on the dollar, staffed them with talented managers, improved operations, and still gone bankrupt if no one bought his steel. His early experience in Indonesia, however, alerted Mittal to the pent-up demand for steel in emerging markets. Mittal noticed a hunger for steel that arose as market reforms increased disposable income for hundreds of millions of consumers, spurring demand for more houses to live in, cars to drive, and roads to congest.

The rising middle class in emerging markets is not the only change in tastes that creates opportunity. An aging population drives demand for drugs to alleviate the discomforts of old age, investment products to ensure a comfortable retirement, and concerts with classic rockers strutting across the stage despite being old enough to collect social security. Growing concern about environmental sustainability stimulates demand for fuel-efficient cars, alternative technologies, and packaging made from recycled materials. These shifts create new consumer tastes, which, like the Atkins diet, generate new opportunities.

THE PUNCH LINE

This book makes three central arguments. First, turbulence is a fundamental feature of markets characterized by dynamism, complexity, and intense competition. Many people lurch from one "black swan" to the next—from the dot-com boom to Enron's implosion to 9/11 to the global downturn—viewing each as a one-off exception to the stability they crave. Unexpected changes are not bugs in the world's operating system; they are a feature. This book is written, in part, to raise readers' sights from the current crisis to the big picture of a world in a constant state of flux.

My second thesis is that turbulence, despite its obvious risks, has an upside. Contextual forces churn ceaselessly, introducing new ingredients, changing tastes, and enabling novel combinations that create opportunities. Most people fixate so heavily on the downside of turbulence—the risks, uncertainty, and threats—that they, like the U.S. Steel executives, ignore golden opportunities right in front of them. Seeing a turbulent world through threat-tinted glasses invites the dysfunctions of threat rigidity—centralized control, limited experimentation, and focus on existing resources—that stymies the pursuit of opportunity.

The third thesis is that individuals can take practical steps to seize the upside of turbulence. In the past few years, a series of books including *The Age of Turbulence* by Alan Greenspan and *The Black Swan* by Nassim Nicholas Taleb have built a compelling case that the world is turbulent, but left readers with little practical guidance on what they can do. This book picks up where they leave off. Many people assume that entrepreneurs such as Bill Gates and Howard Schultz who thrive in turbulence differ from the rest of us, possessing some genetic endowment that predestines them to succeed where others stumble. After decades of research, however, scholars have failed to find any meaningful link between personality traits and success in pursuing opportunities.[35]

I taught entrepreneurship at Harvard Business School during the dot-com boom and bust. The greatest lesson I learned from studying and working with dozens of successful and failed companies in those heady days was this: entrepreneurs and managers succeed not because of who they are but because of what they do. I have studied how dozens of corporate Davids, such as Lakshmi Mittal, have taken on industry Goliaths. In each case the smooth stone in their slingshot was their ability to see and seize opportunities that arise out of turbulent markets. The skills to do so, I believe, can be mastered by anyone.

2.

TIME, TIMING, AND LUCK

The *Mardi Gras* set forth on her maiden voyage on a Saturday in March 1972 with five hundred passengers aboard, including three hundred travel agents who received a free cruise to experience the newly founded Carnival Cruise Lines firsthand.[1] As the pilot navigated the shallow channel out of Miami Harbor, the ship's stern ran aground on a sandbar at the edge of Government Cut, within sight of the tip of Miami Beach. For most of the people involved, the grounding was a harmless bit of fun. During the twenty-four hours the *Mardi Gras* was stranded, tourists rubbernecked from the beach, while passengers bellied up to the open bar, many quaffing a Mardi Gras on the Rocks, a drink improvised on the spot by a creative bartender. For Ted Arison, the founder of the fledgling cruise line, the maiden voyage was a disaster.

Theodore Arison had survived worse. Arison was born in 1924 in an agricultural settlement near Haifa founded by Romanian Jewish emigrants, underwritten by Edmond James de Rothschild, and located in what was then the British-administered Palestine. While vacationing in Yugoslavia in late August 1939, his father, Meir, who ran a shipping company, feared the imminent outbreak of war would trap his family in Europe. Meir found only one flight back to Haifa, departing the next day from Rome, and it was fully booked. He instructed his firm's Italian agent to pay whatever it took to secure five seats, and packed his family into a taxi for a six-hundred-mile cab ride to Rome. Within days of the plane's landing, Hitler had invaded Poland.

After escaping the Nazis, Ted Arison returned to fight them. In 1940, the sixteen-year-old dropped out of the engineering program at the American University of Beirut to enlist in a battalion of Jewish volunteers from Palestine who fought alongside the British Army in Italy and Germany. After a series of business ventures in Israel and New York, in 1966, Arison entered into a joint venture to found Norwegian Caribbean Line (Norwegian), the pioneer in Caribbean passenger cruises, which sailed out of Miami. After that partnership soured, Arison founded Carnival with a single rusted vessel infested with rodents and cockroaches. When Carnival entered the market in 1972, half a dozen established lines already offered cruises to the Caribbean out of Miami, and industry leaders Norwegian and Royal Caribbean controlled seven state-of-the-art ships between them. Competitors derided Carnival as the "Kmart of the Caribbean" and predicted the fledgling line's bankruptcy, since the *Mardi Gras* often sailed with half her berths vacant.

While competitors saw the *Mardi Gras* as half empty, Arison saw her as half full. In the midst of a recession in 1974, he bought control of Carnival for a token dollar (and assumed the company's debt of $5 million). Subsequent decades proved turbulent in the passenger cruise line industry. The competitive landscape churned constantly, with eighty-eight firms entering the U.S. market and seventy-seven exiting between 1966 and 2008 (see figure 2.1 below). Mergers and acquisitions further complicated the picture. Innovations in ship design transformed the cruising experience. Royal Caribbean's *Oasis of the Seas*, for example, spans sixteen decks and features an outdoor amphitheater, a zip line, two rock-climbing walls, and seven distinct neighborhoods. By 2008, passenger cruise ships offered ten times more space than that of ships launched in the early 1970s. Shocks to demand (such as 9/11) and volatility in exchange rates, fuel prices, and the cost of capital further roiled the market.

While other cruise lines came and went, Carnival endured. In 2009, Carnival Corporation was the largest cruise company in the world and controlled not only its flagship line but also Princess Cruises, Costa Crociere, Holland America, Cunard, AIDA, P&O, Ocean Village, Iberocruceros, and the Yachts of Seabourn. The company provided nearly one-half of all cruises globally, and was twice as large as the number two cruise line, Royal Caribbean. Carnival's rise from a single rust bucket to global leadership illustrates the role of luck in producing opportunities and of timing in seizing them.

THE BACKWARD-L VIEW OF TIME

Business leaders are often pictured as captains of industry, standing at the bow of a ship, peering through a telescope deep into the clear horizon of the future, plotting a course, and proceeding steady as she goes. Turbulence, however, enshrouds the future in a fog of uncertainty that frustrates long-term prediction. Volatility rules out smooth extrapolation of past trends, complex interactions stymie efforts to envision all possible outcomes, competitors thwart the best-laid plans,

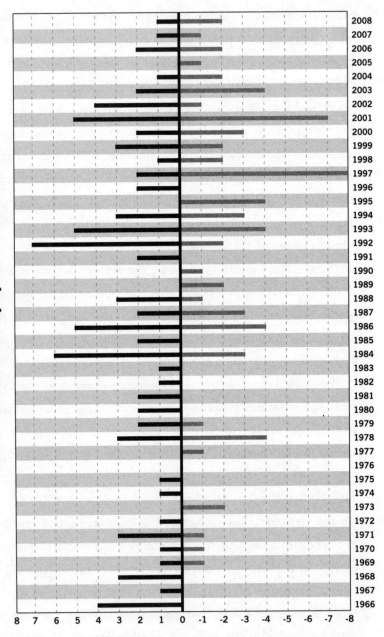

FIGURE 2.1 Number of Firms Entering and Exiting the U.S. Cruise Industry by Year: 1966–2008

and new information forces a fundamental rethink of a situation. In turbulent markets, leaders view the future not through a telescope but through a kaleidoscope.

Arison entered the cruise industry by serendipity, not foresight. After selling his stake in the freight forwarding business he cofounded, Arison was planning to start a business shipping fresh produce when quite by chance he met the owner of two ships that cruised the Bahamas. The owners were wrangling with the firm that managed the ships, and offered Arison the chance to take over the contract and run passenger cruises out of Miami. Arison agreed, although he knew nothing about the industry. A few months later he left for Miami to market cruises to the Bahamas and Jamaica. Before the first cruise left port, Arison faced a crisis when the owners defaulted on debt payments. Creditors auctioned off one ship and confined the other to port. With just a few months before the first cruise would set sail, Arison scrambled to find a suitable replacement and called the Norwegian owner of a passenger ferry. As luck would have it, the ferry had been docked for months, and the desperate owner agreed to the deal over the phone, even though Arison lacked the funds for a down payment and a track record in the industry.

The events that brought Arison into the cruise industry included both lucky and unlucky breaks, but none was foreseeable. In a turbulent world, the future throws out a steady stream of unexpected opportunities and threats. Arison, like anyone in a turbulent market, faced the future like a batter confronting a versatile but erratic pitcher who throws a random mix of pitches—fastballs, cutters, sliders, slurves, screwballs, and knuckleballs. Some pitches offer the potential for base hits, some are unhittable strikes, others are errant throws hurtling toward the batter's head, all interspersed with the rare pitch that could be hit for a home run.

People rarely think of the future as hurtling threats and opportunities at them, in part because of how they visualize time. Most charts depict time as an arrow moving forward from left to right on the horizontal axis of a graph, while plotting another variable—anything from mortgage default rates to gas prices—rising and falling on the vertical axis. This graphing convention yields the familiar L-shaped graph that accompanies articles in the *Wall Street Journal* and populates PowerPoint presentations throughout the corporate world. Figure 2.2, which plots median U.S. housing prices each decade from 1940 to 2000, illustrates the conventional forward-L view of time.

The forward-L graph is so ubiquitous, that people rarely consider the deep assumptions embedded in this diagram. First, the forward-L

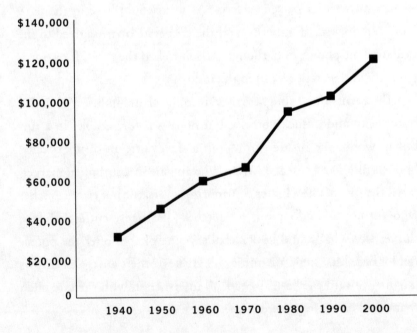

FIGURE 2.2 **Forward-L View of Time**
Median U.S. House Price by Decade, 1940–2000
(in 2000 Dollars)

implies that we stand with our backs to the past and peer—like the captain with the telescope—deep into a clear horizon of the future. The vertical axis—in this case measuring house prices—rises behind, truncating the view before 1940, but implying an unobstructed line of sight into the future. Smooth lines such as housing prices that stretch from left to right, moreover, invite extrapolation of a past trajectory into the future. When taking out a subprime mortgage, many homeowners implicitly assumed that housing prices would rise in the future as they had in the past. Deviations from this projected path are considered unexpected "jolts from the blue," "disruptions," or "black swans," as if the future were obliged to conform to people's desire for predictability.

The forward-L view of time is entrenched, comforting, and highly misleading. Flipping the L provides a more realistic way, in my view, to visualize the passage of time in a turbulent world. In the backward-L view, the arrow of time is reversed and flows from right to left, from an unknown future into a completed past. In this depiction, the vertical axis obscures not the past but the future, leaving executives, politicians, or investors to grope their way forward into a murky future, with limited visibility into what lies ahead.

They can, to be sure, turn their backs to the future and review historical events that have slipped into the past. With the benefit of hindsight, a string of incidents may appear to have been predictable or even inevitable. They are neither. Retrospective lines emerge in the backward-L view of time but guarantee neither continuity nor insight into the future. Like the jagged trace lines drawn by a seismograph recording geological fluctuations as they slip from the present to the past, retrospective chains of events can only describe the past. They remain mute about the future. Events seen in the rearview mirror appear more predictable than they were.

FIGURE 2.3 **Backward-L View of Time**

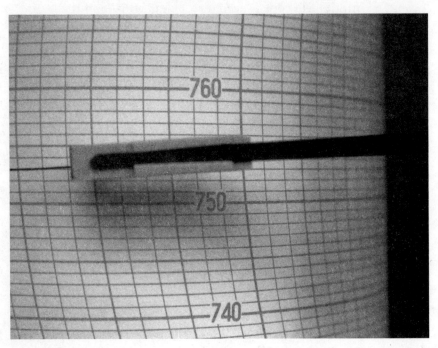

Source: Stock.xchng.

THE INVERSE POWER LAW OF OPPORTUNITIES

Not all opportunities are created equal. The opportunities and threats that emerge out of turbulence vary in magnitude. Over his career, Arison pursued many opportunities—some created no value, others were worth millions of dollars, and Carnival Corporation had an enterprise value of $25 billion in December 2008. I use the term *golden opportunity* to describe occasions when an entrepreneur or manager can create value in significant excess of the cost of the required resources. Whether the opportunity qualifies as golden or not obviously depends on the scale of the business pursuing it: a once-in-a-lifetime opportunity for an Inc. 500 founder may be too small to excite the CEO of a Fortune 500 company.

During the past decade, I have studied the distribution of opportunities and threats across markets and industries and found they follow a pattern mathematicians call an inverse power law, where the frequency of an event is inversely related to its magnitude. This pattern is common across a wide range of complex systems, including weather patterns, earthquakes, and traffic, where events arise out of the complex interactions of volatile variables. In practice, an inverse power law implies that individuals and firms face a steady flow of small opportunities and periodic midsized ones, all punctuated by the rare golden opportunity. Threats follow the same distribution, with many small annoyances scattered among the occasional midsized risk and the periodic sudden-death threat, such as a global downturn, that can undo a company. Figure 2.4 illustrates the distribution of opportunities and threats following an inverse power law.

The lines of the graph represent the magnitude of opportunities and threats over time, much as the traces left by a seismograph record the intensity of earthquakes. Magnitude in this graph is not a

FIGURE 2.4 The Inverse Power Law of Opportunities

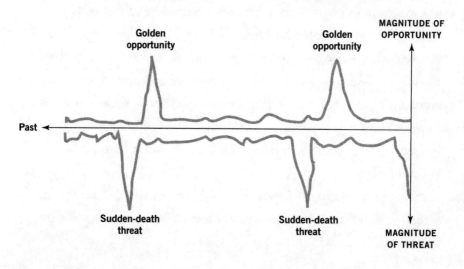

measure of an event's importance to the world as a whole. Rather, the vertical axis measures the impact of an opportunity or threat on a specific firm's ability to create or sustain value. Major world events, such as the rise of the Internet or Lehman's bankruptcy, would appear on this graph only if they directly impacted a particular firm's ability to create value. The 9/11 terrorist attacks created a sudden-death threat for airlines, presented a golden opportunity for security firms, and passed largely unnoticed among Chinese appliance manufacturers. Conversely, an industry-specific change such as a sharp reduction in textile quotas will have no impact on most firms but represent a competitive tsunami for European clothing producers. Rather than describing major events in general terms, such as "black swans," it is more productive to analyze their impact on a specific firm's ability to create and sustain value.

Golden opportunities arise when several windows of opportunity open simultaneously. In Arison's case, demand for cruises exceeded the limited supply; established cruise lines had developed a network of catering and service providers; no existing competitor dominated the market; and the Norwegian owner happened to have a ship sitting in port. Such a favorable confluence of factors is rare. Among the turbulent markets that I have studied, golden opportunities typically occur once or twice in a decade for most companies. Carnival executives seized several golden opportunities since the company's foundation, including a major capacity expansion in 1978 to meet booming demand, a 1987 initial public offering at the peak of a bull market, and the merger with P&O Princess Cruise Lines in the wake of 9/11.

The early industry leaders, Royal Caribbean and Norwegian, lacked Carnival's boldness in exploiting major opportunities as they arose. When, to seize growing demand, Ted Arison commissioned the first new ship in nearly a decade, his counterparts at Royal Caribbean hesitated. They enlarged two of their existing ships by carving them in half with welding torches and inserting a new midsection to increase capacity incrementally. By the time they ordered new ships, Carnival had grasped a sizeable chunk of the growing market.

Managers tend to look for golden opportunities during an economic boom. The best opportunities, however, often arise in the worst of times for the economy as a whole. Distressed sellers must offload valuable assets at bargain basement prices. In 2008, for example, ING Direct snapped up the deposits that Iceland's failing banks were forced to unload, while Spain's Banco Santander acquired struggling British banks Alliance & Leicester and Bradford & Bingley. To conserve cash in a downturn, companies retreat from attractive opportunities, leaving them open for rivals. The global recession may force Adobe Systems to scale back its ambitions in Web design software, creating an opening for a deep-pocket competitor such as Microsoft to exploit. In tough times, firms can also drive hard bargains on tangible assets. Airlines could purchase Airbus A380s on favorable terms in the wake of the 9/11 attacks, a time when most competitors were reluctant or unable to make large commitments.

While golden opportunities matter, they are not a substitute for exploiting the myriad small opportunities that arise every day. Golden opportunities may appear obvious in retrospect, after the founder graces the cover of *Forbes*, but they are rarely apparent in advance. A series of venture capitalists declined to invest in Google, dismissing it as a me-too player in a mature segment crowded with established rivals including Infoseek, Lycos, AltaVista, Excite, Dogpile, Inktomi, HotBot, and Ask Jeeves. Established transatlantic cruise lines sailed between New York and Europe, and their executives observed the rise of Caribbean cruising without grasping the magnitude of the opportunity.

Like waves in the sea, a break that starts out small may swell to a golden opportunity as circumstances shift. When Intel first launched the 8080 microprocessor in 1974, company executives viewed it as little more than a niche product—suitable for traffic lights and cash registers—that should not distract them from their core memory chip business. Their assessment was accurate right up to the point when the personal computer market took off, stimulating massive demand for microprocessors. The rise of the microprocessor may seem inevitable in retrospect, but it was not at all clear at the time. In 1978, an Intel team responsible for selling microprocessors conducted extensive customer interviews and discovered more than fifty potential uses for the new chip. Personal computers did not even make the list.[2]

Small opportunities, moreover, can cumulate to a decisive lead over time. Arison and his team clawed their way to the top of the cruise industry one opportunity at a time. Carnival's marketing department seized a series of moderate opportunities to build demand, debuting, for instance, the first nationwide television advertisement for cruises that featured the then unknown Kathie Lee Johnson (later Gifford). At a time when few tourists had taken a cruise, Carnival sent anonymous "mystery vacationers" to visit travel agencies around the country and ask for a vacation tip without revealing their identity. Any agent who suggested a cruise pocketed a crisp $10 bill. If the travel agent recommended Carnival by name, he or she received $1,000 in cash on the spot.

Many managers equate opportunity with revenue growth. The

true measure of an opportunity, however, is whether it creates economic value, which is the difference between what a customer is willing to pay for something and the cost of all resources (including capital) required to produce it.[3] Opportunities to cut costs are every bit as important to value creation as increasing sales. Founded with a rusty ship, no brand, and the specter of bankruptcy hovering at all times, Carnival executives relentlessly pursued any and every chance to reduce costs. To refurbish the *Mardi Gras* on a shoestring budget, for example, Carnival operations chief Meshulam Zonis found an orphanage in Seville, Spain, that taught orphaned teenagers trades such as carpentry, welding, and electrical work. The priest who ran the orphanage could not find work for his charges in Spain's depressed economy, and Zonis hired more than a hundred of them at one time to work under the guidance of U.S. master craftsmen to renovate Carnival's first ship. Where Royal Caribbean stocked bathrooms with a complementary gift pack with more than a dozen toiletries, Carnival offered a bar of soap.

Individually, none of Carnival's marketing or cost-cutting opportunities could make or break the company, but taken together they filled the ships, increased profits, and allowed Carnival to avoid the financial distress that forced nearly 90 percent of new entrants to exit the industry. I am not arguing for execution of small improvements instead of a strategy of seizing golden opportunities when they arise. In turbulent markets, execution *is* strategic. The relentless pursuit of cost reductions enables firms to outlast less disciplined rivals when sudden-death threats descend. Unrelenting exploitation of small opportunities provide firms with the wherewithal to seize golden opportunities when they arise. A series of small wins enabled Carnival to strengthen its balance sheet and accumulate the cash to invest in new ships and fund major acquisitions. Lulled into complacency by their initial lead, Royal Caribbean and Norwegian, in contrast, lacked Carnival's ruthless discipline in exploiting small opportunities.

PERFECT TIMING

An old joke among academics has two free market economists walking down Chicago's University Avenue when the first exclaims, "Look, there's a $20 bill on the ground." "Impossible," her companion responds without looking down. "If it were there, someone would have picked it up already." Even a bad joke can make a good point, and this one underscores the fleeting nature of opportunity. In competitive markets, where entrepreneurs and firms are always on the lookout for chances to make a buck, good opportunities should be pocketed quickly. Twenty-dollar bills rarely remain on the ground for long.

When pursuing a fleeting opportunity, timing is everything. The variables that influence the nature, magnitude, and timing of an opportunity incessantly shift: one window of opportunity might remain ajar for a while, another widens abruptly, and a third threatens to slam shut at any moment. Arison excelled at darting through the windows of opportunity in the early years of the cruise industry. In 1978, Carnival commissioned the *Tropicale*, the first new cruise ship built in nearly a decade and by the far the most expensively built to date, with an estimated price tag of $110 million.

That Arison's company, six years old and barely eking out a profit, could afford such an expensive ship in the midst of a recession shocked the industry. But Arison's timing was impeccable, as he exploited shifts in the broader context. After decades of healthy growth, Denmark's economy suffered stagflation in the late 1970s. The Nordic country's economic growth rate fell by two-thirds and unemployment jumped fourfold. To bolster its shipping industry, the Danish government offered low interest loans to finance up to 70 percent of the cost of ships built in local yards.[4] Carnival was first to take advantage of the new financing opportunity, and it built a ship large enough to capture scale economies and luxurious enough to increase customers' willingness to pay for a cruise.

Other shifts in the broader context created demand for the *Tropicale*. In October 1978, President Jimmy Carter signed a bill deregulating the U.S. airline industry. With the stroke of a pen, Carter enacted changes that drove the average price of a domestic ticket down by nearly one-third by 1990 and triggered a doubling of passenger miles flown.[5] Cheaper flights to Miami stimulated cruise demand. Deregulation followed the 1977 launch of *The Love Boat*, ABC's weekly television series that introduced cruising to many Americans and served as a decade-long unpaid advertisement for the industry as a blend of fun, romance, and sex. During *The Love Boat*'s ten years on the air, Caribbean cruise demand nearly tripled.[6]

Timing was critical again when Micky Arison, who succeeded his father as president in 1979, sold a stake in Carnival in an initial public offering (IPO) on the American Stock Exchange in July 1987. The stock sale netted Carnival $400 million while leaving the Arisons with a controlling stake of 80 percent. Equity analysts covering the traditional cargo shipping sector struggled to explain the cruise industry. During the heady days of the 1980s bull market, however, investors swallowed whatever misgivings they might have had about the new industry and snapped up Carnival shares. In October of 1987, Norwegian announced its intention to go public as well, but it withdrew its offering the following Monday, when the Dow Jones Industrial Average lost nearly one-quarter of its value (the largest one-day drop in history to that time). Black Monday slammed the bank window shut for Norwegian.

Micky Arison wasted no time putting Carnival's cash to good use. Within a few months of the IPO, he initiated discussions to acquire Royal Caribbean. When that bid fell through, he bought Holland America, the first in a series of acquisitions. Royal Caribbean maintained its independence by selling a stake to the Pritzker and Ofer families, but delayed any major acquisitions until nearly a decade later. Lacking Carnival's funds, Norwegian could match its rival in neither acquisitions nor ship building, and watched the industry consolidation from the side lines.

Good timing is not the same thing as being first. Too early to seize an opportunity can be as bad as too late. Carnival overtook a host of cruise lines that entered the industry earlier, including not only Norwegian and Royal Caribbean, but also Flagship Cruises, Prudential-Grace Lines, and Eastern Cruise Lines, firms whose names have slipped into the annals of shipping history. Had Ted Arison commissioned the *Tropicale* five years before the *Love Boat* and deregulation, he might not have filled the ship. Had Micky Arison tried to float Carnival in the early 1980s, the company's shorter track record and the less buoyant capital markets might have lowered the stock's valuation or precluded an IPO altogether.

Getting the timing right distinguishes opportunity from innovation. Innovators, according to the conventional wisdom, can whip up a value-creating combination at the time and place of their choosing, heedless of what is happening in the larger competitive context. Professors W. Chan Kim and Renée Mauborgne, authors of *Blue Ocean Strategy*, an influential best seller on innovation, for example, argue that the "structure and market boundaries" of any industry "exist only in managers' minds." Managers who accept the *Blue Ocean* approach "do not let existing market structures limit their thinking. To them, extra demand is out there, largely untapped. The crux of the problem is how to create it."[7] Citing examples such as Southwest Airlines, the authors contend that managers can impose a creative business model in the stodgiest of industries anytime they like. All they need is the creativity to think outside the proverbial box and the courage to impose their new vision.

I'm not convinced. Innovation is important, and *Blue Ocean Strategy* is one of the more helpful books on the subject. Vast swaths of the innovation literature dangerously underestimate how external forces dictate the optimal timing to pursue an opportunity. Professor Costas Markides, one of the most insightful scholars of innovation, notes that Charles Schwab, Sony, Texas Instruments, Gillette, and Amazon are household names, while K. Aufhauser, Ampex, Bowmar, Auto-Strop, and Charles Stack remain unknown.[8] The difference? The unknown companies first introduced innovations that the well-known firms later commercialized. The pioneers were more creative. They were also too early, arriving before willing buyers, necessary technology, and supporting infrastructure were in place to commercialize their innovation. The winners timed their entry to match market conditions.

Carnival owes its success, in good measure, to a long list of external forces beyond Arison's control, including the completion of Miami's new port in 1964, Danish stagflation, *The Love Boat*, airline deregulation, and a Wall Street boom. Ted and Micky Arison and the management team they assembled were talented, alert, and tenacious. They excelled at seizing opportunities. But they could not have forced or foreseen the contextual shifts that allowed them to prosper. The windows of opportunity exist in reality, not only in our minds. We cannot open them at will.

Leaders should, of course, influence context as much as they can—for example, by lobbying governments, preempting competitors, or shaping industry standards to their company's benefit. Ted Arison lobbied local officials to expand Miami's port, and Carnival's aggressive marketing accelerated consumers' awareness of cruising as an attractive vacation alternative to Orlando or Las Vegas. But leaders should also recognize that the forces dictating the timing (as well as the form and magnitude) of opportunities often lie beyond their grasp. Managers cannot conjure up a golden opportunity just because sales are falling, investors are clamoring for growth, or the CEO read the latest book on innovation.

A narrow focus on innovation not only underestimates the importance of the external context but can also lead managers to value novelty for its own sake. Royal Caribbean wins praise for its shipboard innovations, such as rock climbing and ice skating. But not every innovation boosts customers' willingness to pay enough to offset the additional costs it imposes. For all the company's innovation, Royal Caribbean's profitability, return on equity, and market capitalization have lagged Carnival's. New initiatives should be measured against the yardstick of value creation, not creativity alone. The focus on novelty can also distract people from mundane opportunities, such as subsidized government financing for ships or low-cost labor, that create significant value despite lacking the glamour of the novel.

THE LUCK OF THE DRAW

When considering an officer for promotion, Napoleon reputedly asked whether the candidate was lucky. Soldiers cannot always choose the battle they must fight. Nor can entrepreneurs or managers control the shifting contextual variables that give shape to opportunities. Whether they find themselves in the right place at the right time to encounter specific opportunities is largely a matter of luck. The confluence of external circumstances produces opportunities. Entrepreneurs and managers must be alert to notice the opportunity and tenacious to seize it, but luck places it within their grasp in the first place.

Ted Arison was lucky to bump into a shipowner desperate for a new manager, lucky to be between jobs at the time, lucky to have some cash on hand, and lucky to find another ship when his first two were seized. Lakshmi Mittal was lucky to run a steel mill in Indonesia as governments around the world privatized their plants and emerging market growth stimulated demand for steel. Mittal or Arison might have succeeded a decade earlier or later, but not with the specific opportunities that made their fortunes.

Admitting the role of luck in success may strike you as obvious; it certainly seems unarguable to me. Nevertheless, the shelves at airport bookstores sag under the weight of best-selling business books that select successful companies, study what they did, and conclude that anyone who does the same thing will reap the same rewards. But these studies overlook how churning external forces set the context for success. A review of ten management best sellers found that none deemed the topic of luck (or chance or timing) important enough to deserve an entry in their index.[9]

Perhaps the most profound thinker on the role of luck in human affairs was Niccolò Machiavelli, who estimated that fortune accounts for half of success or failure, leaving the other half in our hands.[10] Machiavelli's approximation acknowledges the role of both luck and agency without falling into the trap of false precision. It is true that Mittal and Arison were lucky, but it is equally true that they weathered bad breaks and exploited opportunities much better than others.

In a world where chance matters, is there anything we can do to improve our luck? The most common answer to this question is some variation on Arnold Palmer's observation that "the more I practice, the luckier I get." The "practice makes lucky" approach works well for opportunities that fall within the scope of past experience. Decades of finding ways to reduce costs, for instance, helped Carnival managers spot new opportunities for further efficiency gains.

The juiciest opportunities, however, often differ significantly from what worked in the past. Ted Arison knew a lot about freight forwarding and a little about cargo shipping but nothing about cruising when he moved to Miami. Honing established routines can blind people to opportunities that arise from unexpected places. Despite decades of experience, most established cruise lines failed to redeploy their ships to the Caribbean routes, even as the rise of transatlantic flights decimated their traditional business. Transatlantic cruise executives saw Miami as a minor port compared to New York and cruises as a frivolous distraction from the serious work of ferrying passengers across the Atlantic. Practice blinded them to the opportunity that could have salvaged their dying industry.

Machiavelli offered three images of fortune, and each conveys an important insight about snatching opportunities out of turbulence. Comparing luck to the wheel of fortune, a popular image in the Renaissance, Machiavelli notes that the low may be lifted and the mighty humbled. This wheel of fortune implies nurturing hope during the dark days (apt advice in the depth of a global recession) and avoiding the hubris that leads the mighty to fall. Living in a less enlightened era, Machiavelli also likened fortune to a fickle woman who yields her attention to the bold suitor over the timid advances of the tentative beau. The implication of this image is to strike boldly when an opportunity presents itself. Lady Fortune favors the bold.

In one of his most vivid images, Machiavelli wrote that fortune "resembles one of those violent rivers that, when they become enraged, flood the plains, tear down trees and buildings, lift up the earth from the side and deposit it on the other; everyone flees before them, everybody yields to their impact, unable to oppose them in any way."[11] Although we cannot control the torrent, Machiavelli argues, we can limit its damage by constructing embankments—what modern business parlance might describe as mitigating identifiable risks. An optimist might even spot an opportunity to build a hydroelectric plant.

In thinking about how to seize the upside of turbulence, I propose a different image of fortune. In the era before engines and electronic navigation replaced mast and compass, a sailing ship's progress, and indeed its survival, depended on elements beyond its control. Not even the best seaman—think Captain Jack Aubrey in *Master and Commander*, for example—could predict the elements with accuracy, let alone raise the winds or calm the waves. A seasoned captain could, however, still master the sea. Not in the sense that a trainer masters a horse, by bending the beast to his will, but rather by harnessing favorable winds when they gust, riding out the inevitable storms, and remaining ever alert to the shifts in weather that demand a change in tack.

THE MAP PARADOX

On June 15, 1919, Karl Popper left his family's Vienna apartment to join several thousand demonstrators marching to demand that the government free a group of jailed communists. Half the protestors were communists, others teenage boys. The sixteen-year-old Karl Popper was both. Just before noon, the crowd broke into a run and approached Vienna's Hörlgasse shouting for guards to release the prisoners. In that narrow street, the protesters collided with a cordon of police on foot and horseback, breaking the wave and leaving them facing off with the police.[1] The police would later be criticized for their brutality, but they had every reason to fear the worst. The previous evening they had arrested more than a hundred communist leaders based on a reliable tip that they planned to incite demobilized troops to a putsch the next day. A month earlier, a demonstration by thousands of unemployed workers and ex-soldiers in front of the Parliament had turned violent, costing several policemen their lives.

Vienna had been in turmoil for much of the past year. As World War I drew to a close the preceding year, the Austro-Hungarian military disintegrated, losing a series of key battles and suffering widespread mutiny among the troops. The Allied forces, to end the war more quickly, quarantined Vienna to starve the Austrians into submission, causing food riots and near famine.[2] After the war, the victorious Allies carved the former Hapsburg Empire into independent states including Hungary, Czechoslovakia, Poland, and the State of Slovenes, Croats, and Serbs. "Austria," the French prime minister Georges Clemenceau observed acidly, "is what is left," with a population one-sixth its former size. The country suffered from widespread unemployment and hyperinflation. The currency lost half its value in the first six months of 1919 and would go on to lose 90 percent by the end of the year, decimating a lifetime of savings for many Austrian citizens.[3] Joseph Schumpeter, who later coined the phrase "creative destruction," was the minister of finance until he was sacked in November of that year.

As the protestors grew agitated in the Hörlgasse, the police commander warned them to refrain from violence. According to eyewitness accounts, a teenage boy wearing a brown suit and hat approached a mounted policeman and tried to unseat him. When the officer resisted, the boy pulled a pistol hidden inside his jacket and fired one shot at close range, hitting the policeman in the stomach. Several other protestors produced handguns and shot at the police. The officers maintained their discipline, firing three warning shots into the air, but when the mob failed to disperse, they opened fire. Most of the crowd—including Popper—was unarmed and unaware of the planned putsch. Popper fled during the exchange of gunfire, but not before witnessing fellow protesters fall yards from where he stood.

MENTAL MAPS

In plotting their putsch, Vienna's communists followed a path laid out decades earlier by Karl Marx and elaborated by later thinkers. A political theory, such as Marxism, is an example of what I call a *mental map*, a model that represents reality and serves as a guide to action. Maps are not limited to politics: scientists formulate theories to focus their data collection and experimentation; generals develop strategies to deploy troops; coaches draw up game plans to neutralize opponents' best players; entrepreneurs write business plans to secure funding and focus their limited resources. Some mental maps are explicit, others largely implicit, but all perform three specific functions: they emphasize important categories, clarify relationships among variables, and suggest appropriate action.

Mental maps draw selected variables to the fore while nudging less important factors into the background or leaving them off the map altogether. Socialist theory emphasized different classes—for instance, capitalists, workers, and the lumpenproletariat (whom Marx defined as the "flotsam of society"). Categorizing people by economic class rather than, say, religious affiliation or nationality, highlighted the gap between wealthy owners and struggling laborers.

The choice of categories depends on what the user hopes to accomplish. A driver will choose a city map showing streets and highways, while a politician might represent the same terrain with a house-by-house analysis of political party affiliation and past campaign donations. Managers looking to increase their firm's profits might adopt Professor Michal Porter's model of competitive strategy, which specifies five forces that influence the profitability of companies within an industry.[4]

The most useful mental maps not only highlight important variables but also spell out interactions among them. In socialist theory, class struggle described the ongoing battle between different classes to control the means of production, such as factories and mines. Conflict rather than cooperation drove progress, according to this map, and could only end in complete victory for one class. Porter's Five Forces model assumes a similar zero-sum competition for profits, where suppliers, competitors, and customers struggle for a larger slice of a finite profit pie.

By charting the terrain, mental maps suggest effective action. The socialist theory of class struggle ruled out compromise and exhorted activists to bring latent class conflict to a head through violence. Hence Vienna's communists plotted a putsch rather than running for elected office. The Five Forces model suggests that managers first choose a profitable industry to enter and then erect barriers to entry to keep rivals, suppliers, and customers from capturing a disproportionate share of profits.

QUESTION MARX

When Popper joined the communist party in the spring of 1919, he failed to conduct intellectual due diligence on the mental map that guided the party. At that time, a host of contending movements, including anarchism, fascism, and pacifism, offered competing explanations of the turbulence that plagued Europe in the opening decades of the twentieth century. By 1919 socialism had emerged as an article of faith among Vienna's intelligentsia, and Popper accepted it without critical analysis.

After the demonstration, Popper scrutinized the theory that left corpses in the street. How, he wondered, could the communists be so sure their comrades' sacrifice was justified? How did they know that the fall of capitalism was inevitable or that socialism would be better? In the course of his analysis, Popper discovered that Marxist thinkers saw socialism not as utopian idealism but as hard science. They claimed class struggle was an inevitable law of economics—not a socially constructed law, like a speed limit, but a law of nature akin to gravity. Beneath the fiery rhetoric of the revolution lay the cool certainty of science.

When Popper looked under the hood of Marxist theory, he was appalled to find neither science nor truth but a creed riddled with obvious "gaps and loopholes and inconsistencies."[5] Not only did the doctrine suffer from deep theoretical flaws, but the most critical predictions failed real-world tests. Marx predicted that manufacturing-intensive countries, such as England and Germany, would produce the class conflict required to usher in socialism. These countries failed to follow Marx's script, however, and the only revolution of the time took place in agrarian Russia, one of the least industrialized economies in Europe. Despite theoretical flaws and faulty predictions, millions of people clung to Marxism. Angry with himself for embracing a flawed doctrine, Popper rejected it.

In 1919, events conspired to undermine not only political certainties but also most of the established truths that might, in a more stable era, have shaped Popper's future. The dissolution of the Hapsburg Empire demolished bourgeois confidence in the link between hard work and middle-class security. Popper's father, Simon, was born in modest circumstances in a small Czech town and later migrated to Vienna, where he rose to prominence in legal circles. Contrary to the modern stereotype of the workaholic lawyer, Popper's father relaxed by writing poetry and translating Greek and Roman literature into German.[6] When Simon Popper turned sixty-three in 1919, he looked forward to a retirement spent in his personal library. Instead, the collapse of the Austrian currency decimated a lifetime of savings and forced the elder Popper to continue working. Karl Popper moved to low-cost student housing to ease his family's financial burden.

As if it weren't enough that the apparent certainties of Marxism, empire, and middle-class security were upended, that same year saw the laws of physics overturned as well. In November 1919, the *Times* of London, a paper not prone to hyperbole, ran the headline "Revolution in Science, New Theory of the Universe, Newtonian Ideas Overthrown."[7] For two centuries Isaac Newton's laws of motion and universal gravitation had been accepted as a true representation of nature. In 1905, Albert Einstein, a patent clerk working in Bern, Switzerland, proposed a new view of the universe in which gravity could distort space. Based on his theory, he predicted that light passing by a massive object should curve slightly toward it rather than follow a straight path, as Newtonian physics predicted. On May 29, 1919, the English astrophysicist Arthur Stanley Eddington conducted an elegant experiment that proved light did indeed bend when it passed the sun.

PROVISIONAL KNOWLEDGE

Taken together, the events of 1919 seared a single insight upon Karl Popper: that all maps leading into the future—be they political agendas, personal plans, or predictions based on scientific theories—are provisional. They remain subject to rejection in light of disconfirming evidence. His experiences, Popper later wrote, "taught me the wisdom of the Socratic saying, 'I know that I do not know' . . . and impressed on me the value of intellectual modesty."[8]

Any map that makes predictions about the future, according to Popper, whether derived from scientific theories such as Newtonian physics or political doctrines such as Marxism, resemble a working hypothesis, which people adopt not because it is true but because it approximates truth closely enough to guide action. These working hypotheses provide imperfect representations of a complex and fluid world. Popper compared them to nets woven to catch portions of reality as it swims by, while letting everything else pass through the mesh.[9] Working hypotheses are always flawed because they reduce complexity to simplicity, omit critical variables, and remain stable as the world turns.

If you scent a whiff of intellectual paranoia here, trust your nose. Popper's views on provisional knowledge imply that all our maps eventually let us down. Millions of passionate believers in Marxism did not make the creed true, just popular. Widespread consensus did not mean that Iraq possessed weapons of mass destruction, nor does it prove that the earth's temperature will continue to rise in the future. Our theories about the future, without exception, remain subject to revision or rejection in light of new knowledge that might arise in the future. All our theories will let us down; we just don't yet know how or when.

In the early twentieth century, most scientists viewed hypotheses as theories that had not yet been proven. Popper turned this view on its head and argued that any theory—even one as well established as Newtonian physics—was simply a hypothesis that had not yet been disproved. For Popper, science was a Darwinian struggle, where competing theories, all flawed in some way, struggled to survive rigorous testing in the real world. Scientists frame a hypothesis, submit it to severe investigation, and abandon their theory if it fails the test. Rigorous testing weeds out the weaker theories, leaving only the strong to survive, until further experiments expose their flaws and they too are replaced by even stronger theories. Science, for Popper, was permanent revolution.

THE CYCLE OF CONJECTURE AND REFUTATION

The engine that drives scientific revolution, in Popper's view, was a cycle that iterated between conjecture and refutation.[10] The cycle begins when a scientist bypasses a theory's explanatory strengths to search out its weak spots. Prior to formulating the special theory of relativity, Einstein studied both mechanics and electrodynamics with an eye to identifying their limitations. These shortcomings typically manifest themselves as anomalies, unusual findings that fall outside existing categories or defy explanation by established theory. An anomaly points in the direction of a mismatch between a simplified theory and complex reality, and flags a productive spot for further exploration.

In the next step, the investigator formulates a working hypothesis to explain the anomaly. This stage demands the intellectual courage to break cleanly with conventional wisdom and the imagination to envision a creative alternative. Popper idolized Einstein for having the audacity to conceive of an alternative view of the universe while working as a patent clerk. Popper separated problem identification from hypothesis formulation, but he recognized that they often co-evolved in practice, with a hypothesis suggesting a fresh look at the original problem from a different angle.[11]

Popper termed the third step in the cycle "error elimination." In this stage, the researcher submits her working hypothesis to severe testing to expose its flaws. Error elimination includes scrupulous analysis of a theory to unearth logical inconsistencies—recall Popper's critique of Marxism. Error elimination also entails real-world experiments, such as Eddington's test to determine whether gravity bent light. The best way to eliminate errors, Popper argued, was to design experiments to refute a theory rather than find supporting evidence.

Popper placed particular emphasis on error elimination. He noted an asymmetry between what scientists can prove and what they can disprove. Spotting the millionth white swan, to use one of his best known examples, does not conclusively prove that all swans are white. A single black swan, however, disproves it conclusively.[12] "Human reason is unlimited with regard to criticism," Popper argued, "yet limited with regard to its powers of prediction."[13] Popper spent much of his career critiquing the work of others and earned a reputation as an intellectual giant-killer. Many Marxists considered Popper's critique the most devastating ever written, while his scathing appraisal discredited the popular philosophical movement known as logical positivism. (Ironically, Popper detested criticism of his own work, forbidding editors to tweak his prose, shunning colleagues who critiqued his work, and browbeating doctoral students in an atmosphere resembling Senate inquiries under Joseph McCarthy.)[14]

PROVISIONAL KNOWLEDGE IN THE REAL WORLD

Popper's insight that all knowledge of the future is provisional belongs to a branch of philosophy known as epistemology, which explores the nature and limits of knowledge—what we know, don't know, and cannot know. Hard-nosed readers might dismiss these questions as obscure, at best suited to arcane discussions among philosophers of science, at worst relegated to late-night bull sessions in a college dorm room. Popper, however, considered the question of what we can and cannot know profoundly practical. Indeed, one of the best introductions to his thinking is entitled *Philosophy and the Real World*.[15] Popper spent seven decades teasing out the implications of provisional knowledge for a range of real-world questions: How do scientists know when to reject their theories? Is communism a better way to organize society than capitalism? How can governments avoid imposing disastrous policies?

Few people think of themselves as applied epistemologists. Yet whether they succeed or fail in a turbulent world depends to a large extent on how well they manage the cold reality of provisional knowledge. Take entrepreneurship, for example. Many start-ups begin when an entrepreneur glimpses a potential gap in the market and a way to fill it. Entrepreneurs can jot their map on the proverbial cocktail napkin, create a PowerPoint pitch for investors, or write a business plan replete with market surveys and pro forma projections. These differences in form should not obscure their fundamental similarity—all are mental maps, subject to revision or rejection in light of new information. The definition of the opportunity and the plan to pursue it entail assumptions about the evolution of technology, customer adoption, competitive response, and availability of funding, among others. If these assumptions are wrong, the entrepreneur must rethink the hypothesis or abandon it altogether.

Studies of start-up survival confirm that most entrepreneurs follow flawed maps. Research across a broad range of industries, countries, and time periods finds that more than half of all start-ups go out of business within four years.[16] Just because the others survive does not mean the founders got their map right. Start-ups can limp along for years, barely breaking even, without creating significant value. Those that survive completely revise their map as flaws in the plan become evident. A systematic study of three hundred start-ups found that persisting with the initial business plan was the best single predictor of failure one year after founding—nine of ten entrepreneurs who stuck to their initial business plan without revision failed.[17] To be clear, provisional knowledge is not always bad. Technologies sometimes solve an even bigger problem than the targeted one, markets prove larger or grow faster than expected, and competitors occasionally doze off at the wheel.

Popper's cycle of conjecture and refutation can help entrepreneurs cope with their provisional knowledge, particularly in a venture's early years.[18] Aaron Kennedy decided to start Noodles & Company, a chain of restaurants specializing in cooked-to-order noodle dishes from around the world, after he noticed an anomaly. While dining at a pan-Asian noodle restaurant in Greenwich Village, Kennedy was struck that the format was not more common given its healthy fare, speed, and value for money. After spotting a gap in the market, he formulated a conjecture about how to seize the opportunity, and opened one restaurant in Denver and another in Madison, Wisconsin, to test his hypothesis in two different markets.

Noodles & Company's initial experience was not auspicious. The spring of 1996 brought a scathing review in a Madison newspaper, disappointing financial results for both sites, and flooding in the basement of the Madison restaurant. Kennedy and his team drove from Madison to Chicago to tour successful noodle shops, compare them to their own restaurants, and decide whether to quit or revise their business model. They stuck it out, but only after identifying fifteen changes to their initial plan. They switched from steam tables to sauté lines to increase freshness, for example, and warmed up the restaurants' color scheme. The Noodles & Company team tested the modified business model in the existing sites and two new ones over the following two years. Once the revised model gained traction, Noodles & Company scaled rapidly.

The venture capital industry has institutionalized the conjecture-refutation loop by staging investments in rounds. Entrepreneurs sometimes bemoan repeated rounds of fund-raising as a distraction from real work. Painful as it may seem in the short term, this iterative approach can help balance execution with revision. Between rounds of fund-raising, an entrepreneur can go into head-down execution mode to test her hypothesis. The need to raise another round of financing forces the entrepreneur and potential investors to reexamine the map and decide whether to plow forward, revise the plan, or cut their losses. This approach works better than questioning the business model every day or pursuing a plan without revision. The box below describes some ways entrepreneurs and managers can design more effective experiments.

ENTREPRENEURIAL EXPERIMENTS

Entrepreneurs and managers can consciously design experiments to surface flaws in their mental map. In the entrepreneurial context, an experiment is a test designed to reduce uncertainty before committing additional resources. Common examples include customer research, prototypes, and beta customers. Based on the results of these experiments, entrepreneurs may decide to cut their losses, revise their plan and run another experiment, or harvest the value they have created. Below are some practical examples.

Identify deal-killers. Every plan includes countless assumptions. Rather than worrying about all of them, an entrepreneur should identify potential deal-killers, variables that could prove fatal. Deal-killers vary: In commercial real estate development, title disputes or environmental liabilities could scotch a deal, while a software start-up faces a deal-killer if a deep-pocketed rival has a valid claim on the underlying intellectual property. Deal-killers are often discernable early on, and managers and entrepreneurs should try to surface these critical sources of uncertainty early.

Know what you are betting on. In turbulent markets, multiple variables in-fluence an opportunity's payoff. Entrepreneurs should identify the key drivers of success. One way to do that is to pose the question "What are we betting on here?" It could be a better mousetrap, access to a brand or technology that others lack, a critical relationship, or the ability to move quicker than established players. A venture's big bet is not the inverse of deal-killers. In developing a new drug, for example, the big bet is on the compound's therapeutic benefits, while the deal-killer is potential tox-icity.

Design partial experiments. Partial experiments test a single variable, typi-cally a deal-killer or key bet. A real estate developer could test a deal-killer by commissioning an Environmental Protection Agency assessment before buying land, while an entrepreneur could run a patent search to ensure that her intellectual property rights are secure. Partial experiments can also test the big bet. The founders of Kingsley Management marketed an automated system to wash cars thoroughly without damaging the exterior finish. They bet that their solution would appeal to consumers across different climates and not be limited to markets where extreme winters and salt on the roads necessitate frequent trips to the car wash. The founders used their first round of funding to test consumer adoption in markets with different climates.

Design holistic experiments. Holistic experiments test multiple variables and interactions between them on a small scale. Typical examples include a test launch before wider rollout—recall how Noodles & Company got the first two restaurants right before adding more—or building a prototype for an early customer. Such experiments can reveal unexpected interactions among vari-ables. An MIT professor founded E Ink to commercialize a technology that replaced paper and ink with an electronic display. The start-up introduced a prototype for signs in grocery store aisles to update prices remotely. These experiments revealed an unexpected result: metal roofs and aisles of metal cans blocked the wireless signals required to refresh the signs.

Explicitly consider trade-offs. Entrepreneurs can design experiments that are cheap, fast, or certain but not all three. In designing an experiment, entrepreneurs should consider which dimension is most important in their own situation. For medical devices, certainty about product safety is critical, and entrepreneurs must accept expensive and time-consuming clinical trials. If several companies are pursuing the same opportunity, a well-funded start-up might sacrifice certainty and frugality to get a prototype in front of customers quickly. Any entrepreneur bootstrapping a company must look for the cheapest experiment possible, sacrificing both certainty and speed.

Stage your experiments. Entrepreneurs can take a page from the venture capital playbook and stage investments by starting with low-cost tests of deal-killers or big bets before proceeding to more expensive holistic experiments. The Food and Drug Administration's human clinical trial process for testing new drugs illustrates the logic of staging experiments. The first and least expensive step tests new compounds for toxicity, while subsequent and more expensive trials test benefits relative to established drugs.

Avoid experiment creep. Experiment creep occurs when a test drags on too long, costs too much, or loses clarity about intended results. Those running an experiment often become vested in its success, lose objectivity, and cast findings from their tests in the most favorable terms possible. Inviting outsiders—such as investors or customers—to actively participate in designing experiments and reviewing their results can mitigate experiment creep.

WHAT POPPER MISSED

Popper presented a compelling vision of science as endless cycles of conjecture and refutation with fierce competition among theories. Thomas Kuhn, in an influential study of the history of science, describes a reality different from Popper's idealized vision in every important particular.[19] Instead of competing theories, Kuhn finds that scientists rely on a single paradigm—such as Newtonian dynamics or Einstein's theory of relativity—to guide their research. The typical scientist is not the lone genius like Einstein, but rather a card-carrying member of a tightly knit community defined by its adherence to a single paradigm. Most scientists resemble devout members of a religious order bound by their vows to a common doctrine. Instead of seeking anomalies, scientists spend most of their time in head-down mode, plugging away at problems that their paradigm deems worthwhile.

When anomalies arise, scientists typically overlook them, ignore them, or patch existing theory with ad hoc tweaks to accommodate the incongruity. Rather than break with the status quo to formulate bold conjectures, scientists spend their days and years practicing "normal science," extending established knowledge step by incremental step. The history of science, as depicted by Kuhn, consists not of constant revolution but rather of long stretches of normal science within the tight boundaries of the dominant paradigm. Over time, the cumulative pressure of unresolved anomalies grows, and once in a great while it precipitates a crisis where competing theories vie to plug holes in the existing paradigm. After a new paradigm emerges, it grows to dominate the field, and the head-down work of normal science resumes. Revolutions are rare, short-lived, and atypical of how most scientists, in most fields, spend most of their time.

The gap between Popper's vision and the reality described by

Kuhn arises not because practicing scientists fail to achieve a lofty ideal. Rather, Popper's view is flawed because it overlooks the commitments required for scientific inquiry. A scientific paradigm must represent reality, but it must also induce the long-term commitments required to explore that paradigm. Science cannot progress without major investments of time, attention, and cash. Governments, universities, and scientists themselves seek a stable paradigm before committing these resources.

Consider the funding required to make large-scale investments, such as the €5 billion to construct the Large Hadron Collider in Switzerland. Governmental agencies find it much easier to justify an expenditure based on a stable and widely accepted paradigm. Designing experiments for the collider and interpreting the results involve thousands of scientists and engineers from around the world. A shared commitment to the standard model of particle physics provides them with a common language and framework to decide which experiments are worthwhile and to interpret results.

Scientific progress requires collective action sustained over time, and progress is impossible without stable mental maps. Scientists must invest decades of their lives mastering a body of arcane knowledge, honing highly specialized skills, and building a reputation and network within their fields. Few make such commitments unless they believed the paradigm will persist long enough for them to earn a return on their investment. Persevering within a paradigm sometimes allows scientists to resolve stubborn anomalies. The moon's actual perigee (the point in its orbit when it is nearest to earth) was twice that predicted by Newton's theory, a glaring anomaly that stumped scientists. Rather than abandon the model, however, scientists continued to work within the Newtonian paradigm for decades. Their persistence paid off when a French mathematician worked out that past applications of the theory, rather than the theory itself, accounted for the discrepancy, and resolved the anomaly.

Popper saw scientific theories as nets to capture reality, but Kuhn recognized that they play another role as well. Mental maps attract the funds, effort, and attention required to explore the map. Every mental map, from a start-up business plan to a presidential policy agenda, is both a flawed representation of reality and a tool to secure long-term commitments. These two roles work at cross-purposes. To represent a turbulent world, the ideal map is complex enough to encompass a multifaceted reality, fluid enough to adapt as circumstances change, and loosely held enough to be discarded when proven wrong. To secure commitments, however, a map should be simple enough to communicate widely, sufficiently stable to induce long-term commitment, and firmly held enough to inspire confidence. The two roles tug a map in different directions—turbulence calls for constant change, while commitment demands stability.

"The test of a first-rate intelligence," F. Scott Fitzgerald noted, "is the ability to hold two opposed ideas in the mind at the same time and still retain the ability to function."[20] The conflicting roles played by mental maps produce what I call the *map paradox*: in a turbulent world, people must make long-term commitments based on a mental map they know to be flawed. The paradox arises in any situation where progress requires both long-term commitments from many people and adaptation to changing circumstances. In other words, the map paradox arises when grappling with most important issues, including health care reform in the United States, repairing the global financial system, reversing climate change, and negotiating peace in war-torn regions, as well as the personal concerns of running a company or raising a family. There are exceptions, of course—mutual-fund managers face turbulence but can easily reverse their positions.

By and large, however, anything worth doing in a turbulent world requires people to act as if their map is right, know it is wrong, and retain the ability to function.

The map paradox is not a new problem. It has dogged philosophers for millennia. Consider the Skeptics, a school of philosophy in ancient Greece who first articulated the problem of provisional knowledge. The Skeptics distrusted all knowledge and feared seduction by accepted beliefs. Skeptics honed techniques to resist uncritical belief. They raised objections to arguments others accepted blindly. The Greek word *aporia*, often translated as "roadblock" or "impasse," described the objections Skeptics threw in the path of any speaker making an argument. Skeptics reminded interlocutors that "for every argument there is an opposing argument of equal weight."[21] The Skeptic philosopher Sextus Empiricus, for example, would set out the arguments in favor of and against any proposition with equal rigor, regardless of which side he believed. The practice of eliciting arguments on both sides helped check the tendency to accept arguments because they were popular, comforting, or supported by a powerful advocate.

Over the centuries, many rulers, soldiers, and administrators adopted a skeptical stance toward knowledge but faced a practical challenge—how to act decisively in the face of provisional knowledge. Tallying up both sides of an argument often results in a draw, indecision, and inaction. A constant onslaught of objections can bring an argument to a grinding halt. Rigorous skepticism, while intellectually honest, hinders action. To avoid this dilemma, some ancients relegated their skepticism to metaphysical matters, refusing to commit to a view of God, for instance. Faced with the demands of daily life, where they had to commit time, attention, or money, they conformed to established custom and tradition.

Blindly following the crowd in practical affairs, however, eliminates whatever benefits skepticism might bring in practice. The Scottish philosopher David Hume believed dogmatism, an unshakable belief in a doctrine, was unavoidable. To him, people were incapable of reconciling the provisional nature of knowledge with the practical demands of everyday life. If people took seriously the incomplete nature of what they believed, Hume argued, "all discourse, all action would immediately cease, and men remain in a total lethargy, till the necessities of nature, unsatisfied, put an end to their miserable existence."[22] People could not afford to recognize the provisional nature of knowledge, Hume argued, and instead must pretend that their maps were truth. Absent this fiction, they could not function.

Is the map paradox, in the end, unmanageable? Are we destined to choose between skeptical indecision and dogmatic action? Must we continue to lay down horrendous sacrifices at the altar of false theories, like Vienna's communists? Can the extraordinary genius alone manage this tension, leaving the rest of us a choice between two deeply flawed alternatives?

The map paradox cannot be eliminated, but it *can* be successfully managed. Indeed, seizing the upside of turbulence demands it. It is easy to simplify the paradox by ignoring either the reality of provisional knowledge or the necessity of commitment. Scarred by his experience with socialism, Popper considered commitment to any point of view "an outright crime," excluded commitments from his model of science, and avoided binding ties in his professional life.[23] The next chapter will argue that commitments are unavoidable, detail their specific form, and outline how they harden over time.

Nor can people seize the upside of turbulence by ignoring the provisional nature of knowledge. All mental maps are static representations of a shifting situation, simplifications of a complex world made without the benefit of knowledge that will only emerge in the future. They remain always and everywhere provisional, subject to revision or rejection in light of new information. The paradox of the map demands a delicate balance between commitment and revision, stability and flexibility. Striking the balance is difficult, but possible, and chapters 5 through 11 of this book suggest practical steps to help strike this balance.

4.

ACTIVE INERTIA

A year into the recession, demand for vehicles continued to fall, major manufacturers went bust, and a sense of despair spread throughout Detroit. For Harvey Firestone, 1896 was turning out to be a very hard year.[1] Firestone sold horse-drawn carriages in the Detroit branch of the Columbus Buggy Company, which produced high-priced vehicles until the recession forced the firm into receivership and Firestone out of a job. Firestone worked his network of personal contacts to identify another opportunity, and one afternoon he took an acquaintance for a ride in his carriage to discuss possible start-ups. His passenger commented on the smooth ride, which Harvey attributed to the buggy's solid rubber wheels, the only set in Detroit at the time.

After a few hours of discussion, they concluded that rubber tires represented a marked improvement over wooden wheels rimmed by steel, the standard at the time. Firestone's companion recalled a recently closed shop in Chicago that had specialized in pneumatic rubber tires for bicycles. That same night, the two men boarded a train to Chicago, and within a week they had purchased the bankrupt company's equipment and supplies and began fixing rubber tires to buggy wheels. They focused their sales efforts on delivery firms and undertakers, who made frequent journeys with heavy loads. When the economy picked up in 1897, the rubber tire business boomed. The newly inaugurated president, William McKinley, spurred demand when he installed rubber tires on the carriages he brought to the White House.

Although the business boomed, Firestone was forced out of the company by his partners. Firestone, now thirty-one years old, was determined to sell rubber tires, and decided to relocate to Akron, known as America's rubber capital, to start another tire firm. When Firestone arrived, eight existing rubber factories employed one-quarter of Akron's labor force, and the city was known for the tang of molten rubber that hung in the air, and snow blackened by factory smoke. Akron was a boomtown, growing faster than any other city in the United States between 1910 and 1920. The number of residents at times exceeded available beds, forcing tire workers to sleep in shifts.[2] Firestone worked for a few months selling rubber-cushioned horseshoes and solid rubber tires before splitting off to found his own company in 1900.

The rubber tire industry ranked among the world's most turbulent. Tire demand followed the explosive growth in automobile sales. In the first decade of the new century, horseless carriages moved from an expensive hobby to an affordable consumer good after Henry Ford offered the Model T for sale in 1908. In the first twenty-five years of the century, automobile sales grew a thousandfold, increasing tire shipments from a few thousand in 1900 to nearly sixty million twenty-five years later. More than two thousand new companies entered the automobile industry, experimenting with a wide range of power sources (including steam, gasoline, and electricity), designs, and manufacturing processes. The diversity generated widespread uncertainty about which product designs, manufacturing processes, and strategies would ultimately succeed.[3]

Diversity among tire companies mirrored that of automakers. More than five hundred entrepreneurs entered the tire industry, lured by the promise of fame and fortune. The most successful founders, including B. F. Goodrich and Harvey Firestone, became household names, and Akron's tire industry had produced more than a hundred millionaires by 1920. Like the automakers, these companies experimented with a wide range of technologies.[4] In the span of twenty years, the industry passed through three dominant designs for the tires themselves, and two distinct ways to attach them to rims. These product innovations ultimately improved the life span of a tire from five hundred miles in 1900 to twenty thousand miles thirty years later. In the first three decades of the nascent industry, rubber executives contended with technological tumult, patent disputes, the formation and dissolution of industrial trusts, fluctuations in raw material prices (especially for rubber), volatile interest rates, a world war, labor unrest, recessions, and the Great Depression.[5]

Bust followed boom. Overcapacity led to vicious price wars throughout the 1920s and 1930s, when the average price of a tire fell by 80 percent.[6] Competition resembled a limbo contest, with the tire companies bending over backward to cut costs below a price bar that kept slipping lower. The most efficient firms maintained profitability by increasing productivity, including a fivefold increase in the number of tires produced per manufacturing employee.[7] The laggards exited the industry. By 1937, the total number of tire manufacturers had dropped to just over fifty, and the five largest controlled in excess of 80 percent of the domestic tire market. Four of the five leading firms had their headquarters in Akron. Firestone Tire & Rubber survived the shakeout and emerged as the third-largest tire maker in the United States, ranking among the sixty largest American enterprises.

INESCAPABLE COMMITMENTS

The map paradox arises whenever people must make long-term commitments based on an imperfect mental map. In the last chapter we saw that the provisional nature of future knowledge renders all maps imperfect, and in this chapter I will argue that commitments are nevertheless unavoidable. A *commitment*, as I use the word throughout this chapter, refers to any action people take in the present that binds them (or their organization) to a future course of action.[8] Common commitments include official declarations such as President George W. Bush's decision to invade Iraq, signing a contract, investing in specialized resources such as a tire factory, or deepening a relationship.

People crave certainty about the future before making long-term commitments. A newlywed couple shopping for their first house would like to know future real estate prices, interest rates, and their own incomes before taking on a mortgage. Turbulence, however, clouds visibility into the future and can sap the confidence to commit. In 1910, Harvey Firestone had to decide whether to invest the company's available cash in rubber for the next year's production, without a clue about future demand, prices, or raw material costs. "I have never known a time when I was so undecided," Firestone fretted. "It places you in a position where you are afraid to buy and afraid not to buy."[9] Investors who considered equities in 2009 would recognize Firestone's predicament.

In Firestone's position, many executives might be tempted to avoid commitments altogether to keep their options open and avoid making a mistake. Others might resort to tentative commitments to hedge their bets—recall how Royal Caribbean executives sliced their ships in half to extend capacity rather than commission a new ship, as Carnival did. The absence of certainty, however, does not eliminate the need to commit. Even in the most turbulent contexts—a nascent industry, war, or geopolitics—people must make commitments that are consequential and difficult to reverse, for the reasons outlined below.

Commitments can convince others to provide necessary resources. Scientists need government grants to fund research, presidents needs allies' support to fight wars, and entrepreneurs require cash, labor, and technology to build a company. Lacking certainty about the future, the resource owners may dither, reluctant to invest in a risky undertaking. A bold commitment can induce them to commit. Henry Ford hesitated to give Firestone a large share of his business, fearing the start-up could not keep pace with Ford's growing demand for tires. In 1910, Firestone decided to build a new factory, among the largest in the world at the time, to assure Ford that his company could meet the automaker's needs. Firestone agonized over the decision but in the end concluded the massive plant was the only way to convince Ford to give him the business. Skilled rubber workers, to give another example, had their choice of employers in Akron's overheated labor market. To attract and retain crucial workers, Harvey built Firestone Park, a community with hundreds of houses that workers could purchase at below-market rates provided they stayed with the company.

Commitments also maintain focus on critical concerns amidst the myriad distractions that arise in churning markets. The corporate name Firestone Tire & Rubber committed the company to a strategy of supplying tires to the booming automobile market. Other early entrants lacked Firestone's clear focus. Some defined themselves as rubber companies, selling rubber products ranging from rain boots to conveyer belts. Serving a hodgepodge of markets distracted them from the booming automobile market. Other entrants produced myriad automotive components and failed to stay on the frontier of rubber chemistry.

People must also commit to building specialized resources to sustain a competitive advantage against competitors. In business, firms create and sustain value to the extent that they control tangible or intangible resources.[10] To create value, a resource must have three characteristics: First, it must create economic value by cutting costs (think Wal-Mart's logistics) or increasing customers' willingness to pay (think of shelling out $5 for a latte at Starbucks). Second, a resource must be rare—if every car included BMW's technology, the German automaker could command no premium. Finally, it must be difficult for competitors to substitute an alternative resource—Saudi Aramco's oil stockpiles will remain valuable until cars can run on alternative fuels. Valuable, rare, and inimitable resources create sustainable competitive advantage outside business. Superior military technology aids the U.S. armed forces, while LeBron James carries the Cavaliers to the playoffs.

Harvey Firestone invested heavily to create valuable, rare, and inimitable resources. In addition to the state-of-the-art plant, he spent lavishly on advertising—Firestone sponsored the winner of the inaugural Indianapolis 500—to build a brand associated with quality and value. He also built expertise in rubber chemistry, tire design, and manufacturing processes. In an era when few U.S. firms had dedicated research departments, Firestone hired the company's first research chemist in 1908 to build a laboratory. In subsequent decades, the company's engineers and scientists produced a steady series of incremental innovations that cumulatively improved product safety, quality, and durability while chipping away at costs. The gains did not come through any single breakthrough. Rather, the research trajectory doled out its benefits over time.[11]

In terms of building expertise, Harvey Firestone's most important commitment was his initial move to Akron. As the tire industry grew, an ecosystem of supporting institutions cropped up in America's rubber capital, including a college that offered the nation's first rubber chemistry course, technical testing firms, and the leading industry trade journal. The Portage Country Club, founded by two B. F. Goodrich executives, provided the social setting where the founders, managers, researchers, and investors in tire companies congregated to socialize and talk shop.[12] By committing to Akron, Firestone ensured that he and his employees remained in the flow of technical and business information, which helped them stay on the cutting edge of rubber technology. Akron firms accounted for more than 80 percent of the major improvements in tire and rim design and nearly two-thirds of innovation in raw materials and tire components through the early 1930s.[13]

Commitments can yield efficiency as well as expertise. Firestone's bold capacity expansion conferred economies of scale, which he passed on to customers through price reductions while still pocketing some additional profit. Firestone committed to standardized manufacturing processes to maximize efficiency. Before building their new plant, Firestone and his engineers built a tabletop mock-up of the factory and spent hours pulling string through the model factory to simulate alternative flows of materials. By tailoring the plant to a specific manufacturing process, Firestone gained efficiency but limited the company's ability to modify its work flow in the future,

Commitments also fortify confidence. Commitments attract

others, focus effort, build sustainable competitive advantage, and increase efficiency. Taken together, these benefits increase the odds of success, and thereby bolster the confidence to make future commitments. Firestone agonized before building his new plant, but once built, the factory reduced costs and secured a large share of Ford's business, emboldening Firestone to make bigger bets in the future. The virtuous circle linking confidence to commitment, and commitment to success feeds upon itself. Success also reassures outsiders. As long as Firestone continued to make bets and win, Ford renewed its orders, bankers made loans, and workers remained loyal. Commitment and confidence are the critical links in a chain that drives progress.

Repeated cycles of commitment and success build momentum. In his first two decades, Firestone was sued three times for patent infringement, was excluded from a cartel, and faced a recession so bad that creditors unseated management at his two largest competitors. Early failures need not spell ultimate defeat, however, and Firestone made a series of commitments that maintained momentum to overcome these setbacks. After founding his eponymous company, it took Firestone a decade to build the first plant, two decades to perfect the tire, and three decades to emerge as a clear winner. Commitments built the momentum to stay the course.

Commitments do not, of course, guarantee success. Not all investments work out. Recall how Internet start-ups like Flooz.com and Boo.com invested heavily to build brands that never increased customers' willingness to pay. Even if a commitment yields anticipated gains, unforeseen shifts in the external context may cause failure. Firestone could have built his plant, secured the economies of scale, and still gone bankrupt if a recession decreased demand or Ford stumbled. Commitments are necessary but not sufficient for success in a turbulent world.

REINFORCING COMMITMENTS

People often equate commitments with major life choices, such as getting married or choosing a profession, where they make explicit vows after considering consequences and alternatives. Many important commitments, however, look nothing like these once-in-a-lifetime vows. Instead, people stumble into commitments without noticing, let alone evaluating them. The scope of these commitments is not spelled out at the outset but takes shape gradually over time and crystallizes long after the initial steps are taken. A single big bet rarely determines the future. Instead, a densely interwoven tangle of commitments, varying in size and form, initially define the details of a mental map, and then reinforce them.

Most mental maps begin as little more than a hunch. When Firestone committed to sell rubber tires, his plan resembled a nearly blank treasure map: X marked the opportunity, but the chart was otherwise devoid of signposts indicating how to get there. Firestone began pursuing the rubber tire opportunity long before he knew exactly what his commitment entailed in terms of marketing, technology, manufacturing, or customers. People rarely fill the blank space of their mental map through systematic long-term planning. Instead, they respond to immediate opportunities and threats as best they can. When the tire rim cartel excluded Firestone, he innovated around their patent and embarked on an uncharted technological trajectory. He built a plant to secure Ford's business and subsidized housing to retain workers. There was no grand design, but instead a series of workable solutions to unforeseen challenges and opportunities. These ad hoc commitments accumulated over time, filled out Firestone's map with greater granularity, and defined the character of an enterprise. A similar dynamic occurs in any new undertaking—whether a new company, scientific community, or presidential agenda.

Commitments do not cease once the details of a map have stabilized. Subsequent commitments, however, reinforce the emerging status quo rather than define it. Reinforcing commitments are actions that buttress an elaborated map, and they come in all shapes and sizes, ranging from bet-the-company investments implicit in a new plant to small steps such as incremental tire innovations. Despite differences in scale, reinforcing commitments build on the past. They resemble the ruts cut by the wheels of carts passing along a dirt path. The established grooves channel the cart's path, and each passing vehicle deepens the rut.

Reinforcing commitments confer important benefits: they focus attention and concentrate effort on what really matters; they attract employees, customers, and partners who fit well with what the company stands for; they decrease costs (maintaining a current customer, for instance, tends to be much cheaper than landing a new one); they help manage risk (refining an established technology is safer than pioneering a new direction). When extant reinforcing commitments are costly to replicate, they prevent competitors from easily securing the same benefits. Whether baby steps or big leaps, reinforcing commitments enhance speed and reliability along established routes—you can't drive 60 mph on a cart path. Five types of commitments—to frames, resources, processes, relationships, and values—reinforce mental maps with particular force.

Frames focus attention within a narrow segment of a mental map. For companies, the choice of geographic scope, for example, demarcates opportunities they consider from those they ignore. U.S. Steel executives defined their market as North America, thereby discounting opportunities that Mittal considered. Specific metrics to measure success are another important frame. Firestone tracked its share of tires sold to Detroit automakers to a tenth of a percent, celebrating any gain at the expense of competitors. Choice of competitors that matter most—Akron tire makers or Miami-based cruise lines—is another important frame that focuses attention.

FIGURE 4.1 **Reinforcing Commitments**

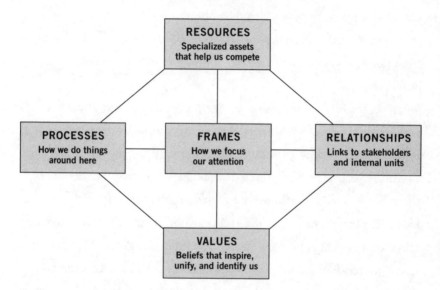

Resources include both hard assets, such as steel factories, and intangible assets, such as Carnival's brand or Firestone's technology. The best resources are not only valuable, rare, and inimitable; they are also aligned with a specific mental map. To ensure distribution in the face of heated competition from Sears Roebuck and other retailers, Firestone increased the number of company-owned retail stores from 9 to 430 in the span of four years. After Harvey died in 1938, his sons, who ran the company for the following four decades, continued to invest in resources to support their father's map. The company integrated backward into a million-acre rubber plantation in Liberia to ensure a secure flow of raw materials at predictable prices.

Processes are the recurrent procedures used to get work done. They include operating procedures, such as logistics or production, and managerial ones, such as decision making and resource allocation. Standardized processes increase efficiency, enable firms to scale, and facilitate coordination among different units. In the 1920s, Firestone's technical team invented "gum-dipping," a manufacturing process that soaked strips of cloth in rubber and then cured them so they assumed a uniform shape. Gum dipping dramatically increased a tire's durability, and the company spread the new process through all of its plants.

Relationships are the associations forged with external individuals and organizations—customers, regulators, suppliers, distributors, and other partners—who provide resources critical for success. Early relationships secure resources and confer credibility. If partners thrive, the relationships contribute to a firm's success. Harvey Firestone befriended Henry Ford, and the ties that bound the two were knotted more tightly when Harvey Firestone's granddaughter, Martha Firestone, married William Clay Ford, Henry's grandson and the largest shareholder in Ford Motors. Sixty years after the Model T, Firestone was still Ford's primary tire supplier, accounting for nearly one-half of Ford's tires.

Values are the shared norms that unite and inspire employees. They are established through both statements and actions. The first people an entrepreneur hires, for example, can leave a lasting impression on a company's culture. Strong values attract employees, fuel their passion, and build strong bonds of loyalty. Harvey Firestone committed to a set of corporate values to bind his company "as a family." In an era of widespread labor strife, Firestone viewed his workers paternalistically. Not only did he draw on the corporate coffers to build subsidized housing, he also introduced an eight-hour workday for all employees and built the Firestone Country Club, open to all employees regardless of rank to provide a setting where employees from all levels could socialize.

FIGURE 4.2 Examples of Reinforcing Commitments

Frames
- Commit to share leadership in core market
- Declare traditional competitor public enemy #1
- Refine existing success metrics

Resources
- Focus R&D expenditure on refining core technology
- Invest in advertising to reinforce existing brand image
- Extend existing brand into closely related markets
- Build specialized facilities to support strategy

Processes
- Codify best practices in process manuals
- Replicate existing processes in new facilities
- Require suppliers to conform to your processes

Relationships
- Invest in technology or capacity to serve existing customers' needs
- Require suppliers and partners to use your information systems
- Integrate backward into components or forward into distribution
- Tighten relationships with partners through joint venture or merger

Values

- Promote people who exemplify core values
- Banish renegades who challenge established culture
- Codify values and distribute to employees

Piling reinforcing commitments one atop another makes it harder to change the underlying map. Fred Smith had the idea for Federal Express while writing an undergraduate term paper about air freight shipping, and translated his map into reality through large investments in brand, trucks, planes, specialized information technology, and a freight handling hub. Rewriting a term paper is much easier than changing a global delivery network underpinned by difficult-to-reverse commitments. The dense interrelationships among established commitments further complicates the difficulty of unpicking one without disrupting others. Eliminating a single route or service for FedEx reverberates through the entire system.

The weight and interconnection among reinforcing commitments is not the only obstacle to modifying a map. Decision makers are also reluctant to admit—to themselves and others—that earlier commitments were wrong.[14] This reluctance to reverse commitments, especially those made with much public fanfare, can lead people to escalate commitment to a flawed map even as evidence piles up that things are getting steadily worse.[15] The United States' escalation in Vietnam is a classic example of escalating commitment. Finally, when mental maps go unchallenged for extended periods of time, they slip into the background of taken-for-granted assumptions that people no longer consciously notice.[16] Maps are most likely to become invisible when they have been held for a long time, have worked well at some point in the past, or are shared by many people.[17]

ACTIVE INERTIA

The hardening of commitments over time locks an organization into a map, which is fine as long as the environment continues to reward progress along the established trajectory. Problems arise, however, when shifts in the external context render the map outmoded or obsolete. After decades of relative stability, the tire industry faced renewed turbulence when French tire maker Michelin introduced the world's first steel-belted radial. The new tire lasted twice as long as the old design, reduced blowouts, rode smoother, and increased fuel economy. Rolling on the strength of its new product, Michelin built twenty-six radial tire factories in Europe between 1960 and 1972, most outside France, and by the early 1970s Michelin led the European tire industry in market share. Michelin's successful assault forced the European tire industry to restructure itself as struggling competitors merged and closed plants. Firestone watched Michelin pummel its rivals from ringside seats, since Firestone had competed in Europe since the 1920s.[18]

The action moved closer to Akron in the late 1960s, when Michelin began selling its radial tires through Sears, opened a $100 million radial tire plant in North America, and convinced Ford to include the Michelin radial as standard equipment on the 1971 Lincoln Continental. Shifting market conditions provided both an opportunity and a threat for Firestone. The company could steal a march by introducing and promoting its own version of the new technology in North America before its rivals. By waiting too long, however, Firestone risked the same fate that befell European tire manufacturers who failed to prevent Michelin's aggressive drive to dominate the market.

Firestone neither seized the opportunity nor mitigated the threat. Instead, the company responded by doing more of what had worked in the past. Executives disparaged the "foreign" technology as unsuitable to American cars and inferior to products designed in Akron. Firestone produced an incremental improvement to its existing tire design that required only minor changes to its production process.[19] This modified tire, known as the belted bias, gained initial market share until customers realized it offered no real benefits and switched to radials. In 1972, Ford announced its intention to place radials on all its models over the following few years, and General Motors made a similar announcement a few months later. Firestone managers responded to Ford's request and approved investments to ramp up radial tire production and introduce the Firestone 500 Steel Belt brand radial tire. To speed the transition, the company manufactured the new tires using a slight variation on its existing production process.[20] Firestone managers failed to close the existing plants rendered obsolete by their investment in the new technology.

Firestone fell prey to *active inertia*, the tendency of established organizations to respond to changes by accelerating activities that succeeded in the past. As turbulent markets throw out new opportunities and threats, organizations trapped in active inertia do more of what worked in the past—a little faster, perhaps, or tweaked at the margin, but the same old same old. With radials on the horizon, Firestone kicked its new product development process into overdrive, extending its established product. When that failed to stave off the radial, the company employed existing processes to make the new tire, and failed to close its redundant plants.

Organizations trapped in active inertia resemble a car with its back wheels stuck in a rut. Managers see market shifts, step on the gas, and race the engine in an increasingly frantic effort to pull themselves out of the rut. Instead of digging themselves out, however, they only dig themselves deeper. The ruts that channel their behavior are the very commitments—now numerous, hardened, and deeply intertwined—that underpinned their historical success. When stale commitments meet turbulent markets, the result is often active inertia. Figure 4.3 lists some common warning signs that commitments have hardened, putting an organization at risk for active inertia. Existing commitments lock firms into active inertia in several ways, described below.

Frames that once focused attention on what really mattered become blinders curtailing the peripheral vision required to spot unfamiliar opportunities and threats. In the late 1960s, the Firestone family still owned approximately one-quarter of the firm, and three of the founder's five sons sat on the board. All of Firestone's top managers had spent their entire career with the company, two-thirds were Akron born and bred, and one-third had followed in their parents' footsteps as Firestone employees. Steeped in the company's traditional map, the team dismissed competitors based outside Akron, remained confident in proven technology, and relied on their longstanding relationship with Ford to weather the storm.

Firestone was neither the first company nor the last to be caught in active inertia as its frames hardened into blinders. When Xerox executives surveyed the competitive market in the 1970s, they saw IBM and Kodak as the enemy, their forty thousand sales and service representatives as crack troops, and patented technology as an insurmountable barrier to entry. Xerox's frames provided the focus to defend its position from repeated attempts by IBM and Kodak to attack its core market. These frames also blinded Xerox to opportunities arising from new technologies, and the threats posed by guerrilla warriors such as Canon and Ricoh, which sold high quality compact copiers to small firms, circumventing the sales force and technology that protected Xerox in large companies. When frames harden into blinders, executives, like generals, tend to fight the last war.

FIGURE 4.3: **Warning Signals of Active Inertia**

- **Cover curse.** Your CEO appears on the cover of a major business magazine. Of the first seven *Forbes* companies of the year, none subsequently outperformed the stock market, and three of the CEOs who graced the cover were fired. Praise from the press reinforces management's attachment to their commitments and may breed hubris.

- **Guru jinx.** Management gurus single out your company as outstanding. The seminal management best seller *In Search of Excellence* identified a series of companies including Atari, Wang, and Data General, which subsequently stumbled. Public praise can reinforce management's confidence in their existing commitments. No organization is immune to active inertia, and successful companies mentioned in this book, including Mittal and Carnival, will stumble unless they too adjust their commitments as circumstances change.

- **CEO writes a book.** Executives write a book articulating the secret of their success, and thereby link themselves publicly to past commitments. Backing away from a conspicuous and explicit statement of commitments is difficult. Publishing a book after retirement, as Jack Welch and Lou Gerstner did, is safe.

- **Edifice complex.** Building a grand corporate headquarters often signals that executives have declared victory and wish to commemorate their triumph. Executives who build grand monuments to their success are rarely in the frame of mind to question the commitments that got them there. The most dangerous buildings contain indoor waterfalls, feature heliports, or win architectural awards.

- **Name a stadium.** Rather than building new monuments, companies sometimes place their names on professional sports venues, including Compaq, Ericsson, Conseco, and Enron, not to mention PSINet, CMGI, Network Associates, and several airlines, including United, Continental, American, Air Canada, America West, and Emirates.

- **Competitors share the same zip code.** Entire communities of similar companies can fall prey to active inertia. Examples include Akron's tire companies, automakers in Detroit, steel producers in Pittsburgh, minicomputer firms along Boston's Route 128, Korean conglomerates headquartered in Seoul, and investment banks on Wall Street. Densely interwoven professional and personal networks tend to reinforce existing commitments and limit fresh information and new ideas.

- **Top executives look like clones.** A homogenous group of top executives often selects and promotes other executives based on their adherence to existing commitments. They also lack the diversity to envision alternatives.

Shifts in the market can devalue once valuable resources and leave them hanging like millstones around a firm's neck. Firestone's initial delay in building new radial plants was based in part on a rational desire to protect its existing asset base. The investment in radial production cut the total number of plants needed in half, because radials lasted twice as long as the tires they replaced. The new factories, moreover, required massive capital expenditures for uncertain returns. Transatlantic cruise lines faced the problem of "millstone" resources. When flights between Europe and America undercut their business, a few established lines tentatively explored Caribbean cruises. Their ships, however, were designed for a rough Atlantic cross-ing and therefore lacked the exposed deck space required for cruises in tropical climates. The strict separation into first, second, and "steerage" classes ran counter to the shared experience sought by Caribbean cruisers.

Well-oiled processes can lapse into mindless routines, which people follow because they are familiar, not because they are opti-mal. Firestone responded to unprecedented events with traditional processes. The company kicked their established product develop-ment process into overdrive to extend the existing tire design. When that didn't stop radials, Firestone managers employed existing pro-duction routines to make the Firestone 500. McDonald's is another case where long-established routines hindered a company from re-sponding effectively to markets shifts. In the early 1990s, McDon-ald's had a 750-page operating manual specifying every aspect of the business. For decades, corporate leaders standardized processes to ensure uniform results among franchisees. As consumer preferences shifted to healthier foods and new entrants heightened competition in the 1990s, McDonald's was trapped by its old routines. The com-pany's single-minded focus on refining its mass-production processes stifled innovation that might have bubbled up if franchisees had en-joyed more leeway to experiment with alternative procedures.

Relationships become shackles that prevent a firm from adjust-ing to shifts in a turbulent market. Harvey Firestone's personal friendship with Henry Ford lifted his tire company to industry leader-ship. But when circumstances shifted, that relationship hindered Firestone's freedom to respond. Firestone depended on Ford for vol-ume to keep its plants full and therefore felt compelled to produce radials when its largest customer demanded them, even though Ford refused to pay higher prices to help offset the required capital investment. Firestone executives maintained a cozy oligopoly with other Akron tire makers. Firestone executives often golfed in a foursome with their counterparts at General, B.F. Goodrich, and Goodyear, joking that Uniroyal could never relocate to Akron because it's awkward to golf in a fivesome. Deep relationships with competitors hindered Firestone executives from breaking rank and marketing radials ahead of the other U.S. tire makers.

In the late 1990s, Compaq Computer was ensnared by its existing relationships. The company had risen to leadership in the personal computer industry through tight relationships with distributors, which resold Compaq's PCs. Dell then began selling computers directly to consumers, first by telephone, and later over the Internet. Compaq executives recognized consumers' growing preference to shop online and the cost advantages of Dell's model. Moving to a direct model, however, would alienate the distribution partners responsible for Compaq's rise to industry leadership, and still accounted for the vast majority of their sales and profits. The handshakes that once enabled success now acted as handcuffs hindering Compaq's response.

Values ossify into stone-cold dogmas that channel behavior into existing ruts. Replacing the old tires with radials that lasted twice as long meant U.S. tire manufacturers would need to close obsolete factories. American tire makers ultimately closed twenty-nine of the fifty-seven domestic plants making bias tires in 1972. Although Firestone accounted for nearly one-quarter of domestic production, the firm closed far fewer than its share. Firestone's cumulative pretax loss from delaying necessary plant closure exceeded $300 million, twice the magnitude of the Firestone 500 write-off.[21] Top executives could not reconcile Firestone's "family values" with layoffs. When addressing investors, Firestone's CEO repeatedly referred to employees and communities as part of the "worldwide Firestone family" and requested shareholders' patience while management tried to increase profits without harming employees or communities. Although "family values" are understandable and even admirable, dogmatic adherence to them can prevent executives from making difficult changes.

The British fashion house Laura Ashley provides another example of hardened dogmas. Laura Ashley founded the company that bore her name to protect the traditional British values that she saw as under siege during the 1960s. She created a series of frilly frocks that embodied the conservative values and modesty she held dear. These clothes, and the values they exemplified, appealed to a large number of women around the world—many bought Laura Ashley clothes, and a few signed up as franchisees. As more women entered the workforce, however, demand for Laura Ashley's floral dresses dropped. The company struggled to adapt its hardened values to the new realities, and it now struggles on in a weakened form.

The costs of active inertia proved high for Firestone. By 1979, the company's financial condition had grown acute, and it faced bankruptcy. More than seven hundred irate investors crowded into the company's 1979 stockholders' meeting, including one dissident investor who proposed firing top management, liquidating the company, and distributing the proceeds to owners. Within a year, the CEO retired at age fifty-seven for "personal reasons" and was replaced with an outsider, who saved the company from bankruptcy without restoring it to competitive health. Japanese tire maker Bridgestone subsequently bought Firestone.

When companies stumble in turbulent markets, their leaders are often accused of failing to see the changes coming. That is almost never the case, as the Firestone case illustrates. Michelin's entry and the possible consequences were undeniable after the French tire maker routed its European rivals, opened an American plant, and sold radial tires through Sears. Firestone executives had ample evidence that their existing map no longer corresponded to changed market realities. A series of events surprised Firestone executives, including Ford's decision to mount radials on the Lincoln Continental, Detroit's abrupt switch, and failure of the belted bias tire to fend off the radial. These events showed up nowhere on their well-creased map, and indicated that something was amiss.

Firestone executives were also surprised by problems when the Firestone 500 tires experienced blowouts.[22] In 1978, the company agreed to a voluntary recall of 8.7 million Firestone 500 tires at a cost of $150 million after taxes, the largest consumer recall in U.S. history.[23] Firestone top executives also lost the ability to anticipate future earnings.

The gray bars in figure 4.4 plot the profits Firestone executives budget a year earlier, while the black bars note the actual profitability. In the first few years of the decade, the management team forecast profitability with better than 90 percent accuracy. In later years, the gaps between their forecasts and actual results widened. Their long-established map no longer provided a reliable guide to a more turbulent market.

Firestone's decline was understandable but far from inevitable. Crosstown rival Goodyear was led through the 1970s by a CEO who spent his entire career with the company, but nearly all of it in international operations. Having lived through the European experience firsthand, he revised Goodyear's map to incorporate radial technology. B. F. Goodrich brought in a CEO from outside the industry who quickly concluded that radials were bad for the tire

FIGURE 4.4 **Firestone After-Tax Profit: Budgeted (Shaded) and Actual ($ Million), 1971–1979**

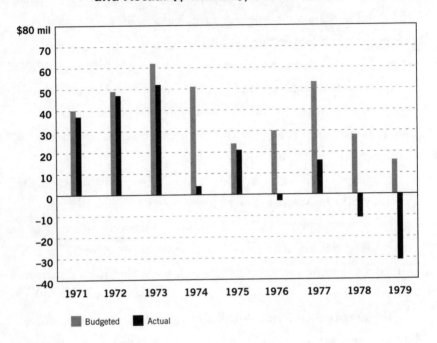

business. B. F. Goodrich limited investments in the tire division, redeployed resources into more promising business units, and ultimately divested the tire division. The first step, in both of these cases, was management's willingness to acknowledge that their map no longer represented the terrain and to explore the discrepancy in greater depth, the subject of the next chapter.

5.

MIND THE GAP

Forty members of the Black Rebel Motorcycle Club—all clad in identical black leather jackets emblazoned with a skull over crossed pistons—maintained a tight formation as they rode their British-made Triumph 650s into a small California town. Sherriff Harry Bleeker prepared for trouble, while his brother Frank, who owned the town's bar, prepared for business and put more beer on ice. Both men were right. Within the span of a few hours, Johnny Strabler, the taciturn leader of the Black Rebels, organized a drag race down the town's main road, hit on the sheriff's daughter, and picked a fight with Chino, the leader of the Beatles, a rival club whose members rode Harley-Davidsons.

The fight escalated when a local, frustrated by the sheriff's hesitation to intervene, drove his car into the crowd of bikers. The bikers dragged him out of the car, which they flipped over. At that point, Sheriff Bleeker intervened and arrested Chino, setting in motion a chain of events in which the Beatles cut the town's phone lines, the

Black Rebels trashed a local beauty parlor, and a crowd of local vigilantes seized a biker. The day culminated in a violent showdown between the bikers and the townspeople, in which one local resident hurled a tire iron into the spokes of a passing Triumph, which skidded out of control and killed an elderly bystander. Shortly after the death, the county sheriff arrived with a phalanx of police cars to restore order.

The Black Rebels and the Beatles fought not on the streets of a small California town, but in the 1953 film *The Wild One*, starring Marlon Brando as Johnny Strabler and Lee Marvin as Chino. Loosely based on a 1951 incident, the film exaggerated a Fourth of July clash between bikers and the residents of Hollister, California, a conflict that was in fact free from violence.[1] Despite its inaccuracies, *The Wild One* reinforced Americans' stereotypes of motorcycles in the 1950s as big, dirty, and dangerous—an apt description of their riders, in the eyes of many. Beneath the stereotype lay an element of truth. Most of the motorcycles sold the late 1950s were large, with engines that displaced at least 500 cc of air and fuel, and were used for leisure rather than basic transportation. In the late 1950s, British producers, including Triumph, Villiers, and Norton, dominated the motorcycle market with their outsized bikes.

Against this backdrop, Honda Motor—the established leader in the Japanese motorcycle market—entered the U.S. market for the first time in the summer of 1959.[2] Within fifteen years, Honda led the industry, accounting for 43 percent of all motorcycles sold in 1974. Its market share ranged from just under one-third in larger motorcycles to over 60 percent in smaller machines. Honda's rapid ascent paved the way for Japanese competitors Yamaha, Kawasaki, and Suzuki to enter. By the mid-1970s, these four Japanese producers accounted for nearly nine of every ten motorcycles sold in the

United States. The rapid ascent of Honda triggered a shakeout among incumbent motorcycle makers, with British producers, including BSA, Excelsior, Greeves, Francis-Barnett, Norton, Panther, Royal Enfield, and Velocette, all hard hit.

MAPS AND GAPS

In an effort to salvage what remained of the English motorcycle industry, the British secretary of state for industry commissioned a consulting group to analyze Honda's rise. In 1975 the Boston Consulting Group presented a report that suggested Honda executives had drafted a long-term strategy to guide their U.S. market entry and then followed their mental map closely in the decade that followed. Honda conducted thorough market research, segmented the U.S. market, and identified an unfilled demand for small motorcycles, according to the report.[3] To fill that demand, Honda crafted a systematic plan to win market share through low prices, aggressive marketing, and a novel distribution network. By increasing volume, the company drove down production costs, allowing further price reductions and market share gains. Honda implemented its strategy methodically, starting in California and advancing eastward over time. A Harvard Business School case study based on the report extolled Honda as a model of long-term planning.

Honda managers did follow a mental map when they entered the U.S. market, but it was the wrong map. When Kihachiro Kawashima, a thirty-nine-year-old Honda employee, relocated to Los Angeles in June 1959 to establish American Honda Motor Company, he drew on his previous experience to sketch a road map to navigate the U.S. market.[4] Kawashima, the former head of sales for Honda Motor in Japan, knew that Toyota's Toyopet Crown subcompact had bombed when introduced into the U.S. market a few years earlier. Kawashima concluded that small bikes, like Toyota's small car, stood no chance in the U.S. market, although both were popular in Japan. Honda's biggest bikes had the best chance of cracking the *Wild One* market. The Honda team decided to challenge European producers in the large-engine categories, target macho bikers, and sell through the existing distribution channels.

Honda executives started with a flawed map, but they also noticed where it diverged from reality and modified it along the way. They spotted the flaws in their map by exploring anomalies, or surprising outcomes that deviate from predictions. Common anomalies include initiatives that should work but don't, initiatives that shouldn't work but do, a surprising connection among unrelated events, an inexplicable competitive move, demand for a product never expected to sell, or events deemed unlikely or impossible. Such incongruities highlight discrepancies between a mental map and the underlying terrain. Sometimes discrepancies signal a shift that renders an existing map outmoded—recall the inability of Firestone managers to predict profitability. Other times they demonstrate that the map was wrong to begin with, as is often the case with start-up business plans. Either way, anomalies point out where a map is wrong.

Two anomalies showed the flaws in Honda's map. Despite a concerted effort, the company managed to sell fewer than sixty of its large bikes each month, far short of their monthly sales goal of one thousand units. What should have sold didn't. The team continued to promote the larger bikes and managed to peddle a few more units until April 1960, when the larger models began to leak oil, overheat, and seize up. Honda recalled the defective large bikes and sent them back to Japan, where engineers worked around the clock to simulate the failure and repair it. Without larger bikes to sell, Kawashima was forced to deviate from his map and push the low-priced Honda 50.

Surprisingly, the small model flew out the door, and in less than a year it exceeded Honda's aggressive sales targets. What shouldn't have sold did.

People rarely discover anomalies through deliberate search. Most stumble upon them.[5] Entrepreneurs, for example, often spot opportunities when they notice an unexpected gap between an industry map and shifting terrain. Professor Amar Bhidé surveyed the founders whose start-ups made the Inc. 500 list of fast-growing companies, and found that only 4 percent of entrepreneurs had identified a gap in the market through a process of deliberate search. Another 71 percent encountered them in their previous jobs, while a further 20 percent discovered them through serendipity—building a hobby into a business, for example, or developing a family member's idea. One entrepreneur noticed an opportunity while honeymooning in Italy (the study did not report how long the marriage lasted).[6] Another study analyzed entrepreneurs who adopted a technology for printing in three dimensions, for applications ranging from architectural models to artificial bones.[7] None of the entrepreneurs sought out the novel technology, but rather stumbled upon it unexpectedly.

Anomalies are easy to miss. They initially emerge as weak signals that whisper rather than shout. Long before the large bikes broke down, the Honda team attracted interest as they scooted around Los Angeles on their Honda 50s. They wrote off the attention as mere curiosity rather than seeing it as a clue about an untapped market for a nonthreatening motorcycle. When a Sears buyer inquired about distributing the small bikes, Honda managers dismissed the call because Sears was not a traditional motorcycle dealer. Similarly, major steel companies underestimated Mittal for decades because the business started in Indonesia, not a traditional breeding ground for industrial giants.

The human mind is hardwired to reinforce existing maps, even in the face of disconfirming evidence. Psychologists have documented a depressingly long list of cognitive biases that distort how people process new information and prevent them from noticing when established mental models break down. "Confirmation bias" refers to our tendency to notice data that confirms existing assumptions while ignoring or discrediting information that challenges our mental map.[8] The British physicist William Thomson, better known as Lord Kelvin, initially dismissed the discovery of X-rays as a hoax because the new energy source violated his deeply held assumptions about how the world should work.[9]

Despite these obstacles to spotting anomalies, there are steps that help people notice gaps they are not looking for, even when the clues are subtle and the mind resistant. They can recognize common anomalies, avoid practices that obstruct recognition, and actively surface incongruities by plunging into the action.

COMMON ANOMALIES

Anomalies are easy to miss, but familiarity with common incongruities increases the odds of noticing one. Not all anomalies point to an opportunity, but many do. Some recurrent anomalies are listed below.

This shouldn't sell (but it does). One of the most welcome anomalies occurs when a product or service that shouldn't sell, such as the Honda 50, exceeds expectations. Unexpected success points to unmet demand outside the boundaries of an established map. Companies should jump on unexpected success and double down, but business history is littered with examples of companies that stumbled upon an unexpected success and ignored it.[10] A few years ago, a London shopkeeper began selling American donuts, which were among his best-selling and most profitable items. A few months later, he eliminated the donuts. The reason? They sold out so fast that later commuters passing through a nearby underground station complained when they couldn't get one.

There should be a product here (but there isn't). As accessories editor for *Mademoiselle* magazine, Kate Brosnahan spotted a gap in the market.[11] "I knew there was something missing in the market for handbags," she later noted. "At the time there was only a very serious bag, the working woman bag with absolutely no style, or the outrageously expensive designer bag like Hermès or Gucci. I thought there must be something in between."[12] In 1992, Brosnahan quit her job and with her partner, Andy Spade, founded Kate Spade, which filled the breach with fabric handbags combining functionality and fashion. The bags were a hit with women between the ages of twenty-five and forty-five, particularly after celebrities such as Gwyneth Paltrow and Julia Roberts bought them.

This shouldn't be so bad, expensive, time-consuming, or annoying (but it is). Customer pain is a reliable indicator of a potential opportunity, as people will typically pay to alleviate it. Reed Hastings, for example, founded Netflix after receiving a $40 late fee for a rented videocassette he misplaced; Charles Schwab created his eponymous low-cost brokerage because he was fed up with being ripped off by brokers; Scott Cook got the idea for Quicken after watching his wife's frustration as she tracked their finances by hand.

This resource shouldn't be so cheap (but it is). Opportunities for arbitrage appear when a resource is priced below its value in an alternative deployment. The simplest case occurs when an alert entrepreneur observes an underpriced asset, buys it, and then resells it at a profit. Some European real estate investors, for instance, buy vacation properties in cities immediately after a low-cost airline such as easyJet or Ryan Air announces its intention to fly there, anticipating the property will increase in value with the new air link. Other times the entrepreneur or manager must create a new business model to fully utilize the asset. The founders of Infosys, India's pioneering provider of outsourced information technology services, deployed Indian engineers to serve multinational clients, allowing the company to earn good profits on the spread between what they charged clients and what they paid their engineers.

This must be good for something (but we're not using it). In some cases, people stumble upon a promising resource or technology without knowing the best use for it, which prompts a search for a problem to solve. While working on medical devices at Corning Corporation, Dr. Hira Thapliyal had the idea to use radio-frequency energy to dissolve fatty deposits that clogged arteries, thereby clearing a path for a catheter.[13] He founded a company to commercialize the technology but soon discovered that the total market was too small to support his firm. Undeterred by the setback, he explored alternative uses for the technology, and ultimately identified the orthopedics market, with more than two million arthroscopic surgeries per year. Thapliyal's low-temperature process for dissolving damaged cartilage minimized damage to surrounding tissue, and he founded a new company, ArthroCare, to pursue the opportunity.

This should be everywhere (but it isn't). Sometimes people stumble upon an attractive business model that has failed to spread widely despite its benefits. At the age of fifty-two, Ray Kroc invested his life savings and took out a mortgage on his home to acquire the exclusive rights to sell a five-headed milk shake maker, and was surprised when a small hamburger stand by the name of McDonald's placed a large order for his Multimixers. When Kroc visited the restaurant, he was astounded to see the volume of food McDonald's assembly line approach to flipping burgers could produce. Kroc convinced the

McDonald brothers to franchise their concept outside California. Kroc did not invent the McDonald's approach to fast food, but he recognized a good thing when he saw it. He scaled quickly, and within three years his sales surpassed one million burgers, giving him the confidence to buy the business from the McDonalds. Howard Schultz didn't start the first Starbucks, but he glimpsed its potential and rolled the model out worldwide.

Customers shouldn't use our product this way (but they do). Chinese appliance maker Haier uses its extensive distribution and service network throughout China to gather data on how customers actually use their products. Haier repairman, for example, discovered that customers in one rural province used their washing machines not only to launder clothes but to clean vegetables as well. The repairmen relayed this information to the product manager, who spotted an opportunity. She had company engineers install wider drain pipes and coarser filters that wouldn't clog with vegetable peels, modifications that allowed the washing machine to clean cabbage as well as shirts. Haier then affixed large stickers emblazoned with pictures of local produce dancing with clothing on the modified washers. The stickers included instructions on how to wash vegetables safely using the machine. This innovation (along with others, including a washing machine that could also make goat's-milk cheese) helped Haier win market share in China's rural provinces while avoiding the cutthroat price wars that plagued the country's appliance industry.

Customers shouldn't care about this (but they do). In 1987, Qinghou Zong was selling school supplies from a bicycle-drawn cart in Hangzhou when he noticed a striking anomaly.[14] Nearly a decade into China's economic reforms, wealthy parents could shop at well-stocked grocery stores but still worried that their children were malnourished. Zong had lived through famine during China's lean years and could not believe that rich parents would worry about food. After digging further, Zong discovered that Beijing's one-child-per-family policy had produced a generation of "little emperors," whose parents and grandparents indulged their every whim. Spoiled rotten, these kids sated themselves on junk food. Zong spotted a gap in the market to sell nutritional supplements that would stimulate children's appetites, provide vitamins and minerals, and assuage parental anxiety. More than three hundred supplements filled the shelves of Chinese stores, but they all targeted adults and promised to boost vitality and sexual potency. By exploring the anomaly, Zong was able to see where the prevailing map in the supplement industry—selling herbal Viagra to adults—ignored a potentially lucrative segment.

This could work in our industry (but we don't do it). When he died on July 7, 2006, at the age of eighty-seven, Dr. Govindappa Venkataswamy (known as Dr. V.) was credited with saving more than one million Indians from blindness.[15] In 1976, at fifty-eight, Dr V. retired from his ophthalmology practice and opened an eleven-bed clinic in Madurai, India, with two other ophthalmologists. Dedicated to eradicating blindness in India, his clinic grew in the following thirty years to a network of five hospitals. Aravind Clinic treated anyone, asking payment from those who could afford it while providing the same quality service free of charge to the two-thirds of patients who could not. Despite giving away their services to the majority of patients, Aravind bankrolled nearly all of its operations and expansion from its own funds. Despite his success, Dr. V. was frustrated that existing procedures could not clear India's backlog of twenty million blind. The aha moment came for Dr V. while passing a McDonald's during a visit to the United States. Amazed that McDonald's could serve millions of hamburgers daily at low cost and with uniform quality, he wanted to learn whether a standardized approach could be used to remove cataracts, the leading cause of blindness in India. After visiting Hamburger University in Oak Brook, Illinois, Dr. V. refined a model of screening, preparing, and operating on patients that allowed his staff to conduct nearly ten times as many operations per year compared to doctors in the state-owned hospitals.

We should have this at home (but we don't). Sometimes people stumble upon a successful business model abroad and cannot believe it does not exist in their home country. In 1992, Michael Fogelberg, a Swede studying business at Seattle University, wanted to store his belongings while returning to Europe for a year, but found that all the local self-storage facilities were full.[16] Fogelberg researched the self-storage industry for a class paper and discovered an attractive business model characterized by high rents, low turnover, and negligible operating costs. Once he understood the economics of the business, Fogelberg was shocked to learn self-storage was virtually nonexistent in continental Europe, despite a population comparable to the United States and smaller houses that should have created greater demand for convenient off-site storage. Fogelberg convinced his father to fund the opportunity and eventually paired with Shurgard, an established North American self-storage firm, to create a European business.

They shouldn't be making so much money (but they are). Established competitors are often surprised when nonconventional rivals make more money than they should. For decades, Goldman Sachs partners had avoided investment management, which they believed generated lower fees than trading and investment banking.[17] When Donaldson, Lufkin & Jenrette published its financial performance as part of a 1970 stock offering, Goldman partners were startled to discover the stability and scale of their rival's asset management business.

Shortly thereafter, Goldman expanded into managing corporate pension funds and aggressively built their asset management business.

ANOMALY PITFALLS

Anomalies are easy to miss under the best of circumstances. Certain traits and practices blind people to incongruities altogether. Forewarned is forearmed. Below is a list of some common pitfalls to avoid.

The arrogance of expertise. Experts in any field—science, medicine, law, education, government, or journalism—devote years to mastering the mental map that defines their field. Professionals reinforce established habits of thought by associating with like-minded colleagues. Over time, experts grow more secure that their reputation is deserved and more confident that their interpretation is correct.[18] Anomalies challenge more than an expert's assessment of a particular situation; they threaten to undermine the knowledge that underpins their status, legitimacy, and identity. Narrow expertise inevitably excludes important facts while raising the costs of admitting that the expert's mental model is flawed.

To spot anomalies, experts must recognize not only the value of their knowledge but also its limitations. Dr. Kevin Stone, a prominent San Francisco orthopedic surgeon, was surprised to learn that several of his patients took glucosamine in place of the ibuprofen Stone had prescribed for joint pain.[19] Many doctors might have ignored the incongruity, dismissed glucosamine as a fad, or scolded patients for disregarding their sage advice. Stone, however, was humble enough to recognize he might be missing something. He learned that glucosamine was the leading nutritional supplement in Europe, where clinical research supported its efficacy. Veterinarians, he discovered, swore by it, and their patients fell for neither fads nor placebos. Based on his research, Stone founded Joint Juice, a company that produces glucosamine in an easy-to-ingest liquid.

The weakness of strong ties. Academics who study social networks use the term *strong tie* to describes links between people—such as long-term colleagues and family members—characterized by frequent interaction, trust, and intimacy.[20] Strong ties bind the members of tightly knit communities together, and overlaps among these relationships weave a tight network where everyone knows everyone else. Recall how Firestone executives belonged to the corporate family, nestled inside the Akron tire community, and embedded within the ecosystem that supplied components to Detroit. Strong ties breed cohesion and trust, and help members mobilize resources. Unfortunately, the same information tends to circulate throughout these densely interwoven networks, like cabin air recycled during a flight. A dense tangle of tight ties can keep out unexpected data that might jar expectations and signal an opportunity or a threat.

While strong ties bind a community together, weak ties connect it to the outside world. Weak ties, such as casual acquaintances, distant relations, or people you follow on Twitter, often see the world differently and introduce fresh pieces of information that might clash with an existing mental map. Actively cultivating weak ties increases exposure to new information, thereby boosting the odds of surfacing an anomaly. One study found that entrepreneurs deliberately exposed themselves to different sources of information—for example, by striking up conversations on trains or maintaining a diverse range of acquaintances—to increase the odds of stumbling upon an interesting opportunity.[21] Consider the Indian information technology firm Infosys, which could have made a comfortable living serving undemanding local firms. Instead, Infosys executives sought out the most sophisticated global customers, including

General Electric and Nordstrom. These customers made "unreasonable" demands that exposed gaps between the company's traditional mental map and the needs of leading corporations worldwide.

The insulation of power. The world may be flat, but most organizations are not. Large corporations, banks, government agencies, and military services are organized as hierarchies, where information flows up, orders flow down, and power concentrates at the top. The folks at the bottom of the pyramid—the frontline troops, employees serving customers every day—are first to see where an existing mental map clashes with the facts on the ground. In theory, these anomalies should percolate up the organization to the powers that be. In practice, however, many leaders surround themselves with an inner circle that protects the boss from anything he or she doesn't want to hear, especially signs that the chosen strategy may not be working. Consider Dick Fuld, the former CEO of Lehman Brothers, who presided over the largest bankruptcy in history. Fuld rarely visited the trading floors to collect firsthand information on market shifts and surrounded himself with lieutenants who discouraged dissent and excoriated anyone who bore bad news.[22]

Contrast Fuld with Andy Grove, the former Intel CEO, who recognized that the first signals of change emerge far from the boardroom. "Snow," as Grove put it, "melts at the periphery."[23] Grove preached a healthy paranoia about the limitations of Intel's business model. To minimize the odds of being caught off guard, he actively sought the opinion of frontline employees, dissatisfied customers, journalists, and investors who could point out potential flaws in the company's mental map.

The seduction of routine. "Routine," according to the English philosopher Alfred North Whitehead, "is the god of every social system."[24] Standardizing an ad hoc process—from cooking hamburgers at McDonald's to assembling cars at Toyota—increases efficiency, reduces waste, and paves the way for continuous improvement. During the past sixty years, a series of process management tools, including total quality management and lean manufacturing, have spread rapidly. These tools all aim to identify defects, such as burnt Big Macs or defective radios in a Camry. Six Sigma, a process management tool developed by Motorola and used by nearly half of all large corporations, attempts to drive the frequency of defects below four per million possible occasions for error.[25] Six Sigma and similar techniques make perfect sense for improving high-volume activities such as fast-food preparation and manufacturing, where deviations annoy customers.

Some organizations have extended Six Sigma outside the factory and made it a core tenet of their overall management philosophy. Striving for zero defects in all activities is dangerous, however, because it can discourage experimentation and hamper learning. More subtly, it dulls sensitivity to anomalies. Process management instills the habit of viewing all anomalies as defects to be eliminated rather than clues to be explored. Process management has its place—typically the factory or the back office—but excessive devotion to routinization devalues the incongruities and serendipity that often signal opportunities. Motorola pioneered Six Sigma but still missed golden opportunities that Nokia and Samsung seized. An excellent study by Professors Mary Benner and Mike Tushman found that a heavy commitment to process management decreased a firm's ability to seize new opportunities.[26] Managers are beginning to realize the limitations of process management tools. A recent study by the management consulting firm Bain & Company found that dissatisfaction with Six Sigma was growing and many companies were abandoning the tool.[27]

GET WRONG FAST

Few institutions in the world face greater turbulence than the U.S. Marine Corps. As America's force-in-readiness, the Marines' missions include not only combat but also evacuations, humanitarian assistance, peacekeeping, and counterterrorism in some of the most unsettled spots on earth. The end of the Cold War made the world more, not less, turbulent for the Marines, which deployed every five weeks on average during the 1990s, a threefold increase in deployment frequency.[28] In the late 1980s, Marine commandant Albert Gray initiated a fundamental rethinking of Corps doctrine to accommodate new realities. The resulting document, entitled *Warfighting*, recognized that no plan survives contact with turbulence. "In the heat of battle," according to *Warfighting*, "plans will go awry, instructions and information will be unclear and misinterpreted, communications will fail, and mistakes and unforeseen events will be commonplace. It is precisely this natural disorder which creates the conditions ripe for exploitation by an opportunistic will."[29] To seize opportunities born of disorder, Marines identify flaws in their map quickly so they can fix them fast as well.

Plunge, don't plan. Generals can plot strategy in the map room, but troops win or lose in the field. Marine Corps officers plan, of course, but they also recognize the limitations of those plans in battle. No general, no matter how experienced or well informed, can foresee how an engagement will unfold. Rather than spend endless hours honing the perfect plan, Marines develop a good enough plan. Many follow the 70 percent solution—if they have 70 percent of the information, do 70 percent of the analysis, and feel 70 percent confident, then a plan is good enough and they proceed. The important work begins when they test their map and adapt it in light of facts on the ground. Marines don't succeed by getting their map right the first time but by finding out where it is wrong (and fixing it) quicker than the enemy.

Plunging into the fray trumps extensive planning in a variety of turbulent contexts, including entrepreneurship. One study of German entrepreneurs found that more time spent planning *decreased* the odds that a start-up would survive.[30] In the late 1980s, Taiwanese food companies eyed the booming Chinese market. Instant noodle leader Uni-President carefully planned its strategy to enter the mainland market from the comfort of its Taiwanese headquarters. By contrast, at Ting Hsin, a cooking oil company, three of the four Wei brothers who ran the company moved their families from Taiwan to China to immerse themselves in the local market. The brothers built a housing complex with nearly three hundred villas to attract other managers to China.

Reconnaissance pull. In reconnaissance, a forward unit advances ahead of the rest of the troops to assess an unfamiliar situation, including terrain, weather, civilian support, road conditions, and enemy deployments ahead. Reconnaissance, at its heart, is a process of stumbling forward into a shifting situation, observing circumstances, and modifying a map in real time. Although troops do not know exactly what they will find, by plunging forward they turn up new information quickly and use it to adapt their plan. Recognizing that their current map must remain subject to revision, reconnaissance troops remain alert to anything that is out of place. The advance is pulled forward by reconnaissance rather than pushed forward by dogged adherence to a preexisting plan.

When entering the terra incognita of the American market, Honda's managing director, Takeo Fujisawa, did not try to dictate a detailed strategy. Instead he chose a trusted subordinate, sent him to study the U.S. market firsthand, and gave him wide latitude on how he increased sales. The Wei brothers continuously adapted their recipes, distribution, and advertising as they advanced and learned more about the new market. Uni-President, in contrast, attempted to replicate its existing model in China and crafted a marketing plan to sell the same products, at premium prices, through similar distribution channels to those they used in Taiwan. Uni-President doggedly stuck to its plan, ignoring evidence that Chinese consumers preferred different flavors, had less money to spend, and shopped differently than their Taiwanese counterparts.

Send out multiple probes. When advancing into turbulence, a prudent Marine officer sends out probes in different directions to broaden the search for new information. Executives and entrepreneurs should likewise avoid betting the company on a single path forward. Ideal probes are inexpensive and quick, to avoid dissipating resources. Sending out multiple probes rather than plowing full steam ahead in a single direction requires leaders with the intellectual humility to recognize that any plan, no matter how good it sounds in theory, is flawed. Managers often staff probes with "expendable" troops, short on talent and long on free time. This tendency is a mistake. Successful reconnaissance requires outstanding people who combine the alertness to spot anomalies, the humility to modify their map, the tenacity to stick with it, and the boldness to seize an opportunity should it arise. Honda president Fujisawa chose one of his most promising managers to lead the North American probe, while three of the four Wei brothers moved to China to evaluate the market.

Pass surfaces and swarm gaps. Marines use the term *surfaces* to describe an enemy's physical stronghold and moments when the adversary is on guard, and *gaps* to describe physical weaknesses and windows of opportunity when an enemy is on its back foot. Marines

sometimes compare reconnaissance to groping their way blind-
folded along a wall of resistance, tapping to find where the wall is
strongest and where cracks exist. They "pass surfaces" by sidest ɔ-
ping entrenched resistance rather than trying to punch th.   ay
through, and "swarm gaps" by piling into any breach they discover,
calling additional troops to follow them.

Passing surfaces and swarming gaps produces a fluid advance,
which military thinkers liken to water wearing away at an obstacle.
"If we watch a torrent bearing down on . . . [an] earthen dam in its
path, we see that it first beats against the obstacle feeling and testing it
at all points. Eventually it finds a small crack at some point. Through the
crack pour the first driblets of water and they rush straight through . . .
simultaneously the water behind pours straight through the breach."[31]

Honda passed a surface by pulling back from the big bikes and
swarmed the gap for smaller bikes. The Wei brothers first tried and
failed to sell premium cooking oil, then egg rolls, and then biscuits,
hit resistance in these segments, and moved on in each case. Then the
youngest brother stumbled on a gap. On an eighteen-hour train ride
to Beijing, he opened a package of instant noodles from Taiwan. He
was shocked when the aromatic noodles, so common in Taiwan, attracted hungry glances from other passengers, some of whom asked to
sample the noodles. Quick-and-dirty market research revealed that
China's instant noodle market was divided into two extremes: low-
quality products in shabby packaging at one end and at the other
premium imported noodles sold as luxury goods in airports and bou-
tiques.

Finish strong. Multiple probes, light taps, and quick retreats
can degenerate into a tentative advance that hinders troops from
exploiting opportunities with vigor. To avoid the risk of missing

opportunities, managers must be prepared to switch from an exploratory advance to a strong finish, yanking resources from other uses and concentrating them to exploit an opportunity to the hilt. Honda executives recognized that the small bikes represented a golden opportunity to expand sales, and finished strong by expanding distribution and buying expensive television advertisements.

The Wei brothers believed high-quality instant noodles at an affordable price for the mass market represented a golden opportunity. They formulated flavors that appealed to different tastes in different Chinese provinces and priced their product above low-end noodles but still within the average consumer's budget. Their test market in Beijing succeeded beyond all expectations, generating orders for three months' production in the first day. To secure an early lead, the Wei brothers raised capital, launched a nationwide advertising campaign, invested more than $300 million in production capacity, and built distribution throughout China. By the time Uni-President executives admitted their plan was flawed, they found themselves far behind the Wei brothers in terms of brand, production, and distribution.

All mental maps are flawed, and anomalies point out gaps between a simple model and a complex reality, the discrepancies between a stable representation and a situation in flux. Although people cannot know in advance where their model is flawed, they can recognize common anomalies, avoid pitfalls that blind them to discrepancies, and plunge into the fray to surface anomalies faster. Finding anomalies is necessary to updating a plan but is not sufficient. To keep a map fresh, one must incorporate new information, reject some old assumptions, rethink others, and reconfigure how the pieces fit together.

Anomalies, for many, are an annoyance at best and a disaster at worst. In this view, they represent a malfunction in a mental map akin to a car breaking down on the highway. If the story ends there, with the map abandoned like a broken-down car on the roadside, anomalies are bad news. But anomalies need not mark the end. They can also spur a fresh twist to an old story. The next chapter explores improvisation to show how to incorporate anomalies into an existing map and keep it fluid as circumstances shift.

6.

KEEPING THE MAP FLUID

You are standing on a stage before a rowdy audience, many of them pretty liquored up. Four other people are on stage, and you are about to play a game where the group tells a story together. The first person begins, the second adds to the story, and so on. Audience members shout suggestions for a title, many bawdy, and you choose "The Day I Went to the Zoo." The game begins. You have no script, no director, no time to rehearse. Your mouth goes dry and your heart pounds as the audience falls silent and stares at you to see what happens next. What do you do? Freeze up? Panic? Leave the stage? Many people consider this their worst nightmare. For improvisational comedians, it is just another day at the office.

Improvisation is the art of making it up as you go along. It differs fundamentally from traditional theater, where the script dictates what happens, directors guide the action, and rehearsal ensures that actors know what to expect from one another. Actors can interpret a role differently in traditional theater, to be sure, but everyone knows how the play proceeds word by word. None of this is true in improvisation. Lacking a script, players must keep the action flowing with no clue as to how it will unfold. The group cannot turn to a director for guidance but must work things out among themselves. They must, in real time, incorporate unexpected twists, recycle old material, and weave disparate elements into a seamless narrative.

Some critics dismiss improvisation as frivolous. Serious actors, in their view, follow a script, while improv is for jokers. Similarly, many citizens expect leaders—including executives, politicians, and soldiers—to craft a long-term plan and methodically execute it. Democratic lawmakers and bankers criticized Treasury Secretary Henry Paulson for lacking a clear plan to rescue the U.S. banking system and derided his approach as improvisation.

In fast-changing situations, however, circumstances often demand improvisation, whether people like it or not. Even the most thoughtful mental map simplifies complexity and omits relevant information. The more rapidly circumstances shift, the faster the flaws emerge. To seize opportunities and mitigate threats arising from turbulence, people must incorporate new information, reuse existing insights, and rethink how pieces of the puzzle fit together. In a turbulent world, responsible leaders acknowledge the need to improvise—the U.S. Marine Corps incorporates this insight into their mantra, "Improvise, adapt, overcome." Dogged pursuit of a map often signals intellectual rigidity rather than superior leadership.

Improvisation can keep a mental map fluid, but requires a rethinking of the notion of a map. Rather than envisioning a map as drawn on a single sheet of paper, it is better to picture it as assembled from separate pieces, like a jigsaw puzzle. Unlike most puzzles, however, there is no single "right" configuration, but rather many possible combinations of existing pieces. Keeping a map fluid requires three things. First is alertness to anomalies that signal important new pieces of information. Second, improvisation necessitates the reuse of existing pieces in new ways, since important pieces of the puzzle, such as an established brand or long-standing customer relationships, cannot be discarded whenever circumstances change. Finally, keeping a map fluid requires periodic reconfiguration into new patterns that recycle existing pieces of information while incorporating new ones.

DISCOVER, DON'T IMPOSE

Keeping a map fluid amidst turbulence is hard work. Fortunately, improvisation provides practical insights for making it up as you go along. Starting from a single theater in a Chicago tavern in 1955, the improvisational community has pioneered a new art form and produced well-known comedians, including Tina Fey, Mike Myers, Bill Murray, the Belushi brothers, Gilda Radner, and Chevy Chase. Through five decades of performances in smoky bars and college theaters, improvisational comedians experimented with many techniques, discarded what failed, and incorporated what worked into their repertoire. This Darwinian process of variation, selection, and retention of what works has produced countless helpful tips on how to improvise (some of which are discussed below) and one big idea: discover, don't impose.[1]

Seasoned improvisers attempt to discover a pattern that emerges in the course of a skit, rather than imposing a preexisting idea on the action. "The Day I Went to the Zoo" skit might begin with one player saying her car wouldn't start, and the second bemoaning the bus drivers' strike. By observing what teammates say and do, comedians discover a pattern during the initial interactions—in this case, unlikely obstacles that prevent a trip to the zoo. Other patterns might include each player trying to outdo the others with their adventures—wrestling bears or swimming with the sharks, for example—or insisting they had a good time despite a long list of unfortunate accidents at the zoo. The pattern typically emerges in the early lines of dialogue and provides a loose road map for subsequent action.

Facing the void of an unscripted play, novice improvisers sometimes try to impose a direction on the unfolding action. They might, for instance, try to tell a joke. This tendency, while understandable, stifles improvisation. To follow the emerging story line, seasoned improvisers avoid forcing a preconceived idea, even a funny joke, during a skit. A gag about two amorous porcupines might win laughs on its own but would kill the flow of a skit where the comedians never made it to the zoo. Canned jokes smother the emerging flow by forcing a preconceived punch line onto a fluid situation.

Improv comedians remain open to "tilts" that interrupt the flow and moves the story in an unexpected direction. A skit called "A Night at the Opera" takes an unexpected twist when the violinist introduces himself as Anthony Soprano. Like anomalies, tilts challenge the existing flow and spur efforts to weave the new twist into the ongoing story. When incorporating tilts, improvisers must often rethink the role of existing material. A harmless violin case, for example, holds a machine gun rather than a stringed instrument once Tony Soprano introduces himself. The pattern that emerges early in a skit does not determine the outcome but provides the basis for an open-ended narrative that could take many possible directions.

Closely related to improvisation is the notion of *bricolage*, a French term that describes the process of solving a problem by tinkering with the materials at hand.² A handyman might, for example, fix a building by playing around with odds and ends and whatever else he can find, rather than drafting a blueprint and going to the hardware store to pick out the materials to execute his plan. In the film *Saving Private Ryan*, for example, Tom Hanks's character stuffs socks with explosives and covers them with grease to create a "sticky bomb" to affix onto advancing tanks to knock off their treads. Starting with the materials at hand and seeking novel combinations can spur creative solutions that a preexisting plan would stifle. "Good cooks," according to a culinary adage, "work from recipes, while great chefs work from ingredients."

All domains of improvisation recognize dead ends—"train wrecks," in jazz parlance—as an unavoidable consequence of making it up as you go along. A zero-tolerance attitude toward mistakes squashes the spontaneity required for successful improvisation. Jazz musicians consider the ability to recover from train wrecks a key skill. While good improvisers recover from their mistakes, great ones incorporate train wrecks into their map. One sign of true mastery in jazz is a player's ability to explore an unsuccessful tilt for a promising theme that moves the music forward in an unexpected way. Salsa dancers see every mistake as a new move, a wonderful image of weaving unexpected and disharmonious movement into the ongoing fabric of action.

Some readers might acknowledge that improvisation matters, but doubt they could pull it off because they assume improvisation requires genius, years of practice, flamboyance, and a hardwired trait for winging it. Actors who teach improvisation, however, have found that most people improvise reasonably well when placed in appropriate circumstances and given clear parameters. Some are better than others, to be sure—you wouldn't pit a team of actuaries against the cast of *Saturday Night Live* in the Improv Olympics—but most people are much better at improvising than they think.

The biggest obstacle to improvisation is not lack of talent but fear, as Keith Johnstone, a pioneer in the pedagogy of improvisation, discovered by accident.[3] In the mid-1960s Johnstone was training actors in the Theatre Machine, an early improvisational theater group in London. The players, most classically trained in England's prestigious drama academies, floundered without a script, a rehearsal, or direction. In working with these actors, Johnstone discovered a bundle of fears that hindered them from improvising. They were afraid of the unknown, of course—the chance that a skit might go off track in front of the audience. In the group situations, actors feared losing face among their peers if they said something stupid or banal. They feared they might reveal something too personal and leave themselves vulnerable. The actors feared that they would take the lead and others would not follow, and conversely, they worried about leading people into a train wreck.

Improvisation requires an environment where people feel safe taking risks. It also requires a team small enough to coordinate closely, shared real-time data on the unfolding situation, and frequent interactions. The structure of improvisation, with a small group acting onstage together, meets these requirements. It is difficult to replicate these conditions in a large organization. The Spanish fashion retailer Zara, which surpassed the Gap in 2008 as the world's largest clothing retailer, however, illustrates how even a large corporation can organize for improvisation.[4] Zara leads the world in "fast fashion," a retail category pioneered by European companies including Sweden's H&M and Britain's Topshop, which track fashion globally, spot emerging trends, and translate them into new products. Zara can move a new product from design table to store rack in three weeks, compared to several months for most retailers. Fast fashion retailers like Zara live or die based on their ability to adapt their mental maps of what will sell to rapidly shifting market conditions.

IMPROVISATIONAL TEAMS

In unsettled circumstances, many people instinctively turn to individual leaders to make sense of the situation. The Prussian military theorist Carl von Clausewitz, for example, argued that a defining characteristic of great generals is *coup d'oeil*—the intuitive ability to survey a turbulent battlefield, grasp the essence of the situation, and adjust the plan accordingly. This individualistic view prevails in the fashion industry as well, where star designers, such as Tom Ford or Stella McCartney, observe fashion, spot what they think will be hot the following season, and design products to fill gaps in the market.

A single general or designer can improvise, but so can teams, and they can do so without recourse to an individual genius. A team's size influences its effectiveness, and across different domains—jazz ensembles and comedy troupes—teams typically range between four and eight. The similarity in the size of improv teams reflects a fundamental trade-off. Adding more members enables a team to look at a situation from different perspectives and achieve a richer understanding. The top management team of a start-up benefits from more members talking to customers, observing competitors, tracking technology, and feeling out venture capitalists. As the team grows larger, however, members struggle to achieve and maintain a shared understanding of the situation. A team of a half dozen members (give or take a few) appears to strike the best balance between the benefits of multiple perspectives and the need to maintain a shared view of the situation. Zara design teams, which focus on a specific geography and product category, typically number between three and five members.

Increasing the diversity of members enhances the number of perspectives without increasing the size. Adding another technologist to a start-up team of programmers adds little marginal gain to their collective understanding, while a finance or marketing expert could provide a fresh perspective. The relevant dimensions of diversity will vary, but the most common include functional expertise, professional training, geographic background, tenure with the company, and industry exposure, as well as demographic factors such as age, gender, and race. Zara teams typically include one or two product designers, a marketing manager, and often a production specialist, who oversees material purchasing and logistics. The diverse team members see the situation through their own distinctive lenses—artistic, marketing, and production. Together they paint a multifaceted picture of an opportunity.

Team members need the predisposition and skills to work together. As a matter of policy, Zara avoids hiring design prima donnas. Instead the company selects employees for their ability to work well in teams. In an industry rife with big egos, Zara screens job candidates for their humility in accepting feedback from colleagues and their willingness to share credit. The compensation system at Zara rewards joint effort, with bonuses linked to team rather than individual performance. Informal feedback further reinforces teamwork. Team members praise colleagues for a job well done and exert subtle peer pressure if they produce substandard work.

RUSH DATA

Improvisation requires data that are real-time, unfiltered, shared, and holistic ("RUSH data" for short). Improvisational skits with all actors onstage at the same time provide the same information to everyone, free from filtering or distortion. In turbulent markets, RUSH data serve the same function as a dashboard on a race car by providing real-time information that helps stay abreast of a fluid situation. Pulling together the required data, however, is difficult in dispersed organizations. Zara has taken a series of concrete steps to ensure that its design teams have the information they need, when they need it, to spot opportunities.

Real time. Data should be real-time to spot shifts in the situation and anomalies. Zara design teams receive hard data on sales and inventory from each store on a daily basis, to determine what is selling and what is not. The importance of real-time data is far from new. From the early days of his steel company, Mittal and his team ran their global network of factories using the *partha* system, a set of practices developed in the nineteenth century by the Marwaris, a tightly knit group renowned for their commercial savvy, that produced some of India's leading industrial dynasties, including the Birla and Bajaj families. Originally based in northern India, the Mawaris migrated when the Mongols invaded their territory in the sixteenth century, and extended their trade and financial network throughout the Indian subcontinent. Faced with the need to track performance throughout their far-flung operations, Marwari merchants developed a system whereby they calculated the profits and cash flow for every operation at the close of the day.

Mittal adapted this system to new technology and treated each plant as a stand-alone business, further divided into smaller units, each with its own numbers for profit, cost, price, quality, volume, and productivity. At a time when many major steel companies collected spotty data on a monthly or quarterly basis, Mittal executives had daily data that highlighted deviations from the plan in great detail. Mittal and his team did not use the data to micromanage the operations; indeed, local managers enjoyed much greater autonomy than their counterparts at other steel companies. Armed with real-time data from around the world, however, they could spot early indicators of shifts in price, demand, or raw material costs before rivals who relied on stale data.

Collecting data from customers provides leading indicators of imminent changes. Sun Microsystems monitored selected customers' system uptime to identify emerging issues at the same time as their customers. Capital markets provide another source of real-time data. Equity analysts monitor the competitive environment to anticipate future cash flow for the companies they track. To pick up early warning signals, one Taiwanese technology company monitors equity analyst briefings and changes in recommendations not only about itself but about its publicly traded competitors, suppliers, and customers as well. The Internet also creates unprecedented opportunities to gather real-time data. By tracking searches for "flu" and related words, Google was able to identify regional outbreaks of the virus two weeks faster than the Centers for Disease Control, which relies on a system of reporting through doctors and hospitals.[5] The Cleveland Clinic has experimented with a system known as MyMonitoring that allows patients to transmit data from an implanted device such as a pacemaker to their medical records using the Internet.

Unfiltered. Many organizations deluge employees with more data than they can read, let alone digest. To stem the flood of information, raw statistics are packaged into standardized reports, such as sales pipelines or monthly budgets. Consolidated reports mitigate information overload, but they also filter out anomalies that don't fit into predefined categories. Through regular observation of unfiltered data, employees develop a more nuanced map of a situation.

Upon taking her position as head of Japanese pet food sales for a multinational food company, one marketing manager pored over reams of standardized reports in search of growth opportunities but found nothing interesting. She then spent a week observing pet owners in their homes. She learned that many Japanese pet owners work long hours, cannot make it home to walk their dogs, live in small apartments, and often return home to an unpleasant odor. Some used doggy diapers, but many simply lived with the smell. Based on her firsthand observation, she identified an opportunity for pet food that minimized odor once digested.

Zara management has bucked industry norms to minimize distortion as data move from consumer to design team. While many fashion retailers franchise 90 percent of their stores to scale quickly, Zara franchises less than 10 percent of its outlets. Owning its own stores limits the retailer's pace of growth but keeps communication channels clear. Zara managers found that tensions and misunderstandings between franchisees and the company garbled communication of information. As the company has grown, Zara executives have resisted the temptation to add layers of management between the stores and designers. The marketing manager on any team communicates directly with the stores in his or her region on a weekly basis.

Zara marketing managers gather firsthand data to share with team members. They sift through daily sales reports and call store managers and supervisors of departments within a shop to ask open-ended questions about what customers like, dislike, ask for, and wear to the store. Marketing managers stay close to the field by visiting their stores regularly and working alongside shop floor staff during Zara's major sales. Most marketing managers spend at least six months working in a store before taking a position in headquarters, to ensure that they understand the operations intimately, know which questions to ask, and recognize what the answers mean.

In many organizations, employees filter out bad news to ensure the boss hears only positive reports. Managers can circumvent these screens by spending time in the field observing a situation firsthand. Ralph Alvarez, president and chief operating officer of McDonald's, spends much of his time on the road, visiting the company's restaurants, talking to customers and franchisees, and studying competitors.[6] Alvarez dons sunglasses and a baseball cap to maintain anonymity on these trips.

Shared. In many organizations, information is fragmented because it rises through functional silos or because managers hoard it as a source of power. Fragmentation breeds misunderstandings based on divergent data, confusion about market conditions, and suspicions of hidden agendas. By sharing data, as Zara does across clothing categories, functions, and regions, employees start with a shared set of facts, and can focus their attention on understanding what the data mean. Sharing data also facilitates coordination. The Cleveland Clinic uses an electronic medical record available to all doctors, nurses, and medical technicians within the system to ensure that they have the most up-to-date information on a patient, and extend the system to the primary care physicians who refer patients. The referring doctor can monitor a patient's treatment online as it is updated in real time, intervene based on her prior knowledge of the patient, and resume follow-up care with an uninterrupted understanding of the patient's treatment history.

Zara design teams use physical prototypes to anchor their discussions around a shared representation of a product. Zara teams produce a paper blueprint, which the pattern department can convert into a fabric model the same day. After asking a colleague to model the prototype, the design team assembles an impromptu focus group of coworkers to discuss how an item looks. To come to a shared view of how a product will look from a customer's perspective, the design team can go to the basement, which holds Zara's Fashion Street, a 24,000-square-meter arcade with full-scale shops. The window displays, layout of the store, displays, and soundtrack playing all match the actual Zara stores, which share a consistent look and feel everywhere in the world.

Holistic. Finally, information should be holistic, describing a situation from diverse perspectives, so team members can form a multidimensional mental map. The Cleveland Clinic's system consolidates data from multiple specialists treating a patient to provide an integrated view of his or her health, and flags dangerous interactions among drugs different doctors prescribe. Holistic data is not the same thing as shared information. A Korean automobile components maker, for example, posted manufacturing quality statistics throughout the organization. Employees only saw part of the picture, however, because they knew nothing about the company's financial, customer, or competitive position.

Zara team members share sales statistics, financial data, marketing reports, and tidbits picked up in casual conversation. Like their counterparts in most fashion houses, Zara designers supplement internal data by scanning the environment to spot emerging trends and fads, frequenting trendy nightclubs and the world's fashion centers. They keep a close eye on what is happening in the music scene, in the movies, and on television. When watching the Academy Awards, for example, a designer might look for patterns among the dresses: are they long or short, wide or narrow, floral or geometric, pastel or bold? They also subscribe to online sites that photograph and post the latest fashions within hours of their debut on the catwalks. Zara marketing managers review data aggregated at the country and world markets to spot emerging trends beyond the stores they oversee.

Software vendors pitching their wares claim that producing RUSH data requires enormous investments in sophisticated systems, which go by a baffling array of acronyms, including CRM, EPR, BI, and SCM. Zara spends much less than rivals on information technology. Whether measured by information technology workers as a percentage of total employees or total spending as a percentage of sales, Zara's IT expenditure is less than one-fourth the retail industry average.[7] Zara's systems were so basic that up until 2004, store managers used floppy disks to collect sales data from cash registers and sent the data to headquarters using a dial-up Internet connection. Companies can produce RUSH data with a modest investment, once they understand the characteristics of information required to keep a map fluid in a turbulent market.

CONTINUOUS INTERACTION

Improvisational performers can keep a performance flowing, reinterpreting old material in light of the new in large part because they observe everything their fellow players say or do and respond on the spot. Continuous interaction is harder, but not impossible, in an organization with thousands or hundreds of thousands of employees spread around the world. Many fashion retailers scatter the individuals involved in design around the globe. The Gap, for example, locates many designers in New York, marketing managers in San Francisco, and prototype production in Asia. Zara, in contrast, co-locates approximately 250 members of design teams together in the company's A Coruña headquarters, in northwestern Spain.

Members of Zara design teams work in one of three rectangular halls, one hall dedicated to designing clothing for women, men, or children. There are no enclosed offices anywhere in the halls. Marketing managers sit at a row of desks that runs like a spine through the center of each hall. On either side of the desks are large rectangular work spaces, bordered by waist-high racks and shelves packed with sample products. Designers spend most of their time at large tables that dominate the work spaces, discussing designs, experimenting with fabrics and colors, and comparing different items. At the end of the hall sits the prototype department, where a team of skilled seamstresses can mock up a sample in a few hours, a capability that many other retailers have outsourced to Asian factories, thereby saving money but losing time.

Physical co-location in an open office helps team members from different backgrounds establish a shared map of the market, rather than glimpsing it from their narrow perspective. Frequent discussions, overheard snippets of conversation, and visual observation of who is working on what help employees intuit the overall situation and understand how their own work fits into the bigger picture. The topography of most large organizations—where finance occupies one floor, for example, and marketing another—reinforces the functional silos that an open office chips away at.

An open office also permits a fluid understanding of a situation in flux. Daily face-to-face meetings and impromptu chats allow team members to talk through market feedback or bounce ideas back and forth in real time. Frequent discussions blend into an ongoing conversation about unfolding events. A continuous flow works much better than an episodic tempo where participants must wait for the next regularly scheduled meeting or conference call to resolve an issue or discuss an idea. It is much better to view a turbulent market as an uninterrupted movie rather than as a series of snapshots presented in intermittent formal meetings. Finally, the open layout allows for the serendipity of chance encounters, when designers or marketing managers bump into colleagues from other departments and exchange insights that might provide a missing piece of information that allows them to reformulate their map.

Physical co-location in an open office is not possible or even desirable in every context. Continuous interaction means continuous distraction. For employees working heads-down on discrete activities—such as processing routine insurance claims or providing technical support over the telephone—the costs of constant interruption may outweigh the benefits of frequent interaction. An open office is best suited to what I call *heads-up work*, complex tasks that require frequent coordination with others and ongoing adaptation to changing circumstances. Designing new products at Zara qualifies as heads-up work. So does starting a new company or fighting a war. When engaged in heads-up work, people should remain alert to anomalies, shifting circumstances, and what others are doing.

The sheer number of employees impedes continuous interaction in large organizations. There exists an upper limit on the number of people—no more than 250, in my experience—who can productively work in an open environment. Above this threshold, it becomes difficult to maintain the frequency of interaction and visual monitoring to maintain a shared mental map, ensure continuity of discussions, and allow serendipity. Large organizations can partition their operations to create smaller groups below this threshhold. Organizations can be subdivided by activity (at Zara, design is co-located but not manufacturing) or by market segment (Zara has separate halls for women's, men's, and children's clothing). New technologies, including instant messaging, chat, and Twitter, may help foster continuous interaction across locations and geographies. Rather than ban these communications technologies as distractions from work, executives should experiment with them as tools to facilitate continuous interaction among dispersed team members.

MAKE IT SAFE

Like the classically trained English actors, many people refrain from improvising because they are afraid to speak up. In a series of studies, Professor Amy Edmondson has found that fear of repercussions often stifles open discussion, even when the resulting mistakes have fatal consequences, such as drug errors in hospitals.[8] In organizations, as in the theater, employees have much to fear, including losing face, taking the lead and finding no one follows, saying something stupid, leading the group in an unproductive direction, or disagreeing with the boss.

A few years ago, I was working with the top management team of a global bank to help them identify growth opportunities. The CEO kicked off the meeting by exhorting everyone to "brainstorm" and "think out of the box." Within a few minutes, an investment banker raised her hand and proposed a creative approach to boost the bank's energy trading profits. Before she had finished her point, a senior banker cut her down with a high-handed comment about another bank that had failed in a similar initiative. The CEO let the exchange pass, and the curtain went down before the show began. The meeting carried on, of course, but as a tedious discussion in which the usual suspects proposed more of the same. The problem was not that people lacked creative ideas; they just didn't feel safe deviating from the accepted script.

Keith Johnstone, the theater director who taught improvisation, discovered that even the most stilted thespians could improvise when placed in situations where it was safe to let go. He had the actors wear masks to improvise anonymously, for instance, and framed his exercises as games rather than performances to minimize the perceived risk. Many of the unofficial rules of improvisation encourage participation by lowering the perceived risk of getting it wrong. The golden rule of improvisation, for example, is "yes, and . . . ," whereby actors accept and build on anything another says. This rule contributes to a climate of safety because each actor knows others will follow their lead. Professor Edmondson defines "psychological safety" as a shared belief that team members can take risks without fear of negative repercussions. She found psychological safety promotes learning and rapid recognition of potential errors, and that it can vary widely across teams even within the same organization. In organizations, of course, people must sometimes disagree and challenge assumptions—unconditional acceptance is not possible or desirable in all contexts. When keeping a mental map fluid in a turbulent context, however, people must feel safe to introduce incongruous information and fresh interpretations.

Downplaying the importance of formal hierarchy is one powerful way to stimulate improvisation. In many organizations, deference to hierarchy stifles open discussion, as when the boss dominates the debate, asserts the "right" answer, and dismisses (or ignores) dissenting opinions. Zara executives minimize the censoring effect of hierarchy in several ways. No team member, regardless of responsibility or tenure, has an enclosed office. Instead, everyone works at identical desks. Although each team has a clear leader, the company has dispensed with formal titles to avoid the stratified aristocracy of vice presidents, senior vice presidents, and executive vice presidents. Zara executives cultivate an informal atmosphere to encourage everyone to speak their mind, and use RUSH data to ensure that facts rather than managerial opinion inform decisions.

There are, of course, risks to minimizing hierarchy. Absent a clear chain of command, Zara's teams could devolve into talk shops, where team members endlessly discuss issues without making decisions. Zara team leaders, however, retain clear responsibility for making decisions if the team cannot reach consensus after discussion. Twice each week, the teams must assemble their offerings for presentation to store managers, and these offerings dictate a tempo that forces regular decisions.

Cutting the cost of failure is another mechanism to stimulate improvisation. Zara sends its products to stores in small batches. If an item sells better than expected, the company can make more the following week, or launch derivative items. When a product does not sell well, in contrast, the limited inventory minimizes the cost of markdowns. Zara pursues an evolutionary approach to style, where the design teams tweak their initial line, modifying and adapting the products in light of new information.

Improvisation is often evoked as a loose metaphor to guide action in a turbulent world, but it is much more than that. Improvisation provides a set of hands-on techniques to incorporate anomalies, reuse existing material, and reconfigure the pieces to balance continuity and change. The prerequisites for improvisation onstage—a small team, continuous interaction, appropriate data, and a safe setting— also enable teams starting a firm or fighting a battle to keep their map fluid as circumstances change. Adapting a mental map is useless, however, if an organization cannot adapt its commitments to follow the new coordinates. The following chapters explore how agility can help organizations pursue a shifting map.

7.

THE ESSENCE OF
AGILITY

As the Korean War began, the situation looked bleak for the U.S. pilots and their allies fighting under the United Nations flag. North Korea, along with the Soviet Union and People's Republic of China, could field more jets, and also flew superior planes. The American-made F-86 Sabre had entered active service only the preceding year and was unproven in combat. The Sabre's swept-back wings cut a fine profile, but few experts considered it equal to its Soviet-produced counterpart, the MiG 15, which matched the Sabre on most performance dimensions and surpassed it on a few critical attributes. The MiG could ascend quicker than the Sabre, operated better at high altitudes, and had a large advantage in its thrust-to-weight ratio, a critical measure of power. The MiG also packed a bigger wallop, carrying three cannons with two hundred rounds, each capable of blowing an enemy out of the sky. The Sabre, in contrast, came equipped with six machine guns and eight rockets.[1]

The North Koreans and their allies also enjoyed superior position. The communists massed large formations of MiGs on the Chinese side of the border with Korea, lay in wait, and scrambled to attack passing Sabres from high altitudes. If the MiGs won the upper hand, they could pursue the UN pilots back to their base. But when the MiG pilots got into trouble, they could retreat to the safety of Chinese airspace, off-limits to UN pilots. In the heat of battle, UN pilots sometimes disregarded these orders and pursued their adversaries across the border, but the deck remained stacked against the UN fighters.

Facing more planes, better planes, and superior position, military experts predicted heavy losses for the Sabres. In the early days of the conflict, UN pilots were expected to lose ten planes for every MiG they shot down in battle—in military parlance, a ten-to-one kill ratio. As the conflict proceeded, the kill ratios were indeed lopsided, but it was the UN fighter pilots who outgunned the MiGs by a ratio of ten to one. The official U.S. Air Force reports tally 792 MiGs shot down to 76 Sabres over the course of the Korean War.[2] How could this be?

Among the top brass, the lopsided victory in the Korean War inspired more pride than understanding. The advantages that typically confer victory—superior resources or position—clearly didn't account for the surprising results. The UN forces had inferior planes and fewer of them, and they flew from less secure bases. In the end, the Air Force brass attributed the success to superior pilots—a facile explanation that said everything, explained nothing, and ignored the reality that seasoned Soviet pilots flew most of the missions.

WINNING THROUGH AGILITY

The Sabre's success remained a mystery for well over a decade. By the late 1960s, however, a loosely organized group, known as the "Fighter Mafia," fought to secure funding for two new fighter planes, the F-15 and F-16. John Boyd, a leader of the group, revisited the results of the Korean War to garner insights to help design the ultimate fighter.

Boyd was uniquely qualified for the job.[3] He had flown two dozen sorties as a wingman in the Korean War and then served as a student and later an instructor at the Fighter Weapons School, the most selective fighter pilot training program in the Air Force, which served as the model for its navy counterpart, popularized in the film *Top Gun*. During his tenure as an instructor, he earned the nickname "Forty-Second Boyd" by issuing an open challenge to any pilot to engage in mock combat. The competition began with the adversary in the superior position. Boyd promised to gain the upper hand in under forty seconds or pay his challenger $40. Although many of the world's best fighter pilots took the bait, Boyd never lost a bet.

During his tenure at Nellis, Boyd literally wrote the book on aerial combat. His 150-page *Aerial Attack Study* codified maneuvers in aerial combat and formed the basis for subsequent air-to-air combat doctrine within the air force. In a later posting, he developed a mathematical formula that allowed, for the first time, a systematic comparison between different aircraft. Lacking a mandate to test his model, Boyd appropriated computer time without official authorization. Discovering his theoretical contribution and his unsanctioned computer usage at the same time, his superior officers put in the paperwork for both a medal recognizing his breakthrough and a court-martial for misappropriation of government resources. In the end, the court-martial proceedings were dropped and Boyd received not only a medal but official awards for his contribution to aeronautical engineering.

Despite his many contributions to the air force, Boyd never rose above the rank of colonel. His intensity in flying spilled over into discussions, where he underscored points by poking his finger—or the lit end of a cigar—into his adversary's tie, a tactic that stressed his point but ruined his chances to wear a general's stars. He remained an influential voice within the air force, however, particularly when it came to designing the next-generation fighter jet. To design the new plane, Boyd reexamined the Sabres' unexpected success in the Korean War and rethought how it had won so many dogfights.

He discovered that early comparisons with the MiGs overlooked two structural attributes of the Sabre that proved decisive in the dogfights over the Korean peninsula. The Sabre featured a bubble canopy made of see-through plastic, which provided the pilot with complete 360-degree visibility of the situation, while the MiG pilot peered through a smaller window encased in thick armor that protected the pilot from hostile fire and reduced wind resistance. Pilots compared looking out the MiG's smaller window to peering through the bottom of a Coca-Cola bottle. Surrounded by the bubble canopy, the UN pilots could spot opportunities to strike ahead of their enemies.

Better visibility to spot a gap in the enemy's defenses, however, is valuable only when combined with the ability to seize fleeting opportunities. The Sabre enjoyed a second advantage that allowed pilots to exploit opportunities as they emerged in battle. The American-made fighter included full hydraulic controls, which enabled pilots to switch from one action to another in the heat of battle. The MiG-15, in contrast, had only partial hydraulics and demanded great upper-body strength from pilots, many of whom lifted weights between sorties to better manhandle the plane in combat.

The Sabre pilots enjoyed greater autonomy to choose maneuvers than their Soviet counterparts, and they used their freedom to improvise. By repeatedly shifting from one tactic to another, the UN pilots neutralized the MiGs' advantages in any specific operation. The ability to climb more quickly did not help the MiG pilot when the Sabre's quick change in maneuver deprived him of a clean shot. With each successive change in operation, the UN pilot gained a slight advantage, no more than a fraction of a second, but as the number of shifts mounted, the cumulative advantage grew. The MiG pilot found himself on the back foot, responding to the Sabre's initiatives. The gap between the Sabre and the MiG grew larger with every twist and turn.

Boyd's analysis broke with the mental map of how to win wars that then prevailed within the U.S. military. Rather that smothering uncertainty with massive resources, Boyd argued, combatants should seek out turbulence, and when possible create it to generate opportunities. Seizing these opportunities, however, required agility, an aircraft's ability to rapidly shift from one action to another in order to exploit gaps in the enemy's defenses.

THREE TYPES OF AGILITY

Agility is a broad notion that applies not only in combat but in any other domain—including business, sports, and software programming—characterized by turbulence, opportunities, and competition. Leaders increasingly recognize the importance of agility. A survey by the consulting firm McKinsey & Company found that nine out of ten executives ranked organizational agility as both critical to business success and growing in importance over time.[4] Boyd's ideas have grown more influential in the military in recent decades, particularly within the U.S. Marine Corps, which embraced his insights as the core of maneuver warfare, the approach discussed in chapter 5. Among engineers, agile programming has become an important technique to develop software when users cannot predict their future needs.

Despite widespread understanding that agility matters, there is less clarity on what it is exactly. I define "agility" as the capacity to identify and capture opportunities more quickly than rivals. Different terms can describe the same notion—the Marines and U.S. Army prefer "maneuverability," while some management writers prefer "nimbleness" or "flexibility" to describe the same idea. The specific wording does not matter, but the underlying idea does. Agility can help organizations seize a wide range of opportunities. Respondents to the McKinsey survey, for example, identified a host of potential benefits from enhanced agility, including higher revenues, greater customer satisfaction, improved operational efficiency, faster time to market, and greater employee satisfaction.

Agility is not raw speed. "The fast beat the slow" (or its Darwinian version, "The fast eat the slow") has entered the conventional wisdom of strategy. This is incorrect. The best way to enhance raw speed is to develop a crystal-clear long-term vision and send the troops off at a dead sprint in pursuit. If the vision is wrong or the world changes, however, this approach only guarantees that an organization arrives at the wrong place before anyone else. People often forget this basic insight in their rush to secure "first-mover advantages" or to "get big fast." Recall how pioneers like Charles Stack were too early to seize opportunities that later entrants like Amazon successfully exploited. Timing matters more than raw speed, and too early can be just as bad as too late.

Instead of increasing velocity, agility improves timing, the ability to do the right thing at the right time. Recall how Carnival timed its new ship construction and initial public offering, neither too early nor too late. Agility breaks the flow of time into smaller segments, allowing for more frequent reassessments of a changing situation. As the Sabre pilots pulled ahead of their counterparts and passed from one maneuver to the next they could wait for the ideal moment to strike. Agility increases the odds of matching the correct action to the situation at hand.

Any single opportunity seized through agility may confer modest benefits, but the cumulative effect of successive small wins can be decisive. It was not any single action that brought the Sabres victory, but rather their ability to shift from one maneuver to another more quickly than the MiGs. A series of tactical victories—operational improvements, cost cutting, incremental product extensions—that are linked to clear strategic goals and executed faster and better than rivals can cumulate to large leads over time. A 2007 survey of 769 CEOs from forty countries found that excellence of execution ranked first among 121 concerns, and sustaining execution in the future ranked as the third most important issue they faced.[5] These executives recognized relentless execution—piling up lots of little wins—as the key to success.

A more agile competitor shapes the circumstances to which a rival must react. As the dogfights advanced, North Korean pilots found themselves responding to the UN pilots' initiative, rather than dictating the flow of the battle themselves. It is often easy to identify an organization, army, or athlete who is winning through agility. They anticipate opportunities and threats that surprise rivals. They set the agenda their rivals must adapt to; time seems to slow down for them, while accelerating for their less agile opponent. The less agile rival despairs as the gap grows larger over time, and often loses any hope of closing it. Most of the MiG pilots who were shot down abandoned all hope of reversing the situation even before their defeat was inevitable.

They gave up before their planes gave out. The psychological drain of responding to a more agile rival and watching the situation deteriorate saps competitive will.

It is important not only to define agility clearly but also to disentangle its various forms. Over the past decade I have researched dozens of firms that thrived in volatile markets, and identified three distinct types of agility. The first is operational agility: a company's capacity, within a focused business model, to find and seize opportunities to improve operations and processes. These opportunities need

FIGURE 7.1 **Three Ways to Be Agile**

Organizations can achieve agility in three distinct ways. They can see and seize a series of opportunities in their core business faster than competitors, reallocate resources out of declining businesses into promising ones, and seize periodic golden opportunities that can propel them ahead of rivals. Below are some factors associated with each type of agility.

	Operational	Portfolio	Strategic
Defined as an organization's ability to:	Within a focused business model, consistently identify and seize opportunities more quickly than rivals	Quickly and effectively shift resources out of less promising businesses and into more attractive opportunities	Identify and seize major opportunities as they arise—
Examples	Wal-Mart Southwest Airlines Toyota Tesco	Procter & Gamble Samsung Group General Electric	Banco Santander Oracle

	Operational	Portfolio	Strategic
Organizational enablers	Shared real-time market data that are granular and credible	A diversified portfolio of independent units	A strong balance sheet and a large war chest to finance big bets
	A small number of corporate priorities to focus effort	A cadre of general managers who can be transferred across units	A governance structure that permits executives to seize opportunities more quickly than rivals
	Clear performance goals for teams and individuals	Central corporate control over important resources, such as talent and cash	
	Mechanisms to hold people accountable and to reward them		Owners and executives with a long-term perspective
		Regular, unbiased evaluation processes	
		Structured process for decreasing investments or selling off units	
Leaders should	Stay in the flow of information	Make unpopular calls on reallocating resources	Be willing to take risks
	Sustain a sense of urgency	Base portfolio decisions on rational rather than emotional or political criteria	Maintain the confidence of owners
	Maintain focus on critical objectives		Mitigate downside risk on big bets
	Recruit entrepreneurial staff	Invest heavily on promising opportunities	Wait for the right opportunity

not be sexy. Cost reductions, quality improvements, or refinements to distribution processes can be just as valuable as introducing new products and services—as the success of Wal-Mart, Toyota, FedEx, and Southwest Airlines illustrate. Chapter 9 describes how to build operational agility within an organization.

Portfolio agility is the capacity to quickly and effectively shift resources, including cash, talent, and managerial attention, out of less promising units and into more attractive ones. A recent study of more than two hundred large enterprises found that the reallocation of resources to faster-growing segments within a company's portfolio of businesses was the largest single driver of revenue growth.[6] Diversified enterprises such as Johnson & Johnson, Procter & Gamble, and the Samsung Group have used their portfolio agility to succeed over long periods, while private equity groups such as Blackstone, KKR, Carlyle, and TPG have earned high returns for their investors by actively managing a portfolio of businesses. Chapter 10 explores how organizations can enhance portfolio agility.

Recall that turbulent markets typically produce a steady flow of small opportunities, intermittent midsize ones, and periodic golden opportunities to create significant value. Strategic agility is an organization's capacity to spot and seize major opportunities when they arise. Such opportunities include scaling a new business, aggressively entering a new market, betting heavily on a new technology, or making significant investments in capacity. The agility to make a big bet quickly does not, of course, guarantee that the gamble will pay off—recall AT&T's cable acquisitions. But companies that avoid big bets altogether risk falling behind more aggressive competitors. Chapter 11 examines strategic agility in greater detail.

FROM LINES TO LOOPS

Boyd viewed the dogfights over the Korean Peninsula as the distilled essence of all combat, where a more agile combatant defeats a better endowed enemy by seizing the opportunities that arise out of turbulence. Boyd was not the first warrior to recognize the importance of agility, a central theme for Sun Tzu, Napoleon, and the architects of the German blitzkrieg. He was, however, the first to conceptualize battle as a series of iterative loops, in which the pilots cycled through four steps: observe, orient, decide, and act.[7]

The cycle begins when a pilot observes the situation, including the hundreds of readings from the cockpit instruments and outside signals—the glint of the sun off a turned wing or an unexpected

FIGURE 7.2 **Boyd's OODA Loop**

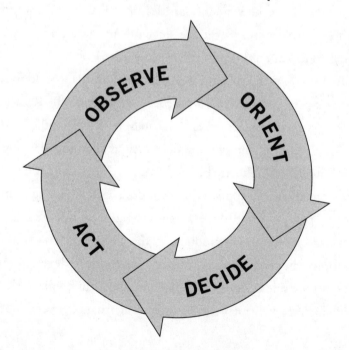

vibration. The bubble canopy opened the Sabre pilots' vista. In the second step, the pilot orients himself by forming a mental map of the situation, including the terrain, location of enemies, and wind. Based on his map of the circumstances, the pilot decides what to do, and acts. The Sabre's hydraulics allowed pilots to translate decision into action faster than the MiG pilots could. After moving through the loop, the pilot would observe the new situation and go through the cycle again.

Boyd referred to this cycle as the OODA loop, to denote the constituent steps of observe, orient, decide, and act. Boyd believed that the dynamic of two fighter pilots cycling through the OODA loop applied more generally to armies clashing on land or navies engaged at sea. The absolute tempo is slower for an infantry battalion or fleet, to be sure, but victory still went to the army or fleet that moved through the loop faster than their adversary. Boyd used the loop to illuminate how smaller armies prevailed in battles ranging from the Greek victory over the Persians at Marathon in 490 BC through to recent conflicts in the Middle East.

Boyd was not the first thinker who used an iterative loop to explain action in the face of turbulence (see figure 7.3). Recall Karl Popper's loop of conjecture and refutation. Boyd studied Popper closely and built on the philosopher's insight that knowledge grows through iterations.[8] Shortly before Boyd developed the OODA loop, W. Edwards Deming applied the plan, do, check, act cycle to manufacturing process improvement, while engineers adopted iterative processes to develop new products in the 1950s. Variations of these early approaches later evolved into agile methods of developing software.[9] At the same time, venture capitalists institutionalized the process of staging investments in rounds to alternate between working through a business plan and testing it in the real world. Precursors undermine Boyd's claim to novelty but reinforce the validity of the OODA loop. Engineers, venture capitalists, and scientists working in separate domains independently concluded that some variation on an iterative loop could help them act more effectively in the face of turbulence.

The iterative approach contrasts with the linear approach many leaders follow when they attempt to predict the future, craft a long-term plan, and implement it methodically over time. This linear approach confers the illusion that leaders have conquered turbulence to gain control of a situation. Throughout history, the apparent rationality of linear planning has attracted leaders, including French generals who plotted attacks on World War I trenches to the last bullet, CEOs who formulate elaborate long-term visions, Soviet central planners micromanaging an entire economy, and software programmers attempting to plot out a detailed plan for a multiyear software development project.

The ritual of predict, plan, and implement may allay anxiety about the future, but it is a crummy way to advance into an unknowable future. A linear approach forces planners to lock into a mental map without benefit of information that will emerge in the future. New information can be safely ignored when circumstances remain relatively stable. Writing a grocery list works because people know what they like to eat, retailers seldom change formats from one week to the next, and neighbors don't corner the market in steaks to foil a planned barbecue. In stable contexts, the costs of strict adherence to a preconceived plan are not tragic—a rigid shopper may miss a special on fish or fresh blueberries. Running a start-up, fighting a battle, or designing novel software, however, is nothing like a trip to the grocery store. The ceaseless

FIGURE 7.3 Comparison of Iterative Approaches

	Key Advocates	Objective	Steps in Process	Important Insights
Experimental loop	Karl Popper (1930s)	Create and test theories	Define problem	Experiments should seek to disconfirm a theory
			Develop tentative theory	Anomalies point to productive areas for further research
			Submit to error elimination	Knowledge emerges from trial and error
Deming cycle	Walter Shewhart (1930s)	Improve quality of standardized processes	Plan objectives and process	Processes can be improved continuously
	W. Edwards Deming (1950s)		Do by implementing process	Good data are necessary to identify gaps versus plan
			Check results against objectives	Variations from plan signal opportunities for improvement
			Act to improve the process	Complex systems require ongoing adjustment
Iterative new product development	Various (1950s–present)	Develop products or software that meet customers' changing needs	Vary by approach (e.g., Extreme Programming, Scrum)	Successive prototypes can produce a better product than a predefined plan
				Ongoing dialogue with customers preferable to written product specification

Staged investment in new ventures	Various venture capitalists (1960s–present)	Invest to build promising start-ups	Evaluate and refine business plan Agree on objectives for a round Oversee progress Reassess investment	Break funding into rounds to force revision of plan Identify key risks at each round and take steps to reduce Stage investments, increasing funding as key sources of uncertainty are resolved
OODA loop	John Boyd (1960s–1970s)	Defeat enemy in combat	Observe situation Orient oneself Decide what to do Act	Competitive iteration Tempo defined relative to rivals Turbulence favors the agile
Agility loop	Donald Sull (2005)	Achieve agility in organizations	Make sense of situation Make choices Make it happen Make revisions	Agility consists of four different types of discussion Each type of discussion has distinct requirements and pitfalls Managers can enhance agility by structuring and leading discussions

churning of external forces produces unexpected opportunities and threats, churns up new information, and defeats the best-laid plans.

Software programming illustrates the folly of a linear advance into a turbulent future. Traditionally, large software development projects assessed users' needs, translated them into features, parceled features for coding, and assembled the code at the end. Sounds sensible, but, unfortunately, it doesn't work. In 1995, the Department of Defense published a study reviewing software projects that had cost the taxpayers more than $35 billion, and found that only 2 percent of the code was used as written, with the rest either requiring significant revision or going unused.[10] Software developed for the private sector did not do much better, with less than 5 percent of code used.[11]

The problem was not a failure to deliver the planned features. The same Defense Department study found that half of the software features met the requirements requested by users in the design stage. By the time programmers delivered the software, however, the customers wanted something different. Users changed their minds for many reasons: They struggled to articulate what they wanted until they saw a prototype, software interacted with hardware in unexpected ways, the new software spawned new requirements, or competitors upped the ante.[12] By freezing features too early, the linear approach kept programmers from incorporating new information.

Linear planning is a siren's song that lures leaders to disaster with a seductive promise of control. In a turbulent world, it is better to bend the line into a loop, and proceed through iterations that allow adjustments to changing circumstances. But an iterative approach is easier to describe than implement. A pilot can quickly proceed through a loop, but how can organizations with tens of thousands of people, divided into discrete units spread across multiple continents, achieve comparable agility? The next chapter argues that leaders can enhance agility by structuring and leading discussions to make sense of turbulence, make hard choices, ensure execution, and revise their mental maps in light of new information.

8.

THE AGILITY LOOP

What makes an effective leader in turbulent markets? Many think the secret of effective leadership lies in brilliant strategic insight—the intellectual horsepower to craft a clever strategy. Others stress discipline, believing that superior leaders excel at execution. Still others feel that a great leader is, above all, inspirational—capable of uniting an organization around an exciting vision. Some, and Dilbert comes to mind here, dismiss the phrase "effective manager" as an oxymoron.

Leadership, at its heart, consists of getting things done through discussions with other people. Several studies find that executives spend between two-thirds and three-quarters of their time engaged in discussions—formal and informal, short and long, one-on-one and in groups and increasingly through e-mail.[1] In this chapter, I introduce the agility loop as a framework to help managers structure and run discussions more effectively. Like the OODA loop or Popper's experimental cycle, the agility loop emphasizes iteration and consists of four steps required to advance into an unknowable future: making sense of a situation; making choices about what to do, not do, and stop doing; making things happen; and making revisions based on new information.

The loop can be embedded within formal processes (strategic planning, budgeting, resource allocation, or performance management) or within the informal conversations—including chance encounters at the water cooler—that fill out the typical manager's day. No organization can achieve agility if these discussions are concentrated at the top of the company; they must be distributed throughout the organization.

All too often conversations bog down in an endless series of unproductive meetings in which the usual suspects cover the same ground without forward progress. Frustration mounts as participants spin their wheels or talk in circles. Discussions frequently stall when managers lead the wrong kinds of discussions at the wrong time (see box).

FIGURE 8.1 **The Agility Loop**

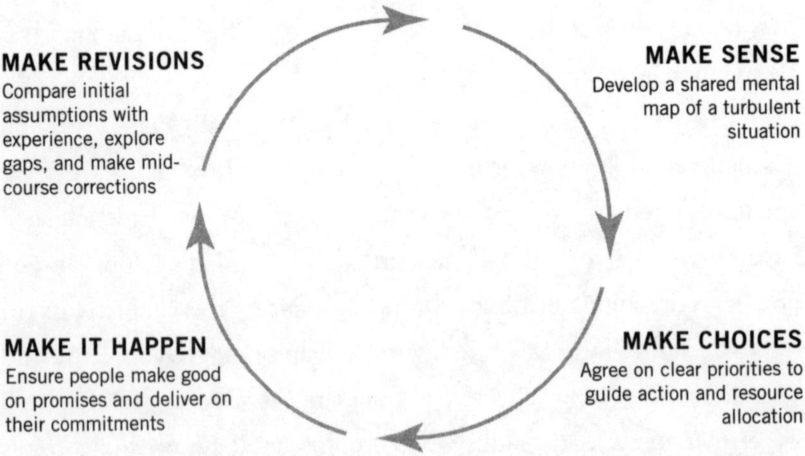

MAKE REVISIONS
Compare initial assumptions with experience, explore gaps, and make mid-course corrections

MAKE SENSE
Develop a shared mental map of a turbulent situation

MAKE IT HAPPEN
Ensure people make good on promises and deliver on their commitments

MAKE CHOICES
Agree on clear priorities to guide action and resource allocation

BEFORE YOU CALL THAT MEETING

The first step in leading through the agility loop is deciding which discussion to have when, who should be involved, and how to lead it. The following simple questions can help improve the quality of discussions.

- **What will we talk about?** This simple question often surfaces a disturbing lack of focus about the objective of a discussion.

- **Are the right people in the room?** Discussions to make sense of a turbulent situation work best when outside viewpoints (from customers or regulators, for instance) are brought to bear, while execution requires that the people who will do the work—rather than their boss or colleague—be in the room.

- **Are we talking about the right thing right now?** Managers must make a call on what conversation is appropriate for the current situation. Are people rehashing assumptions when they should be executing agreed priorities?

- **Does the conversation have the right tone?** Leaders must understand what an effective discussion sounds like at each step. They should establish and maintain a spirit of open inquiry while trying to interpret an ambiguous situation, for example, and promote respectful arguments when making hard trade-offs.

- **Are we skipping key conversations?** Managers must ensure that they are having all the conversations they need. Leaders with a bias for action often shortchange sense-making in their haste to do something, while more cerebral executives may overanalyze strategic issues without ensuring execution.

Although each type of discussion is simple in principle, in practice they break down when people lose sight of what they are trying to achieve, set the wrong tone, lack the appropriate data, or fall prey to common pitfalls.

DISCUSSIONS TO MAKE SENSE

Discussions to make sense should produce a shared mental map of a situation. These conversations should be based on data, specifically information that is real-time, unfiltered, shared, and holistic. Recall that Zara design teams made sense of the fast-moving fashion scene, in large part because they collected both quantitative and qualitative data from the stores daily, shared that information, and considered information not only from a single store but also from the country and world markets to get a fuller picture and spot emerging trends. Absent good data, people default to preconceived notions and un-grounded assumptions.

The best way to make sense of novel situations is to dig into data with an open mind. Unfortunately, participants often make up their mind about what is going on before the discussions begin, and advocate a preformulated point of view instead of exploring alternative interpretations. During the Cuban missile crisis, President John F. Kennedy tried to assess the situation afresh. His military advisors saw the missiles as a prelude to war. They advocated invasion, a course of action they had favored for some time, even though a military strike could escalate into nuclear war.[2]

A tone of open inquiry can minimize the tendency toward pre-baked interpretations. During his successful tenure as U.S. treasury secretary and earlier as co–managing director of Goldman Sachs, Robert Rubin analyzed new situations, from evaluating a risk arbitrage deal to managing an economic crisis, by pulling out a pad of yellow legal paper to write down a long list of questions.[3] Many leaders, in contrast, affirm their authority by claiming to know the answer, no matter what the question. Soliciting questions allows participants to admit they don't know everything, dampens the impulse to commit prematurely to an interpretation, and creates an opening to introduce difficult issues by posing them as questions.

In turbulent contexts, decision makers should avoid anchoring on a single interpretation of a situation. During the Cuban missile crisis, Kennedy's team nearly adopted the "obvious" interpretation that the missiles signaled an escalation of hostilities. In novel situations, however, the best interpretation is rarely obvious, and the most obvious one is often wrong. Participants must feel safe putting forth alternative interpretations. Leaders can stimulate different points of view, rather than passively waiting for them to emerge, by bringing outsiders or iconoclasts into a discussion. Kennedy invited Llewellyn "Tommy" Thompson, a former ambassador to the Soviet Union, who disagreed that Soviet premier Nikita Khrushchev wanted to start a war. Thompson argued that the Soviet leader had backed himself into a corner and was seeking a face-saving way to deescalate the tensions—an interpretation the generals dismissed, but which proved accurate. Kennedy also demanded his advisors generate alternative interpretations and actions, a demand that made it safe to discuss the "soft" options of blockade and diplomatic negotiation that allowed both sides to avoid escalating the conflict

Managers sometimes appoint a devil's advocate to stimulate alternative views. Fierce criticism is a mistake at this stage in the agility loop. Tom Kelley, the general manager of the influential design house IDEO, argues that devil's advocates "may be the biggest innovation killer in America today" because they nip promising ideas in the bud.[4] A fledgling mental map will raise more questions than it can answer initially, but that does not mean it is useless or wrong. Adlai Stevenson, then the U.S. ambassador to the United Nations, viewed the Cuban missile crisis through a diplomatic lens, and favored negotiating with Khrushchev. Kennedy's hard-line advisors savaged Stevenson's view, but the president came to recognize the value of a deal with the Soviet Union as part of his approach to defusing the crisis. A devil's advocate with the license to savage new interpretations can smother discussions to make sense, although this role can enhance discussions to make choices and revise an existing mental map.

Empathy is one of the most critical yet overlooked aspects of making sense. Empathy is not niceness, often used as an excuse to avoid difficult discussions, but rather the ability to see a situation from another person's perspective. Empathy can offset the tendency to see the "other" in abstract terms. Many of Kennedy's advisors believed the Soviets understood only power and respected only force. Because he knew Khrushchev personally, Thompson was aware that the Russian leader despised war. Thompson thought not about what the Soviets would do but what Nikita Khrushchev would do.

In corporations, the "other" often includes competitors, regulators, nongovernmental organizations, and customers. When helping to vet growth opportunities for a large European bank, I jotted down the verbs the teams used to describe what they would do to (not for or with) "the customer," which included "cross-sell," "leverage," "squeeze," "exploit," and "penetrate." At this point I interrupted the proceedings to ask how many customers went to the bank hoping to be "exploited" or "penetrated." This lack of empathy for customers is depressingly common—one leading technology firm referred to customers as "sockets," presumably just waiting to be plugged.

In their haste to do something, teams shortchange discussions to understand what is happening. A bias for action is invaluable in execution but can short-circuit clarifying discussions. Take-charge or gung-ho managers who pride themselves on getting the job often dread the thrashing around necessary to understand a turbulent market. To avoid the ambiguity, they dive into the details of implementation and bypass sense-making discussions altoghter. When action proposals arise, it is best to dig backward to unearth and examine the assumptions that underlie a plan of action. Helpful questions include "If that's the solution, what exactly is the problem?" and "What fresh data would convince us that our interpretation is wrong?"[5]

Executives can separate discussions to interpret a situation from deciding what to do. The top management team of Diageo Ireland breaks the monthly performance management process into distinct meetings.[6] On the second day of the month they assess the market situation and identify potential issues. Five days later, they decide what to do. A leading professional services firm follows a similar logic by considering important issues in three conversations: the first, to discuss alternative interpretations of the situation, the second, to debate a set of alternatives, and the last, to decide on a course of action. Discussions to make sense should answer the question "What is going on here?" while discussions to make choices address "What should we do?" Collapsing them into a single conversation degrades the answer to both questions.

DISCUSSIONS TO MAKE CHOICES

Discussions to make choices aim toward agreement on a small set of clear priorities that focus organizational resources and attention on opportunities that matter most. In turbulent environments, a constant deluge of potential opportunities and threats creates an urge to hedge bets against every foreseeable contingency. Ironically, the spread-your-bets approach increases rather than decreases risk by wasting resources on skirmishes that mean little and by depriving key initiatives of the funds and people they need to succeed. Conversations to make choices conclude when a team agrees on a set of priorities that are consistent with its mental map and concrete enough to guide action and resource allocation throughout the organization.

These conversations are about making difficult trade-offs, and they must allow hard-hitting discussion where team members express disagreements and reservations. Without active efforts to stimulate debate, these conversations drift toward superficial agreement, with unresolved conflict lurking below the waterline. Candor in debate must be tempered with respect for the individuals. When proposals are personalized—"Jane's idea" or "Jack's recommendation"—it is difficult to reject an alternative without bruising the ego of the person who proposed it.

Groupthink occurs when a team converges on a single course of action, and the risk is acute when teams face time pressure and high stakes. Alternative options are not a luxury, however; they are a necessity. During the Cuban missile crisis, Kennedy's advisors quickly converged on military intervention, but the president demanded alternatives. Hard-liners considered these alternatives a waste of time that distracted them from planning the military strike. In the end, Kennedy's call for alternatives produced the blockade that bought both sides time and the diplomatic deal that allowed Khrushchev to save face while removing the missiles. Kennedy, by broadening beyond a single alternative, averted disaster. In her research on effective decision making in turbulent markets, Professor Kathy Eisenhardt found that top management teams did best when they considered at least three alternatives.[7] Multiple alternatives increase confidence that all options have been explored, help to flesh out the full range of possible responses, and provide a fallback if plan A fails.

Discussions to make choices derail when people add priorities without increasing resources or eliminating existing activities. When managers evaluate initiatives in isolation rather than as part of a portfolio of activities, they proliferate priorities. Middle managers in one European engineering group tallied more than fifty so-called strategic priorities that had rained down on them from headquarters in a two-year period. Each goal was worthy, but collectively they overwhelmed local managers seeking clarity on what really mattered. While the corporate executives were quick to add new initiatives, they rarely killed old ones.

To avoid priority proliferation, managers can inject discipline into the prioritization process. At Diageo Ireland, for instance, issues are triaged into one of three categories: "soft" opportunities (or threats), which receive ongoing monitoring but no action; "hard" opportunities, which require immediate action and became a priority within the company; and "nonissues," which are dropped from the agenda altogether. The management team at one technology start-up follows a simple rule: before adding a new priority, they eliminate existing objectives to free necessary resources.

Simple rules can prevent discussions from stalling in a futile quest for complete agreement. Consensus is desirable, but the process takes time, and the costs of delay sometimes outweigh the benefits, particularly in fast-moving markets. Eisenhardt's research on successful decision making found that the most successful firms did not seek complete consensus, but neither did they veer to the other extreme and allow an autocratic leader to call all the shots.[8] Instead, the most successful teams adopted a policy of "qualified consensus," whereby they sought agreement until they recognized complete consensus was impossible, at which time they invoked a set of prespecified rules to break the deadlock. The team in one software company deferred to the functional expert (so the marketing vice president could break the deadlock on an advertising campaign) or they deferred to passion, where two passionate votes in favor outweigh three mildly opposed. The most effective rules are clear and agreed on by the team members in advance.

Teams can also adopt simple rules to guide the prioritization process when they find themselves inundated by alternatives.[9] América Latina Logistica began as a privatized branch of Brazil's freight railway. The new company had only $15 million for capital spending, while managers requested more than ten times that amount to offset decades of underinvestment under government ownership. To select from among countless capital budgeting proposals, management adopted a set of simple rules, including "eliminate bottlenecks to growing revenues," "lowest up-front cash beats highest net present value," and "reuse of existing resources beats acquiring new." These rules helped the team prioritize requests.

Companies often dole out cash, attention, and talent equally across opportunities in a misguided effort to be fair and avoid conflict. The risks were summed up in a memo by a Yahoo executive, who criticized the company for spreading resources like "peanut butter across the myriad opportunities . . . [resulting in] a thin layer of investment spread across everything we do."[10] Companies sometimes confuse a lack of discipline in resource allocation with corporate entrepreneurship. For decades 3M was a byword for corporate entrepreneurship, and the company cultivated a fertile garden of more than a thousand projects.[11] By the late 1990s, however, shareholder returns lagged behind the market. The smooth allocation of resources across opportunities ensured that the most promising initiatives received less funding than they needed to scale, while the worst received more than they deserved.

When an outside CEO joined the company from General Electric, he pruned 3M's overgrown tangle of opportunities. He installed a process to collect data from more than seventy separate laboratories to create a centralized database of all initiatives, including costs, projected sales, risks, and time to market. A group of technical directors ranked projects, then a team of senior leaders from manufacturing, marketing, and product development led a second cull, which reduced the number of projects to approximately seventy-five. These were screened against promising technologies, including nanotechnology, fuel cells, and optical displays. Each project proposal had to discuss risks and cycle times and needed to document a potential market of at least $100 million in annual sales.

FORCING HARD CHOICES IN HARD TIMES

Good times generate abundant cash, which blunts the need to make hard trade-offs, and managers can get away with spreading resources evenly. In a downturn, when cash is scarce, managers should allocate resources with greater rigor. Unfortunately, many managers try to spread the pain of downsizing evenly, demanding an identical percentage reduction in head count or expenditures, for example, across all units regardless of their future potential.

A downturn provides an opportunity to force hard choices. Consider Nokia. After the Soviet Union crumbled, Finland suffered one of the worst recessions in its history, and Nokia, then a diversified conglomerate, faced financial distress. Rather than spreading cuts evenly, Nokia's executives made the hard call to focus on the fledgling telecommunications business, while exiting other businesses accounting for nearly 90 percent of revenues.

(continued)

The Nokia example illustrates important points about making hard choices during a downturn. First, managers must be willing to reverse past commitments. During the 1980s, Nokia executives bet big on consumer electronics, but when that bet did not pay off, the top team was willing to cut their losses to expand the much smaller mobile phone business. Second, Nokia's executives recognized that focusing on telecommunications reduced the group's diversification and exposed the firm to greater risk. To offset the loss of portfolio diversification, they diversified within telecommunications, supplying both handsets and infrastructure, for example, spreading across geographic markets, and achieving economies of scale.

A downturn provides an occasion to make difficult decisions and revisit existing commitments throughout the organization. After the dot-com bubble burst in 2001, Cisco suffered a sharp decline in sales. Cisco's leadership responded by forcing hard choices at every level in the organization, including consolidating suppliers from 1,300 to 420, halving the number of channel partners, culling the bottom third of products, streamlining research and development projects, and sharply reducing acquisitions.

During the boom, Cisco middle managers enjoyed wide latitude to acquire start-ups, with the company snapping up two dozen in 2000 alone. During the downturn, Cisco tightened up the process, creating an investment review board that met monthly to vet acquisition targets. When proposing acquisitions, managers had to present detailed integration plans and personally commit to hitting sales and earnings targets for the new business.

DISCUSSIONS TO MAKE IT HAPPEN

Execution is critical, but the majority of companies struggle to translate strategy into action. Recent studies, including a survey of more than one thousand organizations globally, suggest that 60 percent of organizations fail to execute their strategy effectively.[12] One of the most widespread obstacles to execution is the gap between the nature of work in turbulent markets and the techniques organizations employ to get things done. A century ago, much economic activity could be standardized and took place inside the bounds of a strict hierarchy. Ford Motor Company produced the Model T on an assembly line, with activities from production of components through distribution of cars taking place within the confines of the Ford hierarchy. Such work could be managed through power—employees followed the boss's orders or left—and well-specified operating procedures.

In recent decades the nature of work in developed countries has changed along two dimensions. First, much of the standardized work has been outsourced, offshored, or embedded in software. The work that remains is emergent, where workers must exercise heads-up judgment in execution without guidance from detailed process manuals. Second, many activities take place outside a hierarchy of power. Workers must navigate their way through complicated matrices, alliances, outsourced service providers, and loosely organized supply chains. This is networked rather than hierarchical work. People must coordinate with others who do not report to them. Barking orders and relying on power to get things done doesn't work in a networked world. One study estimated that workers who orchestrate emerging work accounted for 41 percent of the U.S. workforce in 2004 and for 70 percent of new job creation.[13]

While the nature of execution has changed, the tools to get things done have not. Many executives still default to issuing diktats and crafting standardizing process flows, even when power is hard to wield and processes impede flexibility. Recall the study that found investment in process improvement dampened innovation. Standardized processes facilitate high-volume routine activities, but they straitjacket emergent work—such as providing a unique customer solution, dealing with an unprecedented crisis, pursuing a one-off opportunity, or experimenting with a new business model—so critical for agility in turbulent markets.

A simple but powerful mechanism—the promise—provides an alternative way to execute without recourse to standardization or hierarchical power.[14] Promises, or employees' personal pledges within and outside an organization, confer flexibility. Employees can look for the best person to do a job rather than turning to the designated contacts regardless of their competence, interest, or availability. A partner in a large accounting firm working on the nationalization of a global bank could identify partners familiar with each of the bank's global markets. Both parties can exercise creativity and flexibility in agreeing on terms that suit the specific opportunity. The accounting partners could jointly agree on how to structure the project and who would oversee each portion. People can renegotiate as new information arises or priorities shift. Renegotiating promises is not easy, but it is less disruptive than reengineering a well-oiled process.

People often take a legalistic view of promises, defining them according to deal terms, much as lawyers might focus on specific clauses in a contract. The discussions that keep an agreement alive are more important than the specific terms. Both sides must thrash out what the recipient wants and why, how the person making the promise plans to satisfy the request, and any constraints or competing priorities that could derail delivery.

When leading discussions to solicit, negotiate, and monitor promises, managers should maintain a tone of discipline by demanding explicit promises and holding people accountable for delivery. They should temper that discipline with support to ensure that the person making the promise has what they need to deliver. Support can take several forms. A bank president might, for example, authorize the IT department to hire additional engineers or take other projects off the to-do list. Promises have teeth to the extent they are well made. The best promises share five characteristics; they are public, active, voluntary, explicit, and they include a clear rationale for why they matter.

Public. The most effective promises are made in public, to increase the cost of wriggling out of them, and to help employees understand how initiatives relate to one another. When Akin Öngör took over as CEO of Garanti Bank, he noticed that managers often failed to deliver on their promises to colleagues. He published managers' commitments in the company's weekly newsletter, along with updates on their progress. At Mittal Steel's Mexican plant, internal service agreements were posted publicly, including who promised what to whom by when. Public promises clear the fog of anonymity that surrounds collective commitments made to abstract goals such as "capturing synergies" or "filling the white spaces." The person making a commitment has a name and face in mind when executing the agreement, and the recipient knows who is accountable to deliver.

Active. Misunderstandings often arise when people from dissimilar functions, markets, or business units try to achieve a meeting of minds on what needs to get done. Based on their divergent backgrounds, they may understand the same promise in very different ways. Active probing by both sides does not eliminate these miscues, but can surface them eariler. Back and forth discussions clarify requests and produce creative counteroffers when the original request is infeasible to achieve.

The Royal Bank of Canada builds active discussions into its system to monitor opportunities for revenue growth. The person responsible for each initiative actively negotiates the milestones appropriate to the specific opportunity, rather than promising to hit standardized success metrics. They might judge an e-banking start-up by unique visitors to the Web site and revenue growth rather than total profits. The managers meet regularly to discuss progress and to renegotiate as necessary, much as an entrepreneur might with a venture capitalist.

Voluntary. In many organizations, people feel compelled to comply with every request in order to maintain their reputation as a team player, please the boss, or simply avoid looking like a jerk. When the response to every request is yes, it counts for little. A responsible no, in contrast, often signals resource constraints or conflicting priorities. To offset the tendency toward a meaningless yes, managers should legitimize responses other than automatic agreement. One software executive gave his team a set of cards, most of which were marked "yes" or "counteroffer," while three were marked "no." Using those cards, team members could decline three requests per quarter, provided they explained their rationale to the whole team. Commitment-phobic employees will abuse a voluntary system, and keeping them on the team undermines the effectiveness of voluntary promises.

Explicit. A large hydroelectric engineering joint venture recognized the need for clarity of organizational promises. From its inception in 2000, Voith Siemens Hydro Power Generation battled upstart Chinese and Indian manufacturers at the low end of the market and established rivals, including GE and Alstom, at the high end. The company responded by offering integrated solutions—entire power houses, including turbines, generators, and other components. To seize these opportunities, managers needed to revise how employees in different disciplines, departments, and regions managed their promises. The CEO initiated a program to ensure that promises were explicit. Engineers in the various disciplines created and distributed a set of checklists to guide requests and promises. The checklists specified a handful of factors that had to be clear to both parties, including names, dates, underlying rationales for requests, and the skills necessary to get the job done. The engineers established periodic design freezes, during which they would check that everyone shared an explicit agreement on who was doing what by when.

Motivated. People often make requests without explaining why they matter, and the recipient struggles to understand why the work is important. The most effective promises are motivated, in the sense that the rationale for the request is clearly laid out and linked to organizational priorities. It can be cumbersome to explain how a specific initiative fits in the overall corporate strategy, but when people understand why their promise matters, they are more likely to execute it with vigor despite conflicting demands and unforeseen roadblocks. Armed with a clear understanding of the underlying rationale, they can exercise creativity in meeting the spirit of the request instead of blindly fulfilling it to the letter. The U.S. Marine Corps uses mission-based orders, which articulate what the commanding officer wants and why, and why this matters to *his* commanding officer as well. After providing clarity on what to achieve and how it matters, mission-based orders leave the how of implementation to the discretion of the subordinate officer.[15]

DISCUSSIONS TO MAKE REVISIONS

In principle, discussions to make revisions are simple: the team discusses what they expected to happen and what actually happened, explores discrepancies between expectations and reality, and adjusts their mental map accordingly. Many managers, however, skip discussions to make revisions. When things are working, they continue plowing ahead, following the principle "If it ain't broke, don't fix it." They keep their sights fixed on the future and dismiss reflection on the past as a waste of time.

Even clear failure often fails to spur revision of an existing mental map and the associated commitments. People fear that any analysis of what went wrong will degenerate into an exercise in doling out blame rather than distilling lessons. People feel threatened by the scrutiny of their actions, and tend to personalize feedback as criticism of their competence, judgment, or motivation. The blame game is common but not inevitable. Founded and staffed by fighter pilots, the consulting firm Afterburner applies an iterative model used by the U.S. Air Force to help companies enhance their ability to execute. To ensure an honest discussion while debriefing an initiative, Afterburner advocates a "nameless and rankless" discussion, where anyone can bring up any issue. Leaders start the meeting by acknowledging what didn't work for them and inviting criticism from the other team members to set a tone of open discussion.[16]

A fundamental obstacle to revision is the mistaken assumption that a map is right and failure is attributable to unforeseen events or feeble execution. In a turbulent world, it is better to assume the map is wrong. The partners of ONSET Ventures, an early-stage venture capital firm, begin with this premise. They will not seek additional funding for a venture until its business model has changed at least once, nor will they hire a CEO until the business model has stabilized.

Leaders must balance perseverance with the critical distance required to examine and revise a map and the related commitments. Alternating between periods of heads-down execution and dispassionate revision can help manage the map paradox. ONSET's partners meet regularly to pose hard questions about portfolio firms: "If this deal walked in fresh today, would we still invest? Have they delivered what they promised? Why shouldn't we pull the plug?" Before and after these meetings to question the plan, partners support the portfolio companies wholeheartedly, but they periodically shift into revision mode to reexamine their maps.

ONSET partners have built in a system to balance commitment to a map with distance. Founders are long on commitment but often too mired in details to see the flaws in their plan. ONSET partners serve as mentors to help the entrepreneur revisit his or her assumptions. Even partners can fall in love with a deal and lose perspective, however, so their colleagues provide a backstop in the revision meetings. ONSET also invites outsiders, including customers and other venture capital firms, into the revision process. Late-stage investors describe what actions a start-up team could take—such as launching a prototype of the product, validating market size, or lining up early users—to increase its valuation in subsequent rounds. Figure 8.2 summarizes discussions at each stage in the agility loop.

Over a lunch in Qingdao a few years ago, I asked Mianmian Yang, then the COO of Chinese appliance maker Haier, what she looked for in a manager. She explained that most executives focus too much on IQ—intellectual horsepower—and EQ, or the ability to work with people. Both are necessary, she explained, but in turbulent markets such as China's, great leaders differed from good leaders in terms of TQ—a leader's tenacity quotient.

Leading discussions through the loop demands tenacity despite inevitable setbacks. A dogfight with fighter planes will be over in minutes, but organizational agility confers its benefits over decades. Tenacity is often equated with formulating a plan and then sticking to it doggedly; think of Jacob wrestling the stranger, holding on throughout the night. But this rigid tenacity, devoid of revision, often leads to disaster in a turbulent world. Leaders should instead aspire to flexible

FIGURE 8.2 Discussions Through the Agility Loop

	Make Sense	Make Choices	Make It Happen	Make Revisions
Objective	Develop a shared mental map of a situation	Agree on clear priorities to guide action and resource allocation	Ensure people make good promises and deliver on them	Compare assumptions with reality, explore gaps, and adjust the map and related commitments
Appropriate tone	Open inquiry	Respectful argumentation	Supportive discipline	Dispassionate analysis
Information support	Real-time, unfiltered, shared, and holistic data	Ongoing monitoring of the portfolio of priorities	Monitor performance against promises	Variance reporting to spot divergence between the plan and actual results
Required leadership traits	The ability to grasp the essence of a messy situation Curiosity Empathy to see other points of view	Decisiveness Sensitivity to keeping the social fabric intact through hard discussions Credibility to make the call	Trustworthiness Ability to excite the troops about ambitious promises Drive to maintain a sense of urgency	Intellectual humility Sensitivity to anomalies

Common pitfalls	Advocating preexisting positions	Personalize proposals	Private promises	Skip altogether
	Failure to see the situation from other viewpoints	Fail to explore alternatives	Passive agreement	Hold too late
	Anchoring too quickly on one viewpoint	Superficial agreement	Meaningless yes	Blame game
	Bias for premature action	Priority proliferation	Implicit agreements	
		Search for unobtainable consensus	What without why	
		Spread resources evenly		
Killer questions	What fresh data would convince us our interpretation is wrong?	What other options do we have?	What did you promise to do?	What did we expect to happen versus what really happened?
	What is surprising?	What will we stop doing in order to free required resources?	What have you done?	Why was there a difference?
	What is changing?		What is hindering you?	What should we change?
	What opportunities do we see?			Which commitments that worked in the past are holding us back now?

tenacity, which combines urgency in execution with adaptation as circumstances change. Instead of Jacob holding on throughout the night, leaders should emulate Hercules. The Greek hero grappled with Nereus, the old man of the sea, who while wrestling could change shape from lion to serpent to water to a tree. Hercules never let go, but he also adjusted his hold as Nereus shifted from shape to shape. In the end Hercules prevailed.

9.

BUILDING AN AGILE ORGANIZATION

On November 18, 2008, August Busch IV relinquished his role as president and CEO of the brewing company run by his family for five generations, and transferred control to InBev. The combined entity, now Anheuser-Busch InBev, became the largest brewer in the world by volume, revenues, and profit. Busch, a scion of the family that built Anheuser-Busch into the dominant brewer in the United States, had opposed the acquisition, but relented after InBev sweetened its bid to $52 billion.

The press referred to InBev as a European firm, but in fact the company that drove the creation of the world's largest brewer was Brazilian. InBev emerged from the 2004 merger of Belgium's Interbrew and Brazil's AmBev. The Brazilian partner provided the chairman, the CEO, and approximately 90 percent of the senior executives, while the Belgians contributed brands and factories. The Brazilians, not the Belgians, ran the show.

Companhia Cervejaria Brahma, commonly known as Brahma, was founded in 1888 by a Swiss brewer who named the company, according to various accounts, for the Hindu god of creation, the composer Johannes Brahms, or the inventor of the float-and-valve flush toilet.[1] Brahma built a national network over the following century, but it always trailed its larger rival Companhia Antarctica Paulista, known as Antarctica.

A century later, Brahma offered its employees little cause for celebration as its centennial approached in 1988. As the weaker of Brazil's leading brewers, Brahma struggled to maintain market share in the turbulent Brazilian market. By the late 1980s, consumers preferred Antarctica's lager three to one over Brahma's flagship brew, and Brahma lagged its market rival on nearly every operational and financial metric. Brahma's distress attracted the unwanted attention of investors who launched a hostile takeover bid for the company. The company was nearly bust.

In the two decades that followed, Brahma skirted bankruptcy and transformed itself from a Brazilian also-ran to the leading partner in the world's largest brewer. Brahma initiated a series of deals, acquiring its Brazilian rival, merging with Belgian brewer InterBrew, all culminating in the Anheuser-Busch acquisition. Brahma's rise is not a story of grand strategy or vision; indeed, the CEO openly dismissed both. Rather, it illustrates how an organization can achieve the agility to seize opportunities, and mitigate threats, in turbulent markets.

WINNING BY AGILITY

Late in the summer of 1989, a trio of bankers associated with Brazil's Banco de Investimentos Garantia paid $50 million to acquire a controlling stake in Brahma. The partners decided that one of their own, Marcel Telles, would take over as CEO of the brewing company. When Telles joined Brahma in November 1989, few expected him to reverse the brewer's decline, let alone guide it to global leadership. Brahma's financial position remained precarious, and Brazil was heading for a steep downturn. The year 1990 marked the beginning of Brazil's deepest recession in nearly a decade, with the country's gross domestic product shrinking by 4.2 percent that year, accompanied by a sharp increase in unemployment.[2]

Telles was not an obvious candidate to lead the company, having spent his entire career as a securities trader—someone who, as he described the role, "stays in a trading room and has no contact whatsoever with the external world, knows nothing about industry or markets."[3] Telles had never run a business, never worked in brewing (or any other industry), or managed more than half a secretary until the day he took the helm of a brewing company with twenty-five thousand employees. Telles, however, had two advantages—long experience with turbulence and a career at Garantia.

For twenty years, Telles had made his living trading on Brazil's turbulence, and he expected the volatility to continue. He was right. In 1989, Brazilians chose Fernando Affonso Collor de Mello as the first democratically elected president in Brazil after nearly three decades of military rule. The thirty-nine-year-old Collor, a former Brazilian karate champion, won the election despite his image as a playboy. He campaigned with his second wife, a college senior at the time. Once in office, Collor eradicated protective tariffs, unleashing competitive upheaval. Nineteen of Brazil's twenty largest automobile parts suppliers ceased to exist in less than three years. Collor froze individual savings—Brazilians could not make withdrawals from their own bank accounts—sharply reducing consumption.

Throughout the 1990s, Brazilians paid their bills in four separate currencies. Crises in Mexico, Asia, Russia, and Argentina whipsawed Brazil's economy, triggering dramatic swings in exchange and interest rates.[4] Brazilians experienced hyperinflation, with prices rising more than 20 percent each month—the price of a loaf of bread could rise twice in the course of a shopping trip—before the currency stabilized in the mid-1990s.

Telles had learned to master turbulence while working at Garantia, a bank founded in 1971 by Jorge Paulo Lemann.[5] Lemann had returned to his native Brazil after studying economics at Harvard, playing professional tennis (including games at Wimbledon), and working as an intern at Credit Suisse. Lemann and his partners pooled their capital to buy a seat on the Rio de Janeiro stock exchange but lost more than half their capital within a few months when the Brazilian market collapsed. Lemann bought out his initial partners and over time built Garantia into the leading investment bank in Brazil.

As the bank thrived, Garantia's new partners pooled their personal capital and used the funds to buy controlling stakes in companies including a nonfood retailer, a joint venture with Wal-Mart, and a logistics company. The bank and the companies in its orbit shared common practices—they recruited the most talented graduates in the country, rewarded performance with generous bonuses, shared ownership with employees, scoured the globe for best practices, and captured real-time data. The Garantia group companies also shared common values, including internal competition, informality, and a relentless drive to cut costs.

Telles drew on Garantia's practices and values to transform Brahma into an organization that excelled at operational agility, no mean feat considering the state of the company when he arrived. When Telles joined Brahma in 1989, the organization resembled a government bureaucracy that happened to make beer. The brewer had a strict hierarchy, with four separate restaurants, one each for employees, supervisors, middle managers, and senior executives. When a whistle blew at 5:00 P.M., the factory shook as employees stampeded down the steps to clock out. A decade later, however, Brahma was the corporate equivalent of the Sabre jet, able to spot and exploit opportunities consistently faster than market leader Antarctica.

Improvements in Brahma's distribution are a good example of the type of opportunities for operational improvement the brewer exploited. Distribution to small eating places was critical in Brazil because customers consumed three-quarters of all beer in bars and restaurants, rather than buying it in stores. Beer imbibed in bars and restaurants, moreover, generated three times the profit per bottle compared to beer sold in stores. Telles searched around the world for the best ways to run a distribution network and ultimately adopted processes used by Anheuser-Busch. Telles and his team cut off distributors who failed to follow new requirements, and invested heavily in those who embraced the new practices. In less than a decade, Brahma cut the number of distributors in half while increasing the productivity of those remaining nearly fourfold.

Anheuser-Busch distributed its beer in Brazil through Antarctica's network. Despite privileged access to the American brewer's playbook, Antarctica managers dawdled in implementing state-of-the-art practices and pruning less-effective distributors. Antarctica made most of its changes in the late 1990s, years after Brahma had transformed its own network. This pattern played out repeatedly throughout the 1990s. Telles spotted opportunities arising out of turbulence and seized them. Antarctica's managers saw the same opportunities but started a year or two later than Brahma, took longer to execute, and finished later.

In a manner reminiscent of the dogfights between a Sabre and a MiG, Brahma shifted through a series of maneuvers faster than Antarctica, building a state-of-the-art factory, expanding into neighboring countries, exploiting cost efficiencies, introducing new products, and beating Antarctica to the punch in signing a distribution deal with Pepsi. Each opportunity conferred modest benefits, but their cumulative impact proved decisive. Within a decade, Brahma was four times more valuable than its rival.

Brahma's senior executives made four major changes to transform the company from a slow-moving bureaucracy into an agile organization. They secured real-time, unfiltered, shared, and holistic data; they installed the organizational equivalent of the Sabre jet's full hydraulics to translate corporate objectives into action; they developed a cohort of ambitious managers; and they built a corporate culture to underpin agility.

RUSH DATA

As a trader, Telles understood the value of real-time, unfiltered, shared, and holistic information. When Telles joined Brahma he found data that were stale and patchy in scope, and he assigned a key executive to build a management information system that could provide daily profit-and-loss reports by product line for each of Brahma's million points of sale. Antarctica's managers, in contrast, continued to rely on market information aggregated at the state level and reported on a monthly basis.

Like Zara's executives, Telles knocked down the walls. He replaced offices and cubicles with an open workspace modeled on a trading floor, where every executive from the CEO down worked at the same-sized desk in the large open space. The shared space allowed managers to interact continuously to forge a shared mental map. Telles capped the number of total employees in the headquarters at 240, based on the number of traders and investment bankers on the floor at Garantia. A larger group, he feared, would impede the free flow of information. The open office proved so successful that Brahma soon extended the layout to most company operations, including plants and call centers.

"You don't learn anything at headquarters," Telles observed. "It's easy to be fooled by PowerPoint presentations." Instead of bringing field managers to the home office, the headquarters went into the field. Brahma's senior executives spent one or two weeks each month visiting local operations to observe the situation firsthand, identify unexpected opportunities or threats, and agree on midcourse corrections. They also visited suppliers and customers. If they suspected a sales representative was giving them the red carpet treatment only at satisfied customers' locations, they insisted on unannounced trips to random outlets to get a fuller picture.

Brahma executives put the local data into a global perspective. They tracked global trends, visiting leading brewers such as Modelo, Coors, and Anheuser-Busch to identify best practices and understand trends in their markets. Teams analyzed European and North American brewers as potential acquisitions, to dig into their underlying financials. Based on this analysis, Brahma executives concluded the industry was destined for consolidation to a handful of global brewers, and concluded they needed to position Brahma for the endgame. While Antarctica saw the world through the bottom of a Coke bottle, their counterparts at Brahma viewed it through a bubble canopy.

ORGANIZATIONAL HYDRAULICS

To translate insights into action, Brahma executives built the corporate equivalent of the Sabre's full hydraulics. *Organizational hydraulics*, as I use the term, describes the processes that link corporate objectives to individual action throughout the organization, much as an airplane's hydraulic controls translate the pilot's intent into action. Many organizations rely on partial hydraulics, where senior executives must exert heroic efforts to ensure execution. Agile organizations, in contrast, run on full hydraulics, where corporate priorities are converted smoothly into effective action.

Organizational hydraulics start at the top when the senior team sets the agenda and outlines key priorities for the organization as a whole. In many organizations, agility stalls in the boardroom, when top executives proliferate priorities. Recall the European engineering firm with more than fifty so-called priorities. A glut of competing objectives fragments attention, effort, and resources. Across a wide range of settings, cognitive psychologists find that people can store no more than three to four similar items in their primary memory and remember these flawlessly without prompting.[6] More items impede recollection and muddy the issues. If you chase one hundred rabbits, according to a Japanese proverb, you catch no rabbits. The same is true with organizational priorities.

Based on their understanding of the situation at a point in time, Brahma executives established three priorities each year, such as improving distribution, relaunching a low-price brand, or improving productivity. The best priorities are concrete, clearly linked to market conditions, and uncluttered by competing mandates from the top, such as mission, vision, purpose, or ambition. They clarify the company's main effort in any year, prevent dissipation of resources, and offer clear accountability. Brahma executives posted the priorities publicly throughout all facilities to keep them at the top of the mind for employees.

Ensuring execution on priorities requires a system to cascade objectives through the organization. At Brahma, employees at each level met with their boss to agree on their individual targets for the following year, while business unit heads negotiated five objectives for their operation. Quantitative targets trumped qualitative ones, as did objectives that could be tracked on an ongoing basis rather than those that could only be assessed at year-end. Brahma capped the number of targets at five for any individual or unit to maintain focus.

Brahma's information systems tracked performance against objectives at the corporate, unit, and individual level, and the company posted the results publicly. Behind every desk in Brahma's open office hung a chart that listed the employee's objectives, color-coded to denote progress. A green dot indicated on track, a yellow dot meant at risk, and a red dot flagged initiatives off track. The system applied to every manager, including the CEO and senior executives, who also worked at desks in the open office. Repeated failure to meet objectives led to dismissal, but the occasional red dot was tolerated. Carlos Brito, who succeeded Telles as CEO, noted, "It is better to be red once than consistently yellow."

Brahma linked compensation to performance against unit and individual objectives. Brahma's base salary matched the industry average, but bonuses were significantly larger. Telles explained, "A bonus has to be large enough to truly motivate people. If you give it to everybody, it won't be big enough." Top-performing managers earned a bonus equivalent to eighteen months' salary; the next tier earned nine months' salary, while the bottom 40 percent received no bonus. Factories were benchmarked against one another, and employees in the top one-third of plants in terms of relative performance (adjusting for plant size, technology, etc.) were rewarded with bonus payments, while workers in the other plants received nothing.

Annual bonuses encourage a short-term perspective, while individual objectives undermine cooperation. Brahma modified its compensation system to encourage long-term thinking and cooperation. No one earned a bonus unless the firm as a whole hit its numbers. Brahma created a partnership within the company to offset the pressure toward selfish or short-term behavior. Any of the existing two hundred partners could nominate a candidate, and after careful evaluation the partnership as a whole voted, with a unanimous vote required for election. Newly elected partners borrowed money to buy Brahma shares and paid back the loans out of their future bonuses. Repayments consumed three-quarters of the average partner's bonus.

COHORT OF VIKINGS

Agility requires employees alert to opportunities and aggressive enough to seize them; employees that I compare to Nordic Vikings, who took to their longboats, left home, and searched for opportunity. The nineteenth-century entrepreneurs who built Brahma's national network exemplified the Viking spirit, braving floods, hostile natives, extreme terrain, and the occasional outbreak of the plague as they expanded the brewer's reach across Brazil. After they conquered a bit of terrain, however, Vikings often settled down to cultivate it; growing comfortable with their plot of land and losing their edge. Vikings, in short, become farmers. The same dynamic takes place in organizations. As the founders settle down or retire, many firms become comfortable places to work, attracting employees who crave security and repelling those who seek adventure. By the 1980s, Brahma had become a farming community, staffed by employees who valued the company's generous pension plan and job for life, but had little appetite for the aggressive pursuit of opportunity.

I am not arguing that Vikings are good and farmers are bad. Vikings often win the glory and wealth but run a higher risk of heart attack and divorce. Nor should an organization hire all Vikings to the exclusion of the farmers, who bring stability and continuity to ongoing operations. Telles and his team consciously avoided a policy, like that adopted by General Electric, of firing the bottom 10 percent of performers every year. Farmers could till the fields at Brahma. They might not earn fat bonuses, but they need not fear job loss either. Building an agile organization requires getting the balance of farmers and Vikings right.

When Garantia bought Brahma, the company was farmer-rich and Viking-poor. Telles assembled a core team of three outsiders to help him, including a marketing executive from Brazil's leading chocolate maker, a fellow trader as chief financial officer, and Carlos Brito, a twenty-nine-year-old with an MBA from Stanford. The team spent the first few weeks conducting brief interviews with the top two layers of managers, explaining that they would rely on Brahma employees to fill out the management ranks. Based on these interviews, they selected a group of midlevel managers to help drive further changes, and identified managers unlikely to make the transition, who were fired or reassigned.

The senior team tried hiring industry veterans but found them too cynical and political for Brahma's culture. Instead they supplemented internal promotions with new recruits. In 1990, the company launched a trainee program for graduating college seniors, and in the following decade they hired more than four hundred graduates.

Sixty percent moved into management positions, and many became partners. A job at Brahma was among the most coveted positions in Brazil, with more than nine thousand students applying for twenty-five trainee positions per year—making the training program an order of magnitude more selective than colleges such as Harvard or Oxford. Telles and other top executives oversaw the recruiting process, personally visiting leading universities to woo students, and interviewing all final-round candidates.

Brahma selected candidates for their ambition, negotiation skills, ability to work under pressure, fluency in English, and computer skills. Trainees spent their first four months rotating through different units to understand the business as a whole, and then another five months working on a high-profile project. In 1998, voluntary employee turnover among trainees was zero. Candidates, for their part, flocked to Brahma for the opportunities to advance rapidly, to work in an environment where their opinions counted, for access to senior executives, and to seize the financial upside if they did well.

All Brahma managers were expected to spend half their time developing talent within the organization, spending time on activities including recruiting, mentoring, and providing constructive performance reviews twice a year to all direct reports. Telles attributes Brahma's return on investment not to strategy, successful acquisitions, or financial engineering. Rather he puts it down to Brahma's system for attracting Vikings and harnessing their energy to the company's objectives.

Attracting Vikings is one thing, but keeping them is another. The partnership provided a powerful tool for betting on young talent. Every year the partners reserved the right to make up to twenty "bets" by offering partnership to superstars with only a year or two of experience in the brewer, to lock them into the company. Equity alone is not enough to retain Vikings; they also require opportunities to distinguish themselves. Telles compared Brahma (and later Am-Bev and InBev) to a bicycle that can remain upright only while in motion. To retain Vikings, a company must offer them a steady flow of opportunities to excel; otherwise they look outside the firm for adventure. By 2004, most AmBev senior executives were in their thirties and forties, leaving little room for promotions. The Interbrew merger was timed, in part, to ensure a steady flow of opportunities for new Vikings.

CULTURE OF AGILITY

All agile companies that I have studied put five values at or near the heart of their culture: performance, transparency, informality, partnership, and cost consciousness. These firms use different words to express the same ideas—"merit", "achievement", or "execution" might denote performance. Companies manifest the values in different ways. Few companies, for example, post performance publicly, as Brahma did. The core values, however, remain remarkably constant across agile firms.

Performance. It all starts with performance. Agility is not about pulling off one grand strategic coup, but rather about relentless execution sustained over time. Organizational hydraulics translate corporate priorities into individual objectives, while incentives reward their successful completion. A corporate culture that recognizes, prizes, and rewards outstanding performance against aggressive objectives underpins these processes.

Managers can reinforce performance by recognizing achievement publicly. Vikings crave recognition for their accomplishments—the adult equivalent of the gold star on a student's work. Many organizations, however, withhold recognition to avoid alienating the majority of employees whose performance is, by definition, average. Brahma recognized performance in several ways, including public posting of personal performance, election to partnership, and lopsided bonuses. The star performers valued the outsized financial incentives of eighteen months' bonus and equity, but they also appreciated the recognition from their peers that these rewards signified.

Symbolic gestures reinforce performance. In many organizations, status, hierarchical power, tenure, or a personal relationship with the boss determine who gets ahead. Purging status symbols sends a powerful signal that performance matters above all else. Telles eliminated the status symbols, including special dining rooms, parking places, and washrooms for executives, to signal that performance alone would differentiate employees going forward. Brahma also severed ties with distributors run by relatives of current Brahma employees to make clear that distributors would be evaluated exclusively on how well they did against their objectives.

Transparency. Many executives dismiss transparency as an airy-fairy aspiration that sounds nice in theory but could not survive contact with the real world. Wrong. Transparency confers hard-nosed benefits—it builds trust in the compensation system, maintains pressure to perform, and minimizes the risk that employees will take unethical shortcuts. Transparency in performance evaluation, including public posting of objectives and performance, minimizes speculation that executives hammer out bonuses and promotions in a smoke-filled room, favoring their cronies. By all accounts, Brahma's system creates a pressure-cooker environment. Some employees disliked the constant pressure, but even they agreed the evaluation process was fair.

The Brahma team applied the same transparency when setting the corporation's overall financial targets. In 1999, Brahma's finance office analyzed the annual growth in earnings implied in the company's stock price, and estimated that Brahma would need to deliver a minimum of 15 percent growth in cash flows to justify its current valuation, which set the floor for the company's financial objectives the next year. The team communicated not only the goal but how they had arrived at it. Employees viewed the target as ambitious, but not arbitrary.

The combination of aggressive employees, internal competition, and objectives that ratchet upward creates pressure to perform. It also creates pressure to cut corners. Several companies, including Enron, BP, and Drexel Burnham Lambert, built aggressive cultures that rose by agility but suffered from unethical, and in some cases illegal, behavior. Recognizing this danger, Brahma executives took steps to mitigate it. Partners bought stock with their own money, rather than receiving options as a gift. Holding equity exposed them to personal losses if colleagues took actions that could destroy value for the firm as a whole, and heightened their vigilance toward illegal behavior.

Brahma's extreme transparency left few shadows where employees could cheat in private. "Sunlight," as Louis Brandeis observed, "is the best disinfectant." Brahma reported operational and financial performance to employees and outside investors far in excess of legal disclosure requirements. The company's ownership structure combined the Garantia investors who held a controlling stake with two hundred partners observing the business day in and day out, and with public owners who brought an outside perspective. Armed with good data, the three types of owners created a system of checks and balances that mitigated the risk of environmental, ethical, compliance, or safety lapses that could endanger the company's success or even viability. When a company such as Enron or BP overlooks a manager's wrongdoing because he hits his numbers, it sends a strong signal that performance trumps ethics. Firing a high-performing manager for ethical transgressions, in contrast, broadcasts throughout the organization that such lapses will not be tolerated, no matter how well someone performs.

Informality. Agility requires employees to offer divergent interpretations, disagree respectfully, discuss performance frankly, and surface unexpected data. Formality and excess deference to hierarchy imperil these discussions. Hierarchy often breeds a sense of infallibility or self-importance that poisons frank discussions. It is neither feasible nor desirable to eliminate hierarchy altogether—top leaders need the power to set priorities, make decisions, and settle disagreements. That said, it is possible to downplay hierarchical distinctions in day-to-day discussions.

The physical layout of a work space can foster informality. The phalanx of receptionists and locked doors that protect senior executives in most large companies reinforce power differentials, while an open office forces executives to remain accessible. Brahma executives held discussions at round tables, a common choice among leaders trying to encourage informality, because no one sits at the head of a round table. A shift in office layout or furniture alone confers little benefit, but combined with other actions, it can be a powerful symbol to reinforce informality.

Partnership. The Viking spirit turns destructive when internal competition crowds out cooperation. The Viking heaven was Valhalla, where warriors feasted together all night, then hacked their comrades to pieces all day. Brahma mitigated the risk of destructive competition in part through incentives. No one received a bonus if the company failed to hit its targets, and equity provided partners incentives to chip in on initiatives that would create value for the firm as a whole, and ensure their subordinates did the same.

The open office environment promoted frequent interaction, which helped employees see how their work interacted with others'. A marketing manager might have a brilliant idea for a packaging re-design, but a spontaneous discussion with a manufacturing colleague could quickly clarify the costs associated with the innovation. An open office reduces the backstabbing, hiding, and politics that pre-vail when employees work in silos. Relatively frequent job rotations prevent managers from growing too parochial in their outlook, while the partnership reinforces the sense of belonging to a cohort that col-laborates on companywide decisions. These mechanisms do not elim-inate internal competition, but the sense of shared destiny blunts some of its sharper edges.

Cost-consciousness. Many companies veer between periods of un-disciplined growth and brutal cost cutting. During a boom, manag-ers press on the gas pedal to pursue every opportunity in sight. When the economic cycle turns, they slam on the brakes, abandon growth, and slash expenses to free cash. As the economy picks up again, they abandon their newfound cost discipline to pursue rev-enue growth. This stop-go approach is a mistake. In hard times, managers should remain alert to opportunities. They should main-tain a relentless focus on efficiency during booms, when unneces-sary costs sprout like weeds.

Managers can use a downturn not only to cut costs in the short term but also to build processes to maintain cost discipline when the economy rebounds. Facing a deep recession in Brazil, Brahma introduced zero-based budgeting, which required managers to develop their budget from scratch and justify each budget item anew. It not only cut costs that year but also instilled an ongoing cost discipline that carried forward when the recession ended. Carnival Cruise Lines survived the depth of recession in the early 1970s by focusing on efficiency, and maintained that discipline in subsequent decades. Carnival's cost-consciousness allowed the company to earn a 5–10 percent advantage in operating costs as a percentage of revenues over the following decades. Cumulatively, these cost savings provided the cash to acquire rivals, build new ships, and overtake Royal Caribbean as the undisputed industry leader.

THE LEADER'S ROLE

Organizational power, many believe, is a fixed-sum game, where top-down power comes at the expense of bottom-up autonomy. Agile organizations, however, demand both strong senior executives and empowered employees. Viking managers need the leeway to exercise judgment and creativity in hitting their objectives, while senior executives must set these priorities in the first place. Senior executives build the agile organization, including changes to information systems, compensation, and culture that can only come from the top.

Building organizational agility often requires a sharp break from past practices. As a result, leaders need a mandate from the owners and board of directors, who must understand that the process takes years and entails inevitable setbacks. As the transformation shows results, senior leaders can point to their track record to secure support for later changes. At the outset, however, they need support for transformation until the changes produce tangible benefits.

To build an agile organization, leaders must work all the levers—RUSH data to make sense of a turbulent situation, organizational hydraulics to translate priorities into execution, the cadre of Viking managers to execute, an agile culture, and their own leadership style. Managers often pull one or two levers, usually the most accessible or most familiar. That is a mistake. The components of an agile organization reinforce one another and work best in unison. One European telecommunications company invested heavily in information systems to track their environment and hired futurologists to anticipate emerging opportunities and threats. The company, however, failed to reward execution or promote executives based on performance, legacies from its days as a government-owned enterprise. As a result, the company consistently anticipated market shifts, and consistently failed to exploit them.

In building a culture of agility, senior leaders must exemplify the values they expect from others. Brahma's senior executives posted their objectives and performance behind their desks just like everyone else. Although Brahma's top team could have selected employees eligible to buy stock, they instead delegated that decision to the partnership.

Leaders must not only embody the culture but also protect it, especially as a company grows. Rapid growth can dilute a corporate culture as a deluge of new recruits come in, overwhelming veterans' ability to indoctrinate them in the company's values through frequent interaction and example. The leadership of one global professional services firm faced growth opportunities in the 1980s but feared diluting their culture. After a careful analysis of how new recruits came to embody the firm's values, including recruitment, training, apprenticeship, and turnover, the firm's leadership concluded that growth in excess of 20 percent per year would overwhelm the firm's ability to transmit its values, and consequently dilute its culture. They turned away business to keep below the culture-maintaining speed limit. In contrast to most investment banks, which grew by cobbling together disparate acquisitions, Goldman Sachs favored organic growth to preserve its culture.

Agility breeds success, but success breeds complacency. As an agile organization begins to outexecute rivals and win share in the market, employees tend to relax and execute with less urgency. They question the need to push so hard, particularly in keeping costs low. The temptation to ease up is understandable but corrosive. Agility prevails through relentless execution, accumulating small victories over time. Organizations cannot afford to let down their guard. Life-threatening perils, such as the 2008 credit crisis, or major opportunities, like InBev's acquisition of Anheuser-Busch, create their own pressure. Leaders must maintain a sense of urgency in the lulls between the storms. Viking managers, internal competition, and pay-for performance all stimulate urgency, but they are not enough. Leaders must inject pressure in good times to ensure that the organization can survive hard times.

Brahma's rise illustrates the power of operational agility—a company's capacity, within a focused business model, to identify and seize opportunities more quickly than rivals can. The transformation from a slow-moving bureaucracy to an agile organization demonstrates that even the most hidebound bureaucracy can achieve agility. Finally, the timing of transformation, begun in a deep recession, demonstrates how downturns open a window of opportunity to initiate and accelerate a transformation to build an agile organization.

TRANSFORMATION IN A DOWNTURN

Major change efforts are difficult in the best of times. In the midst of a downturn, managers fixate on immediate concerns—declining demand, scarce credit, and layoffs—and view a comprehensive transformation of their organization and culture as a luxury they cannot afford. The worst of times for the economy as a whole, however, can be the best of times for leaders to drive transformation. Brahma began its transformation from a bureaucracy to an agile organization during Brazil's deep recession in 1990. In past downturns, other firms including Toyota, Nokia, Cisco, and Samsung emerged from an economic crisis more agile than when they entered it. Like the mythical Libyan wrestler Antaeus (who regained vigor when thrown to the ground), these companies grew stronger during hard times.

Every downturn opens a window of opportunity to drive transformation. An economic crisis marks a sharp break with the past that lowers resistance to change and cuts through complacency. Observing the discontinuity, employees understand that they cannot continue to do more of what worked in the past. An economic crisis brings latent challenges to a head, and managers can harness the resulting urgency to tackle them. Market crises provide an external rationale—"the recession made me do it"—to justify painful decisions that would appear extreme in better times. Finally, an economic crisis provides managers with air cover to make decisions that incur short-term financial pain for long-term gain, such as culling products, "firing" unprofitable customers, or exiting money-losing businesses. In a downturn, investors, boards, and bosses are more forgiving of long-term changes that incur short-term performance dips.

Downturns offer an opportunity to accelerate ongoing transformations as well as initiate new ones. Change initiatives require

(continued)

eight to ten years to complete in large organizations and often run out of steam along the way. Downturns provide an ideal opportunity to reinvigorate an ongoing transformation. Managers can harness a downturn to renew a sense of urgency, justify unpopular decisions, and shake up complacent employees. After succeeding his father as chairman of the Samsung Group in 1987, Lee Kun Hee kicked off a program to transform the conglomerate from a solid Korean competitor to an agile global leader.[7] Fifteen years later, the group's flagship business, Samsung Electronics, had achieved the chairman's ambition—leading in technological innovation, new product introductions, brand awareness, and financial returns. A careful analysis of Samsung's transformation reveals that most of the critical changes that propelled the group to global leadership were concentrated during two downturns.

After a promising start in the mid-1980s, Samsung's transformation began to run out of steam. Lee used the global recession of the early 1990s to force through a series of difficult changes in short order. He divested businesses, such as sugar and paper processing, that were profitable but slow-moving and incapable of achieving leadership in global markets. Lee concentrated research and development and advertising expenditures on a handful of businesses with the potential to win globally, while cutting expenditures in others. The chairman insisted that subsidiaries measure performance against global leaders, rather than benchmark other Korean companies, and instituted manufacturing processes to produce world-class quality. Finally, Samsung bucked the Korean tradition of basing promotions strictly on seniority, to advance a large number of young executives based on their performance and global outlook.

By the mid-1990s, Lee again worried that the change process was losing traction. While other Korean executives bemoaned the

(continued)

Asian economic crisis, which began in 1997, Lee embraced it as a further opportunity to reinvigorate Samsung's transformation. He divested more units and led a further round of head-count reductions. The chairman increased the autonomy of the remaining businesses by eliminating cross-business subsidies, loan guarantees, and below-market transfer prices. These changes, which marked a sharp break from traditional business practices in Korea, increased the units' agility.

10.

AVOIDING A CORPORATE MIDLIFE CRISIS

Conventional management wisdom holds that companies, like people, must pass through a life cycle.[1] Firms begin life with the rapid-fire experimentation of a start-up, scale the business during the corporate equivalent of adolescence, mature into the dull reliability of middle age, and lapse into inevitable decline. Sometimes companies progress through this sequence as a cohort. Minicomputer makers arrayed along Boston's Route 128 and steelmakers in Sheffield, England, first rose and then fell as a group.[2] Other times a company passes through the life cycle in isolation, as Polaroid or Laura Ashley did. Life cycle, according to this viewpoint, is destiny.

The corporate life cycle framework describes a common progression for many organizations. But life cycle is not destiny. Firestone declined, but its crosstown rival Goodyear survived the transition to radial tires. Brahma was already a century old when Marcel Telles took the helm. Other examples of long-established firms that have managed to renew themselves over extended periods include General Electric, Johnson & Johnson, Procter & Gamble, HSBC, Nokia, and the Samsung Group. These firms, it seems, have found the corporate equivalent of the fountain of youth.

The secret to their success lies in a simple insight: companies do not pass through life cycles, opportunities do. Most firms, particularly large organizations, oversee a diverse portfolio of opportunities that exist at different stages in the life cycle. There are, of course, single-product companies that at first glance resemble one-trick ponies. Even then, a deeper look often uncovers multiple opportunities. Kodak, for example, is best known for its film business. But in the 1990s the company also had a vibrant medical imaging and clinical diagnostic business even after divesting operations in photocopying, chemicals, and pharmaceuticals. There are no mature companies, only portfolios overloaded with mature opportunities. Organizations can avoid a corporate midlife crisis through portfolio agility—the ability to quickly and effectively shift resources, including cash, talent, and managerial attention, out of less promising units and into more attractive ones.

For many managers, journalists, and academics, diversification is a dirty word. Diversified conglomerates—think Daewoo and Tyco—are always a bad idea according to this line of thought. The litany of sins associated with diversification is long: it creates unmanageable levels of complexity, forces profitable units to subsidize the losses of less successful units, and complicates financial reporting. Managers diversify, according to this school of thought, for all the wrong reasons. By buying unrelated businesses, CEOs diversify their personal wealth tied up in company stock, entrench themselves in their position, and increase their power and prestige by controlling a sprawling empire.[3] A series of empirical studies support the hypothesis that diversified firms destroy value.[4] One careful study by Professors Philip Berger and Eli Ofek found that the average diversified firm destroyed 15 percent of the value its component units would have created as free-standing entities.[5] Companies should stick to their knitting, according to this view, and allow investors to diversify their holdings by acquiring shares in a wide range of focused companies. Research in strategy encouraging firms to "stick to their knitting," "focus on their core" reinforce the message that corporations should pursue extreme focus.[6]

This viewpoint ignores some inconvenient truths. Recent research by financial economists has found that diversification per se does not necessarily destroy value.[7] The so-called diversification discount, these studies suggest, arises when managers diversify to escape problems in their core businesses. The resulting conglomerates often underperform because the component units earn low returns, not because they are diversified. Diversification also provides opportunities for growth. Recall the study of two hundred large enterprises that found that the reallocation of resources to faster-growing segments within a company's portfolio was the largest single driver of revenue growth. Indeed, diversified firms such as Johnson & Johnson, Procter & Gamble, and Samsung Electronics have leveraged their portfolio agility to succeed over long periods, while private equity groups, including Blackstone, KKR, Carlyle, and TPG, have rewarded their limited partners richly by actively managing a portfolio of businesses.

A varied set of business units is necessary for portfolio agility but not sufficient. In the early 1980s, the conglomerate Westinghouse rivaled General Electric (GE), but in subsequent decades it faltered and was ultimately dismantled. Portfolio agility requires disciplined processes to evaluate individual business units and reallocate key resources such as money and talent. It is equally critical that the company as a whole, rather than individual units, control talent, cash, and other resources for redistribution. One North American bank paid a management consulting firm millions of dollars to profile its diverse business units in painstaking detail. The resulting research provided a compelling case for shifting resources from two of the established businesses into promising new ones. Unfortunately, the bank was a loose federation of units and lacked the precedent or processes to reallocate resources across fiefdoms. Despite the clear data favoring a reallocation of resources, the bank's cash cows continued to hoard their money, their claims on the IT budget, and their best people, while the promising businesses withered, starved of the resources they needed to grow.

Portfolio agility demands that leaders make difficult and often unpopular choices, particularly when removing resources from a business or reversing previous commitments. The late Reginald H. Jones, Jack Welch's predecessor at GE, had the formal tools to classify the company's strategic business units but shied away from some difficult decisions, such as exiting the Utah International mining company deal, which he himself had advocated. Welch reversed Jones's missteps, cleaning out GE's portfolio in his early years on the job. More impressively, he also fixed his own mistakes, such as selling Kidder, Peabody & Company in 1994, when the acquisition, engulfed in trading scandals, did not meet expectations. Welch allocated resources based on logic rather than emotion. He invested heavily in GE Capital, although he did not always see eye to eye with the leadership of that business. Meanwhile, he fired the head of Kidder, even though he was an old friend.

Before reallocating talent across business units, a company must cultivate a cadre of general managers versatile enough to move from business to business. GE invests heavily in that group of managers, giving them P&L responsibility early on, rotating them through jobs and units, and offering them leadership training. Goldman Sachs rose from a second-tier investment bank with a few products in 1976 to a global leader across a highly diversified product range by the early 1990s.[8] Critical to Goldman's rise was the Investment Banking Services (IBS) unit, staffed with generalists who solicited new business and maintained client relationships. At that time, most investment banks encouraged employees to specialize in a sector, region, or specific product. Goldman's IBS bankers, in contrast, were true generalists, and could therefore move from one geography or sector to another as new opportunities emerged and others declined. Portfolio agility does not mean everyone in an organization will become a general manager. In fact, generalists allow others to increase their specialization. Goldman research analysts and product specialists could build deeper expertise in a sector or financial instrument, because they knew the IBS bankers could bridge their expertise with the client's needs.

To achieve portfolio agility, leaders should view their organization as an array of opportunities at various stages in the life cycle, paying particular attention to promising opportunities. To avoid the corporate equivalent of a midlife crisis, they should recognize common portfolio pathologies, such as the use of the same metrics to assess opportunities at different life-cycle stages or the systematic failure to exit declining units. Only then can they manage their entire portfolio more effectively, seeding and nurturing the right opportunities while exiting those that drain valuable resources.

MAPPING THE FOUR LIFE CYCLE STAGES

The first step in managing a portfolio of opportunities is to map them. The standard method for evaluating a firm's portfolio is to array them using a matrix, such as the Boston Consulting Group's (BCG) popular growth-share matrix.[9] This matrix assumes that success results from increasing volume of products sold to build experience in the sector and scale economies. The BCG matrix focuses on market share and growth, two variables that directly drive volume. The simple matrix provides executives with a snapshot to compare "cash cows" that could fund investments in rising "stars," while avoiding "dogs" and puzzling over "question marks."

Portfolio planning using the BCG and related matrices took hold in many companies, but subsequent research found little evidence that these tools improved performance.[10] Portfolio matrices suffer from two major limitations. First, they provide a static picture that fails to convey how a business unit might evolve over time. Lacking a sense of time, they also omit the critical inflection points as an opportunity passes through the life cycle. In pursuing the opportunity to sell My M&M's, which customers personalize with their own message, executives at Mars had to navigate difficult questions as they moved from one stage of the life cycle to the next: Should they scale this product instead of other promising opportunities? How would they integrate My M&M's with established businesses? A static model neither raises nor answers these questions.

An alternative approach to mapping a portfolio begins by disaggregating an organization into components that correspond to opportunities, recognizing that they vary by stages in the life cycle. Projects in the start-up phase, for example, are often formal development initiatives or skunkwork efforts flying beneath the radar. Mature opportunities are often business units with their own profit-

and-loss responsibilities. Opportunities also vary by industry. In the fast-moving consumer goods industry, opportunities typically cluster around brands within specific geographies. Professional service firms view opportunities as distinct client offerings. The opportunity life cycle framework can be used at various levels within a company to analyze business units or to disaggregate customers and products within a specific unit.

These opportunities can then be placed into one of four stages in the life cycle. (See figure 10.1.) Opportunities begin in the start-up phase when an entrepreneur or manager spots an unmet need in the marketplace and envisions a new way to meet the need. Like youth, the start-up stage is marked by constant experimentation to identify the best segment to target, or the right business model to create value. After validating the opportunity and stabilizing the business model, the opportunity enters adolescence and scales up to seize market share. Then comes maturity, in which the opportunity—now its own business unit—fights for market share against well-known rivals in a clearly delineated market. The final stage is decline, which can come about from a number of sources, including the entry of low-cost competitors, shifting consumer preferences, or the introduction of substitute products.

Opportunities consume different levels of resources depending on where they are in the life cycle. In the start-up stage, entrepreneurs or middle managers can tinker with an idea for years without spending serious money, but rapid growth during the scale stage often demands significant investment. Mature opportunities generate the cash to support their own operations and also fund start-ups and scaling businesses. Units in decline, if unchecked, can consume a disproportionate share of resources, management time, and emotional energy. Different opportunities can be denoted as balls that vary in

FIGURE 10.1 **Life Cycle Portfolio**

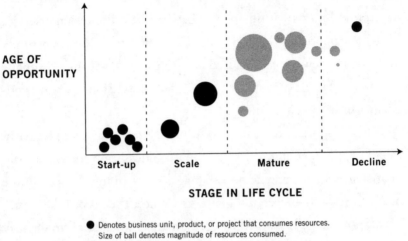

**AGE OF
OPPORTUNITY**

Start-up   Scale   Mature   Decline

STAGE IN LIFE CYCLE

● Denotes business unit, product, or project that consumes resources.
  Size of ball denotes magnitude of resources consumed.

● Denotes business unit, product, or project that contributes resources.
  Size of ball denotes magnitude of resources contributed.

color—black when an opportunity consumes cash and gray when it throws off resources. They also vary in size depending on the magnitude of resources they consume or generate.

The balls can be placed in the appropriate stage in the opportunity life cycle to present a snapshot of a portfolio at a point in time. The vertical axis plots the elapsed time from an opportunity's inception to the present, and the horizontal denotes stage in the life cycle. In this graph, opportunities typically follow an upward-sloping line from young experiments (bottom left of figure) to old, declining businesses (top right). The stages in the life cycle convey an implicit sense of progress over time as an opportunity passes from one stage to another. Plotting actual opportunities against expectations reveals outliers. These outliers, in turn, raise questions that can focus attention on potential issues in the opportunity portfolio. (See figure 10.2.)

FIGURE 10.2 **Outliers Raise Questions**

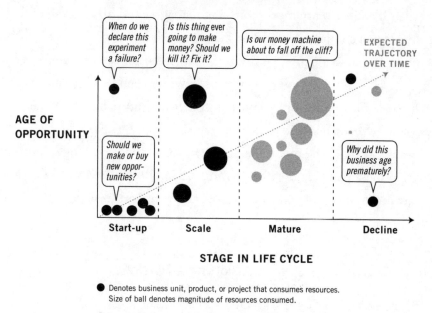

Denotes business unit, product, or project that consumes resources. Size of ball denotes magnitude of resources consumed.

Denotes business unit, product, or project that contributes resources. Size of ball denotes magnitude of resources contributed.

The easiest way to map an opportunity portfolio is to start with financial resources. The operating cash flows consumed or produced by an opportunity in a year determines its size. The basic plotting can be refined in several ways. Managers might plot the net present value of the opportunity to determine the size of the ball. Further refinements include the scoring of opportunities by risk, shadow circles to denote their potential magnitude, and arrows to indicate the speed at which opportunities move from one stage to the next, relative to initial forecasts or industry averages.

This first-cut analysis provides the basis for plotting nonfinancial resources, which vary by industry, and might include engineering hours, production capacity, or information technology resources. The allocation of management talent across opportunities is an important consideration in almost all situations. One global engineering firm identified its twenty most promising managers and marked their initials on the opportunities they managed. All but two of those high-potential individuals were running mature businesses or staunching the bleeding in declining operations, leaving second-string managers to scale the opportunities crucial to the firm's future health. None of these refinements will work in every situation, but they do suggest ways to extend the tool to deepen executives' understanding of portfolio dynamics. Figure 10.3 provides a blank template to conduct a quick diagnostic of your own organization's opportunity portfolio.

FIGURE 10.3 Plotting a Portfolio

Business opportunities typically progress through four stages—start-up, scale, mature, and decline—which are labeled along the horizontal axis. The vertical axis denotes the age of an opportunity, and the expected trajectory for an opportunity over time is shown as the upward-sloping dashed line. The balls represent different opportunities, with the size of each denoting the amount of cash consumed (black) or generated (gray) in a year. By mapping an organization's constituent opportunities, managers can identify imbalances and other trouble spots, and surface important questions about opportunities that deviate from the expected trajectory.

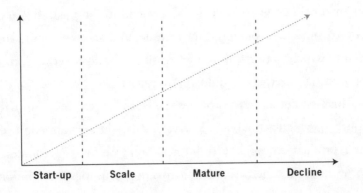

COMMON PATHOLOGIES

The point of the mapping exercise is not precision, but rather to surface important questions. Are resources currently in balance? Can the mature opportunities fund all the start-up and scaling activities being undertaken? Are there enough or too many early-stage startups? Is a core business about to enter a period of decline? Portfolio imbalance is often a symptom of a deeper pathology in how resources are allocated within the firm.

No exit. Professor Joseph Bower and a series of his doctoral students have shown that in most large, complex organizations, resources are allocated through a bottom-up process.[11] Frontline employees closest to the market identify and experiment with potential opportunities at little cost to the organization. To secure the significant resources required for scaling, a well-regarded middle manager must sponsor the project, take responsibility for its execution, and vouch for its ultimate success to senior executives and the board of directors. The middle manager puts her reputation on the line, providing a strong incentive for her to advance only the most promising projects and make sure they deliver.

This bottom-up process of resource allocation promotes investment, but often stalls in reverse because it fails to trigger *dis*investment from opportunities that are not panning out.[12] Managers rarely recommend killing a project that might jeopardize their own reputations or that of their colleagues. The cost of delaying exit from a declining business can be significant. Recall that the losses from Firestone's delay in closing its outdated plants exceeded the cost of the Firestone 500 recall. Delayed exit diverts management attention, as senior executives spend so much time discussing problem children that they lose focus on promising opportunities. When companies allocate their best managers to fix their worst problems, they burn out the most rising stars and deprive them of the chance to scale an attractive opportunity.

The no-exit syndrome is a particularly thorny challenge in the scaling stage. Companies allow opportunities to consume resources even if they fail to gain traction in the market. Like airplanes that taxi beyond the runway without taking off, these businesses advance at high speeds, knocking down trees and buildings along the way. Because opportunities in the scaling stage devour so many resources, they live in the corporate spotlight, increasing the reputational damage their management champions incur if they pull the plug. Managers can smother start-up projects, but killing a project, burning resources to scale, often ends in a public execution.

One European financial services firm tackled the no-exit problem head on. When the CEO appointed an executive to scale an exciting opportunity in Eastern Europe, he also built in checks to ensure that it was possible to kill the initiative if necessary. He insisted the team include senior members from the risk and finance functions to oversee performance against plan. He refused to authorize the expenditures until the group articulated a handful of deal-killer indicators that would constitute clear grounds for terminating the business. He also structured the business as a separate legal entity, even though the firm owned all the shares. This legal structure allowed him to appoint a board of directors, which the CEO staffed with outsiders detached from the business, as well as a director who had scaled a service business and could distinguish typical growing pains from serious problems. When the risks of the new opportunity proved to outweigh the rewards, the CEO orchestrated a face-saving exit for the executive, promoting him to a significant position in the core business and praising his willingness to take on the scaling of a venture in an unfamiliar market.

Overvaluing value-based management. Finance theory instructs executives to invest only in projects that have a positive net present value and return surplus cash to investors. Value-based management puts a premium on credible forecasts of cash flow. The most credible forecasts are those based on low-risk projects in known domains that produce positive cash flows quickly. An investment process that values credibility and low risk above all else will penalize projects with uncertain outcomes, even when they offer a substantial potential upside.[13]

Blue Circle Industries, at one time the global leader in the cement industry, exemplified the benefits, and also risks, of putting too much value on value-based management. It adopted tough annual targets for return on capital employed (ROCE) backed up with business-unit budget contracts and incentives linked to increasing returns on capital. Blue Circle's corporate office ranked potential investments according to prospective net present value, payback, and return on capital. Only those at the top of the list won approval, while those at the bottom were rejected—a break from a past in which interesting projects received token funding to encourage low-cost experimentation. Measured by ROCE, the approach worked. In the second half of the 1990s, Blue Circle's return on capital doubled, producing cash to buy shares back.

But then the competitive landscape shifted. The industry began to consolidate globally, and emerging markets offered some of the juiciest opportunities. Because its capital budgeting process favored reliable cash-flow forecasts, Blue Circle turned down nearly all projects in emerging markets to focus its investments in stable countries with reliable prospects. The insistence on sure-thing investments left Blue Circle a laggard in the race for globalization. Despite a desperate bid for expansion in Southeast Asia in 1997, the company was overtaken by more aggressive competitors, such as CEMEX. It was acquired by Lafarge in 2001.

When executives wake up one morning and realize their organization lacks attractive opportunities for growth, they often attempt a crash course to renew the portfolio through large-scale initiatives, including unrelated acquisitions, large mergers, or a flurry of new products. Like most actions born of desperation, these have a high failure rate. A better approach ensures that the organization has a set of promising new opportunities in reserve, waiting for the day when circumstances favor scaling.

The Beta Group, a business incubator that commercializes promising technologies, evaluates many potential opportunities, sorting them into three categories. Ideas with no real promise land in the Dumpster; those ready for prime-time scale, and promising ideas whose time has yet to come are stored in a "refrigerator." Promising start-ups can be premature for any number of reasons—perhaps the current market is too small, the technology has major kinks, or the business model is unclear. Beta's approach enables the firm to focus its limited resources on two or three opportunities that are ready to scale, while keeping track of the fifty or so refrigerated projects. A company can keep tabs on such proposals by reassessing their viability, perhaps through small-scale experiments or joint ventures to obtain information on how those opportunities are evolving.

Maintaining a healthy stock of opportunities requires active leadership. Even during periods of restructuring and ruthless cost cutting, senior management must nurture promising businesses by providing political cover, framing the opportunities as experiments, or protecting them from corporate antibodies. They must also remain on the lookout for growth even in downturns. The best opportunities often arise in the worst times, as distressed sellers offload assets at bargain basement prices.

Let a thousand flowers bloom. Sometimes the problem is not too few opportunities but too many. At one fast-moving consumer goods company, the top managers mapped their portfolio to understand why significant investment in innovation had yielded disappointing returns. What they found surprised them. The company excelled at identifying promising opportunities, and managers agreed it was reasonably easy to find the resources to scale projects. But of more than a dozen opportunities that the company was funding, most had been scaling for longer than projected without gaining traction in the market.

The root problem was the ad hoc process the company used to select which opportunities received the resources required to scale. Managers aimed for fairness in allocating cash and talented people, but that egalitarian spirit meant the company gave the green light to numerous projects. Indeed, it was attempting to scale more than three times as many opportunities than its main competitor. As a result, none of those projects received the resources required to scale successfully, and they stalled in the market, much like the initiatives at 3M discussed earlier.

One size fits all. Projects at various life cycle stages differ in their objectives, optimal management style, performance metrics, and predictability. A start-up venture works best with an entrepreneurial manager seeking to validate the opportunity and stabilize the business model. Projects' success should be evaluated against milestones tailored to their specific opportunities—number of users for a social Web site, for instance, or beta customer satisfaction for an engineering solution. A mature business, in contrast, requires an active steward focused on generating cash. (See figure 10.4.)

FIGURE 10.4 Managing Across the Life Cycle

Opportunities at different stages in the life cycle require different management approaches and performance metrics, and vary in terms of their predictability. Specialized institutions have evolved in capital markets to focus on these different stages. Many companies, however, attempt to apply a one-size-fits-all approach to managing opportunities through the life cycle.

	Start-up	Scale	Mature	Decline
Objective	Validate opportunity	Scale business model	Produce cash	Reinvigorate or exit
What motivates managers?	Passion for idea	Share of upside	Security of working in an established business	Pay and bonuses for making tough decisions
	Fun and excitement	Satisfaction of building something	Autonomy	
	Recognition		Power	
Who are the best managers?	Scientists and inventors	Experienced builders with clarity of focus and drive to execute	Active stewards adept at spotting and neutralizing threats to core	Turnaround artists who are relentless in instilling financial discipline
	Entrepreneurs			

Which metrics measure progress?	Milestones marking specific achievements (often measuring customer adoption)	Focus on growth and time to profitability	Numerous metrics, typically refined and financial, often extrapolated from the past	Measures of cash released from terminating money-losing activities
How to secure or release resources?	Spread passion for opportunity Bootstrap Limit resources required	Build enthusiasm with exciting growth story Generate fast profits to protect business from skeptics	Generate cash to fund growth elsewhere Protect the core business from any threats	Prune resources to fund growth elsewhere
Predictability (1 low to 10 high)	1–3	4–6	6–8	8–9
Financial institutions that specialize	Angel funding Incubators Early-stage venture capital	Venture capital	Banks Public equity markets	Leveraged buyout firms

In 1999, IBM created the Emerging Business Opportunity (EBO) management system to spur organic growth and protect new opportunities until they were mature enough to stand on their own. EBO drew on a "horizons of growth" model that distinguished between opportunities in the start-up phase, those scaling through rapid growth, and mature businesses.[14] IBM recognized that different growth horizons required distinct approaches to people, strategy, resource allocation, and measurement. The EBO was designed to protect nascent opportunities and identify when they were ready to move from one stage to the next.

EBO's approach to measurement went beyond financial metrics to include milestones appropriate to each stage. Start-up opportunities, for example, might need to win a share of mind, as evidenced in press and analyst reports. Scaling businesses needed to demonstrate progress in trials and early-customer adoption, while mature businesses were measured against strict profitability and sales-volume objectives. The milestones helped executives spot when an opportunity was ready to move into the next horizon, perhaps requiring a change of management as well as different forms of support and incentives from EBO.

Generation gap. The final pathology has little to do with process and everything to do with people. Just as opportunities pass through life stages, so do the people behind them. Across a wide range of organizations, portfolios have decayed when executives gripped the reins of power for too long, blocking up-and-comers from positions of authority. Veteran executives often lack the urgent personal incentives to renew the opportunity portfolio—it is much easier for them to rest on their laurels and bide their time until retirement. When a cohort of seasoned executives have control over which opportunities to scale, they may err on the side of loss aversion, protecting the mature businesses (which they often scaled and ran) while avoiding risky bets on the future. "There are no mature businesses," Warren Buffett once observed, "only mature managers."

To avoid this fate, companies can empower younger managers who have a large stake in the future, as Brahma did with its trainee program. When the forty-seven-year-old John Browne became BP's group CEO in 1995, he set out to place operating power in the hands of the next generation. He and his team broke BP's bureaucratic organization into approximately 150 business units, each overseeing an oil field, a chemical plant, a regional marketing area, or other operation. Browne then handed the keys to these businesses to a new generation of managers, most of whom were in their thirties or early forties. This was a massive transfer of power because those operations collectively generated upward of $120 billion in revenues by 2001 and employed more than one hundred thousand people.

What to do with the heroes from the last war? In many organizations, the biggest obstacle to a generational shift comes from seasoned executives who want to maintain an active role. At BP, many of these leaders became group vice presidents, positioned between the 150 business units and Browne's team. These senior executives coached the next generation, oversaw talent development and succession planning, and negotiated performance contracts with the business unit leaders. This structure left Browne and his team free to focus on branding, the company's stance on environmental issues, geopolitical shifts affecting supply, and other larger, longer-term issues.

According to conventional wisdom, companies resemble organisms that must pass ineluctably through the predetermined stages of start-up, scaling, maturity, and decline. In large, complex organizations, things are not so simple. Business opportunities, not firms, pass through these stages. Most organizations include multiple opportunities arrayed across the different stages of the life cycle. Leaders who understand this distinction can enhance their organization's portfolio agility and thrive in turbulence.

11.

AGILE ABSORPTION

On October 30, 1974, George Foreman, the reigning heavyweight champion of the world, joined hands with his cornermen in his dressing room. The men bowed their heads in silent prayer.[1] In a few minutes, Foreman would enter the ring to defend his heavyweight title against Muhammad Ali, in a bout dubbed the "Rumble in the Jungle," held in Kinshasa, Zaire, and broadcast around the world. The stakes were high for both fighters, who would split a $10 million purse, with the winner carrying away the championship belt. Foreman and his cornermen did not pray for victory, which they took for granted. Rather, they implored God to protect Ali from serious injury in the ring.

Today, the name George Foreman evokes late-night television advertisements in which an avuncular man clad in an apron pitches a low-fat grill. In his prime, the name George Foreman struck terror in his opponents. Foreman's sheer bulk, physical strength, and toughness conferred absorption, or the ability to weather all the punishment his opponent could dish out. Foreman lacked agility, to be sure. In his prefight taunts, Ali compared Foreman to a mummy, shuffling with an awkward gait. Foreman compensated for his lack of bob-and-weave dexterity with his ability to weather blows, waiting for his adversary to tire or drop his guard. Then he unleashed the knockout blow. Foreman arrived in Kinshasa with a record unblemished by loss and stacked with forty wins, all but three by knockout. In the three years preceding the Rumble, Foreman won 90 percent of his fights by knockout or TKO before the end of the second round.

Foreman entered the Rumble a three-to-one favorite, and many thought the odds should have been longer. Foreman had dispatched fighters including Joe Frazier and Ken Norton, who had beaten Ali. Even Ali's cornermen worried about their boxer's safety. Ali's doctor, Ferdie Pacheco, marveled at the way Foreman had knocked Frazier around like a child.[2] Pacheco commissioned a jet to wait near the stadium, its engines running, with a flight plan to the nearest world-class neurological hospital. The young Ali epitomized agility, which enables a boxer to spot an opportunity—the hint of a sagging right arm or upturned chin—and exploit it before his opponent adjusts. Still, entering the Rumble, Ali's agility seemed no match for Foreman's capacity to absorb punishment.

The defining characteristic of the Rumble, or any boxing match, is uncertainty. Fighters can study tapes of past fights or select sparring partners who simulate an opponent's style, but they cannot predict a blow-by-blow chronology of a fight in advance, foresee spikes in confidence, foretell the errant punch that splits an eyebrow, or anticipate a wily foe's tactics. Competing in turbulent markets can feel a lot like entering the ring against George Foreman in his prime—or, even worse, like stumbling into a barroom brawl: The punches come from all directions, include a steady barrage of body blows and periodic haymakers, and are thrown by a rotating cast of characters who change the rules abruptly, swinging bottles and bar stools as well as fists.

The Rumble illustrates that agility, for all its benefits, is not the only, or even the best, way to master turbulence, in the ring and beyond. Absorption—the ability to withstand shifts in the competitive context—is a potent alternative. Agility and absorption are not mutually exclusive, and true champions combine them to achieve *agile absorption*—the capability to identify and seize opportunities while retaining the structural characteristics needed to weather changes.

ABSORPTION

Outside the ring, absorption results from structural factors that permit an organization to survive changes in its environment. Firms can build absorption in several ways, including obvious levers such as size, diversification, and a war chest of cash. Others factors, such as high customer switching costs, low fixed costs, and a powerful patron, can also buffer a firm against environmental changes, although in less evident ways.

Several factors enhance absorption, the most obvious being sheer size. Larger firms that control more resources and a greater market share can weather more storms for a longer time than smaller rivals.[3] General Motors accounted for approximately one-half of all cars sold in the United States in the 1950s. The automaker's large asset base and domestic market share allowed it to survive a steady erosion at the hands of more agile competitors, such as Honda and Toyota, in subsequent decades. Like a slowly sinking ship, General Motors has stayed afloat by steadily throwing ballast overboard—shuttering plants, discontinuing brands, and selling businesses. Initial size conferred the ballast to hold on for as long as General Motors has. At some point, a firm may become "too big to fail," when sheer scale

FIGURE 11.1 **Bulking Up for the Fight**

Source	Benefits from this source of absorption . . .	. . . but beware
Low fixed costs	These can help a firm weather a wide range of changes, such as price wars, higher raw material costs, and declining demand.	Leaders must maintain relentless pressure on costs, especially when times are good.
War chest of cash	Cash is perfectly fungible, so it can be deployed against future contingencies that managers cannot foresee.	Executives must win owners' confidence to stockpile the cash rather than paying it out to shareholders.
Diversified cash flows	Companies can withstand downturns in specific units, and diversified units serve as a store of potential wealth that can be sold later.	Diversification of cash flows, not revenues, confers absorption. A collection of unprofitable subsidiaries resembles a group of drunks leaning on one another for support.
Too big to fail	Large firms can survive by off-loading operations and reducing head count in crises. Size also increases the odds the government, customers, or suppliers will prop up an ailing firm.	Size can breed bureaucracy that impedes agility.
Tangible resources	Valuable resources such as raw material deposits, real estate, and so on serve as a store of potential value.	These resources can reuse internal political struggles within a firm over the distribution of gain instead of an external focus on creating value.

Source	Benefits from this form of absorption . . .	. . . but beware
Intangible resources	Brand, expertise, and technology can insulate the firm against changes in the market in the short and medium term.	Overreliance on existing resources can lull executives and employees into complacency.
Customer lock-in	Switching costs prevent customers from easily jumping ship, buying a firm time when circumstances shift.	Lock-in works both ways: existing customers can drag a firm down as well as buoy it up.
Protected core market	Barriers to entry in a core market provide a safe stream of cash to weather storms.	Hiding behind barriers to entry can dull a firm's competitive edge and leave it vulnerable if the barriers fall.
Powerful patron	A powerful government, regulator, customer, or investor vested in the firm's success can buffer it from changes.	Powerful patrons have their own agendas and may force a firm to pursue objectives not in the firm's interest.
Excess staff	The corporate equivalent of body fat, these employees serve as a store of value that can be shed in hard times.	Excess employees depress profitability and create busy work for others. Worst source of absorption.

raises the cost of failure for governments, banks, customers, and unions, which have high incentives to intervene to prevent collapse. Diversification enhances absorption by allowing an organization with varied sources of cash flow to withstand hard times in one or more of its portfolio businesses. Absorption comes from diversification of cash flows, not revenues, and a collection of money-losing subsidiaries in a conglomerate can no more buttress one another than can a group of drunks staggering down the street, leaning on one another for support. A diversified portfolio also acts as a store of wealth that can be accessed to weather future storms. To subsidize its long decline, General Motors has sold off some of the jewels from its historical diversification, including Terex, Frigidaire, Raytheon, EDS, and Hughes, among others.

Managers build absorption capacity by stockpiling slack resources. In the 1960s, the sociologist James D. Thompson introduced the notion of buffering—activities intended to smooth or absorb environmental fluctuations. Thompson analyzed how manufacturing firms protected their core production capacity from fluctuations in demand by, among other things, maintaining large stocks of inventory and taking steps to smooth demand.[4] Although holding large stocks of inventory has fallen out of favor as a buffering mechanism, firms continue to accumulate cash as a slack resource to hedge against unforeseen events. In contrast to specialized resources, like a brand or technology, cash is fungible—it can be deployed against most contingencies even if a manager cannot foresee its ultimate use.

Brazil's regional jet maker Embraer, for example, used its cash-rich balance sheet to absorb the shock from 9/11, when its customers abruptly refused delivery of $500 million worth of aircraft in the span of a few months. European rival Fairchild Dornier, in contrast, had recently gone private in a leveraged buyout, and went bankrupt because it lacked the financial wherewithal to survive the precipitous fall in demand that followed the 9/11 attacks. Cash reserves are particularly important in turbulent contexts, such as emerging markets or new ventures, where the cost and availability of capital is subject to wide swings, and where funding is often most difficult to obtain just when a company needs it most.

Firms can accumulate not only spare cash but also employees. Over time, firms often build up "latent slack," the academic euphemism for more employees than a company needs to get the work done. Although keeping these employees on the payroll shows up as a cost on the income statement, excess workers and managers represent slack resources that management can recover, through layoffs to free up cash in hard times.[5] Corporate fat, like its human equivalent, serves as a store of energy that can be burned in hard times. Researchers have demonstrated that the benefits of latent slack are greatest when a firm enters a crisis with significant excess staffing and head count reductions are part of a broader restructuring effort.

Companies can enhance their absorption by locking up resources that are valuable, rare, and difficult to imitate. Saudi Arabia's state-run oil company, Saudi Aramco, controls approximately one-quarter of the world's easily extracted oil reserves, a store of resources that enables the company to weather the shifting tides of prices, geopolitics, competitive dynamics, and fuel technology with relative impunity. Companies can also buffer themselves by controlling intangible resources such as a technology or a brand. Coca-Cola controls the most valuable brand in the world. The strength of Coke's brand has allowed the company to survive slowing demand in its core market, aggressive innovation by competitors, tensions with bottlers, and turmoil among the top executives that resulted in a rapid turnover of CEOs. While Coke relied on its established brand, Pepsi proved more agile, seizing opportunities in bottled water, sports drinks, and juice that allowed it to overtake Coca-Cola in market capitalization in December 2005, for the first time in more than a century of competition.[6]

High switching costs can prevent customers from abandoning a supplier even when an attractive substitute arises or rivals offer better terms. Large corporations using Oracle database software face enormous costs, risk, and hassle to migrate systems to an alternative product. They tend to stay put, allowing Oracle to absorb shifts in technology, competitive dynamics, and customer preferences. In many cases these barriers to entry provide a profitable core business that serves as the basis for expansion into new sectors. Oracle has used cash from its database business to acquire applications-software makers such as PeopleSoft and Siebel, while Microsoft's strong position in Windows and Office have underwritten forays into gaming. Few barriers to entry remain impenetrable in the long term, but they can buffer firms from onslaughts in the midterm.

Strong partners vested in a firm's success enhance absorption. During the boom years in the personal computer industry, Microsoft had a strong interest in seeing Intel upgrade its microprocessors to run ever-larger versions of Windows, and both companies supported Dell as it tried to sell more personal computers with Intel and Microsoft inside. Government support is another source of absorption. Emirates Air, one of the fastest-growing major airlines in the world, benefited throughout the 1990s from a close relationship with the ruling al-Maktoum family of Dubai, whose interests in promoting their city-state are interwoven with the airline. Dubai has invested in the infrastructure to support Emirates' growth, encouraged the development of attractions such as indoor skiing in the desert and Dubai World that attract passengers to fly to (and through) Dubai, and put in place policies (such as no personal income tax or labor unions) that helped Emirates attract employees and avoid the union strife, which hampers many airlines. These partnerships rely on the patron's own absorption. A small city-state without significant oil reserves, Dubai itself possesses limited absorption to weather crises.

Low fixed costs also help a firm to survive unexpected shocks, such as price wars, higher raw material costs, and volume declines. The semiconductor design and fabricator Taiwan Semiconductor Manufacturing Company (TSMC) has followed a relentless strategy of lowering fixed costs since its inception in 1987. In 2006 TSMC could break even at a capacity utilization of approximately 40 percent, while its three largest competitors broke even at approximately two-thirds capacity utilization.[7] In practice, this meant that TSMC could maintain its profitability when volume dropped without resorting to low-margin business to fill its fabrication plants.

It is easy to underestimate absorption, which looks plodding compared to agility, but it is dangerous to do so. During World War II, the German army was one of the most agile fighting forces in modern history—by most estimates the typical German soldier was 25–50 percent more effective than his American or British counterpart.[8] The German blitzkrieg was perhaps the best example of military agility in recent history. For all their agility, however, the Germans lost. The Allies' greater absorption allowed them to deploy more troops and hardware, absorb the German forays, and ultimately prevail.

ABSORPTION AND STRATEGIC AGILITY

At first glance, absorption seems purely defensive, but companies can employ it to seize new business opportunities as well as mitigate threats. Firms that rely on absorption solely for defense risk falling behind rivals that use it as offense as well. For over a century, Banco Santander and rival Banco Popular belonged to a protected oligopoly of Spanish banks. When Spain deregulated its banking market, their paths diverged. Santander bulked up in Spain, seized opportunities in Latin America, and expanded into Europe, while Banco Popular played it safe, eschewed foreign markets, and stuck to its domestic market. Popular's domestic focus provided good returns to shareholders but prevented the bank from absorbing changes—such as the housing slowdown in Spain—or acquiring major opportunities outside its home market.

Absorption is particularly valuable in supporting strategic agility, an organization's ability to spot and decisively seize game-changing opportunities that arise out of turbulent markets. Carnival's larger size and lower fixed costs helped the cruise line convince investors to favor it in the battle to acquire P&O Princess. A healthy balance sheet and geographical diversification of cash flows among his existing steel operations allowed Lakshmi Mittal to snap up the Kazakh steel mill and iron deposits.

Golden opportunities are not spaced evenly over time, and absorption can keep a company in the game until its big chance emerges. Apple's iPod is the stock example of agility. The iPod *is* an excellent example of agility, but it was the firm's absorption that kept Apple alive enough to seize the opportunity. During the 1990s, Apple was relegated to the "other" category in the PC market when its share fell to under 5 percent, and its stock remained flat from the late 1980s through early 2004. A small base of loyal customers kept the company in the game long enough for changes in the context to create a golden opportunity.

Absorption also allows companies to outlast rivals in wars of attrition. As Microsoft entered the video game industry, the software giant duked it out in round after round with Nintendo and Sony, losing billions of dollars by some estimates. But Microsoft has also built up enormous stores of absorption over the years—through customer lock-in, brand identity, and cash reserves—that allow it to wear down its gaming rivals through successive periods of investment. Microsoft's absorptive capabilities increase the odds that the company will emerge victorious at the end of the battle for dominance in the video game industry.

While agility allows a company to stake out an early position, absorption allows it to reinforce an early beachhead. In the fast-moving consumer goods industry, both Groupe Danone and Procter & Gamble spotted opportunities in China, Russia, Brazil, and other emerging markets. Lacking absorption, Danone relied on joint ventures to scale quickly despite limited resources. This approach created headaches later on when the partnerships soured. By contrast, the more absorptive Procter & Gamble could afford to staff its emerging market operations with expatriates and then hire local talent and inculcate them in the P&G way over the years.

AGILE ABSORPTION

Managers often see absorption and agility as stark alternatives—the former the domain of established enterprises defending turf and the latter the realm of nimble start-ups looking to grow. Ali's triumph in the Rumble, however, demonstrates the power of combining the two. Ali's training regimen months before the fight consisted of being clobbered by the hardest-hitting sparring partners he could find, to increase his ability to take a punch. During the Rumble he unveiled the now-famous "rope-a-dope" strategy, deliberately placing himself on the ropes to channel the energy of Foreman's blows and allow Ali to absorb more punishment.

Absorption and agility are complements, not substitutes. They resemble yin and yang, the two opposing but complementary forces that coexist in all living things, according to traditional Chinese philosophy. Yin, the passive element, corresponds to absorption, while yang is the active element, resembling agility. The balance between yin and yang is constantly shifting, and their effectiveness increases by getting the combination right, rather than relying too heavily on one or the other. Agile absorption refers to an organization's capability to consistently identify and seize opportunities while retaining the structural characteristics to weather changes in the market. It is the organizational equivalent of Ali in his prime, fleet of foot and hand but able to take a blow.

To assess their organization's level of agile absorption, managers can ask themselves a series of questions: "How agile are we? How absorptive are we? Where does our absorption currently come from? Are these the best sources? Are there alternative ways to boost our absorption that would enhance our agility?" They can also inventory the levels of agility and absorption within their organizations with the survey at the end of this chapter.

At first glance, the structural factors that provide absorption appear incompatible with agility: global scale versus a lean operation, for instance, or legacy assets versus a clean sheet of paper. In fact, however, leaders can achieve and maintain agile absorption, as the examples below illustrate.

More good fats, fewer bad fats. As a first step, executives should recognize that sources of absorption vary in their effect on agility. Like dietary fats, all sources of absorption provide energy for hard times, but some sources are healthier than others. Low fixed costs, for example, are an outstanding source of absorption. They allow a firm to weather a wide range of threats without degrading the ability to seize opportunities.

Other sources of absorption, in contrast, come at an unacceptably high cost in terms of foregone agility. Excess workers, particularly those in staff positions, tend to generate work to justify their existence. Their efforts, however well intentioned, introduce unnecessary complexity and bureaucracy that sap agility. Powerful patrons can drag an organization down as well as lift it up. Government interventions saved many banks, but their salvation comes at the cost of political interference with strategy and pay policy. The government of Dubai might encourage Emirates to grow at a pace that serves Dubai but causes the airline to overinvest in capacity.

Actively manage trade-offs. Executives should manage trade-offs when balancing agility and absorption. Time and time again, General Motors missed opportunities that Toyota seized—for example, by differentiating on product quality and coming out with smaller cars and hybrids. Many factors contributed to GM's decline, but one oft-cited explanation is management's inability to lay off workers when demand slipped. Guaranteed jobs translate labor from a variable cost to a fixed cost, thereby decreasing absorption. Toyota also guarantees its employees lifetime employment; the Japanese carmaker attempted to lay off workers in the 1950s, but encountered massive resistance from unions and the government. Toyota traded the higher fixed costs for flexible work rules, variable job assignments, and employee involvement, which collectively enhanced the company's agility. GM executives, in contrast, gave the absorption away without receiving agility in return.

Many managers believe that corporate bulk is the archenemy of agility. But it is complexity, not size per se, that smothers agility. Companies that pursue a focused business model, such as Wal-Mart, Toyota, or Southwest Airlines, can scale without adding complexity. This extreme focus comes at a cost, however, since it decreases the scope for portfolio agility and leaves a firm vulnerable to shifting consumer tastes (think Laura Ashley) or technologies (think Polaroid).

An alternative approach to achieve scale with agility breaks a large organization into multiple independent profit-and-loss units. Independent units can move quickly and maintain a sense of ownership among employees who might feel adrift in an organization with 200,000 employees. This approach offers the potential to combine operational, portfolio, and strategic agility with a high level of absorption. Firms that have excelled at managing multiple units in the past, such as GE, Johnson & Johnson, and HSBC, have remained industry leaders over extended periods. This approach carries costs as well: independent units often duplicate back-office functions, which increases fixed costs, and executives must invest heavily to promote cooperation among fiercely autonomous divisions.

Build an agile culture on an absorptive asset base. In his early career, Muhammad Ali could bob and weave to victory, but he rose to greatness by combining agility with absorption. Over time, however, the agility seeped from his limbs, and Ali survived his late fights through absorption alone. Many organizations follow a similar arc. Early agility wins them the trappings of success—size, cash, and a secure position. These sources of absorption, however, gnaw away at the cultural roots of agility. Bureaucracy, political infighting, complacency, and arrogance sprout in their place. When the context shifts—and turbulence ensures it will—the bloated organization lumbers through the ring like a punch-drunk heavyweight, absorbing blows it can no longer dodge and missing opportunities it is too slow to seize. The cumulative effect of these blows wears down champions, such as U.S. Steel or General Motors, two companies that once appeared invincible. A similar fate could undo absorption heavyweights such as Merck, Coca-Cola, Microsoft, Citigroup, Royal Dutch Shell, or Sony.

Tendency is not destiny. The decline and fall of a company's culture of agility is neither inevitable nor irreversible. When Mittal acquired state-own mills in Mexico and Kazakhstan, the steelmaker built an agile organization on the absorptive infrastructure of these large facilities. Through subsequent mergers and acquisitions, Mittal has dramatically increased its absorption by bulking up in size, diversifying its cash flows, and acquiring technology. Through the process, however, Mittal Steel has remained more agile than competitors by writing agility software on the hardware of absorption. I hope that the insights in this book help managers throughout the world balance agility with absorption to seize the upside of turbulence.

CAN YOUR ORGANIZATION GO THE DISTANCE?

All organizations combine some degree of agility and absorption. Circle the number that reflects your level of agreement with each of the following statements for your own organization. When you have finished, calculate the average of your scores for both agility and absorption, then plot your score on the matrix to see where your organization falls.

FIGURE 11.2 **Going the Distance Survey**

	Strongly disagree		Neither agree nor disagree		Strongly agree
Measures of absorption					
1. Our size prevents us from failing or being acquired.	1	2	3	4	5
2. Our company's cash flows are highly diversified by business line and/or geography.	1	2	3	4	5
3. We have a strong balance sheet and more cash and marketable securities than rivals.	1	2	3	4	5
4. We own tangible resources that customers pay a premium for and rivals cannot imitate.	1	2	3	4	5
5. We control intangible resources that customers pay a premium for and rivals cannot imitate.	1	2	3	4	5

(continued)

	Strongly disagree		Neither agree nor disagree		Strongly agree
6. We have abundant slack (people who are not creating value in the organization).	1	2	3	4	5
7. Customers are locked into using our product by high switching costs.	1	2	3	4	5
8. Powerful partners (e.g., government, investors) are vested in our success.	1	2	3	4	5
9. We are leaders in a profitable home market with high barriers to entry.	1	2	3	4	5
10. We have low fixed costs relative to our most efficient competitors.	1	2	3	4	5

Average score for absorption = _____

Measures of agility

	Strongly disagree		Neither agree nor disagree		Strongly agree
1. Our systems provide us with market data in real time that are granular and credible.	1	2	3	4	5
2. We consistently spot and exploit changes in the market before competitors.	1	2	3	4	5
3. We have a shared understanding of the situation across units and levels in the hierarchy.	1	2	3	4	5

(continued)

	Strongly disagree		Neither agree nor disagree		Strongly agree
4. Objectives are clear to all, and everyone is held accountable for delivery.	1	2	3	4	5
5. We are not overwhelmed by a large number of key performance indicators and objectives.	1	2	3	4	5
6. Our organization attracts, retains, and rewards entrepreneurial managers.	1	2	3	4	5
7. We maintain the same sense of urgency as a start-up venture even in good times.	1	2	3	4	5
8. Management admits mistakes and does not delay in exiting unsuccessful businesses.	1	2	3	4	5
9. Top executives systematically reallocate cash and top management talent across units.	1	2	3	4	5
10. Top executives have the courage to seize major opportunities when they arise.	1	2	3	4	5

Average score for agility = _____

The survey allows you to assess quickly which heavyweight boxer your organization most resembles. The two-by-two matrix below plots eighteen of the greatest heavyweight boxers of all time in terms of agility (including variables such as hand speed and footwork) and absorption (including size and durability). Foreman defines one extreme, scoring among the highest in absorption and lowest in agility. The 1892 heavyweight champ James "Gentleman Jim" Corbett represents the other, displaying exceptional agility but limited absorption. The boxers who scored well along both dimensions—including Joe Louis and Larry Holmes—are among the greatest of all time.

Using your survey data, plot your own organization in terms of agility and absorption to see which heavyweight boxer your organization most resembles.

FIGURE 11.3 **Boxer Matrix**

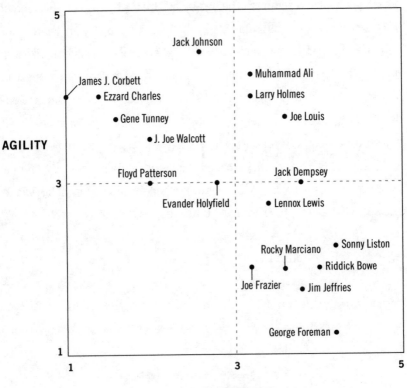

ACKNOWLEDGMENTS

This book is the culmination of thousands of interviews and discussions, with managers, colleagues, and students over the span of a decade. During this time, it has been a particular pleasure to collaborate with former students who became collaborators and coauthors. I thank Martin Escobari, who helped on the Mittal and Brahma cases, and also co-authored a book on companies that thrived in the turbulent Brazilian market. My co-author Stefano Turconi has done an outstanding job of collecting and synthesizing data on Zara, the fast-fashion sector, and the cruise industry, where we have been helped immeasurably by Barbara Muckermann. In my study of Chinese entrepreneurs, Yong (Harry) Wang did an excellent job of supervising research teams based in Shanghai and Beijing, translating company documents, and working with the companies to ensure the accuracy of our data and analysis.

I owe an enormous debt to the executives, owners, and outside directors who were so generous with their own time in interviews, provided company data, arranged interviews with their colleagues, and reviewed our findings for accuracy. A few executives deserve special acknowledgment for contributing above and beyond the call of duty, particularly Carlos Siffert, Luiz Kaufmann, Carlos Alberto Sicupira, and Marcel Telles. In addition I would like to thank Terry Opdendyk, João Bosco Silva, Maurício Botelho, Alexandre Behring, Mário Bavaresco Júnior, Raul Calfat, Sílvio Carvalho, Newton Chiaparini, Renato Cuoco, Ana Maria Diniz, Carlos Ermírio de Moraes, Luís Ermírio de Moraes, Luis Gemignani, Aymar Giglio Junior, Jackson Gomes, Ronald de Jongh, Wilson Kuzuhara, Guilherme Leal, Antonio Matias, Caio Mattar, Ruy Moraes Abreu, Henri Penchas, Antonio Luiz Seabra, Alfredo Setubal, Roberto Setubal, José Tambasco, Fernando Tracanella, Luiz Antonio Viana, Ying Han, Xingsheng Zhang, Ying Wu, Johnny Chou, Ruimin Zhang, Mianmian Yang, Zhidong Wang, Chuanzhi Liu, Mary Ma, Yaochang Yu, Qinghou Zong, Zongnan Wang, Boquan He, Charles Zhang, Ezequiel Sanchez Cascales, Jesus Echevarria, Stefano Sutter, Dilip Patel, Micky Arison, Maurice Zarmati, Bob Dickinson, Roberta Jacoby, Tim Gallagher, Brendan Corrigan, Brenda Yester, Meshulam Zonis, Chris Hayman, Mary Bond, Anne Kalosh, Lakshmi Mittal, and Aditya Mittal; and I am grateful to the others who were so generous with their time, but are too numerous to thank individually.

Among my colleagues I owe a special debt of gratitude to Stanford professor Kathy Eisenhardt, whose work on strategy in uncertain markets has been an inspiration to me over the years. At the Harvard Business School, I thank Carliss Baldwin and Jonathan West, with whom I met twice a month to work through the classic texts about managing in a turbulent world, including the work of Frank Knight, Karl Popper, Friedrich Hayek, Joseph Schumpeter, and others. My former colleagues in the Entrepreneurship Unit at Harvard, particularly Howard Stevenson, Bill Sahlman, and Bob Higgins, provided invaluable insights into the process of pursuing an opportunity. At the London Business School, my colleagues Andrew Scott and Hélène Rey helped navigate the voluminous research about turbulence in macroeconomics. Phil Rosenzweig provided useful comments on my research design. Dominic Houlder and Ben Bryant, now a professor at IMD, both helped enrich my findings on portions of this research. I acknowledge with gratitude funding from the London Business School, the David Rockefeller Center for Latin American Studies at Harvard University, and the Harvard Business School Division of Research.

I am very grateful for the generosity of Keith Johnstone and Neil Mullarkey for their time and insights through many discussions about improvisation. My understanding of John Boyd and his influence on doctrinal change in U.S. Marine Corps benefited immensely from the insights and comments from Jim Murphy, Brigadier General Robert Schmidle USMC, Will Duke, Chet Richards, Colonel Michael D. Wyly USMC (ret.), Scott Gebicke, Victor Meyer, and Brigadier General Charles Campbell USAF (ret.). I thank Steve Fuller for reviewing the chapter on Karl Popper.

The executive participants in Achieving Strategic Agility, London Business School's week-long "boot camp" on managing in turbulent markets, have provided invaluable insights, examples, and challenges on how the ideas in this book play out in practice. I benefited immensely from discussions with executives from Oracle, Emirates, Standard Chartered Bank, BT, SKF, and Mars, who participated in the Global Business Consortium. Several students have contributed their time and effort to research and write case studies or conduct projects related to this research. I thank Aaron Wen, Nelson Liu, Ying Zhang,

Liyang Jin, Yong Yuan, Jason Hu, Charles Xu, Allen Qian, Julia Zheng, Greg Ye, Alex Araujo, Fernando Martins, Andre Delben Silva, Marcella Escobari, Mauro Goncalves de Oliveira Filho, Cinnamon Russell, and Giles Jepson.

Ben Loehnen, my editor at HarperBusiness, did an outstanding job. In addition to suggesting the title, Ben pinpointed weaknesses in earlier drafts and explained clearly why passages didn't work. Researching, conceptualizing, and writing this book have been an all-engrossing effort for a decade. I thank my wife, Theresa, and our children, Charles, Phillip, Elizabeth, and Genevieve, who tolerated endless dinnertime discussions about "the book," and extended periods when research and writing consumed much of my time and energy.

NOTES

CHAPTER 1: THE STONE IN DAVID'S SLINGSHOT

1. Brian Apelt, *The Corporation: A Centennial Biography of United States Steel Corporation, 1901–2001* (Pittsburgh, Penn.: Cathedral Publishing, 2001); Kenneth Warren, *Big Steel: The First Century of the United States Steel Corporation, 1901–2001* (Pittsburgh, Penn.: University of Pittsburgh Press, 2008).

2. Mark Houser, "The Fall and Rise of the Mon Valley," *Pittsburgh Tribune-Review*, September 9, 2007.

3. Martin Woertler et al., *Global Steel: Breaking the Stalemate*, Boston Consulting Group, 2002.

4. Warren, *Big Steel*, table A9.

5. Most of the data on Mittal draws from Donald Sull, "Spinning Steel into Gold: The Case of Ispat International N.V.," *European Management Journal* 17, 4 (1999): 368–81. Other helpful sources include Simon Clark and Matthew Craze, "Man of Steel," *Bloomberg Markets*, July 2005, and various equity analyst reports and SEC filings.

6. Woertler et al., *Global Steel*.

7. For a detailed description of these studies, see the research design and methodology appendix in Donald N. Sull, *Made in China*, (Boston: Harvard Business School Press, 2005), and the introductory chapter of Donald N. Sull and Martin Escobari, *Success Against the Odds*, (London: Elsevier/Campus, 2005).

8. In his outstanding book *The Halo Effect*, (New York: Free Press, 2007), Professor Phil Rosenzweig describes a set of factors that obscure our ability to distinguish the underlying sources of corporate performance. These include the halo effect created by superior performance, which leads observers to view every aspect of an organization—from strategy to culture—in a positive light. Many variables, moreover, are closely correlated with one another, frustrating our ability to untangle causal relationships. Scholars studying corporate performance cannot ignore Phil's trenchant analysis, but nor should they abandon the search for actions that can increase the odds of success. My own approach was to treat the paired-case

research findings as preliminary, and submit them to further scrutiny as described in the text.

9. John Y. Campbell et al., "Have Individual Stocks Become More Volatile? An Empirical Explanation of Idiosyncratic Risk," *Journal of Finance* 56 (2001): 1–43. Campbell and colleagues found no increase in aggregate stock market volatility, confirming the finding that aggregate stock market volatility has remained essentially flat between the 1920s and the late 1990s. See G. William Schwert, "Why Does Stock Market Volatility Change over Time?" *Journal of Finance* 44 (1989): 1115–53. Recent research argues that idiosyncratic volatility has not followed a steady upward trend, but rather switches between periods of relative stability and higher volatility. See Michael W. Brandt et al., "The Idiosyncratic Volatility Puzzle: Time Trend or Speculative Episodes," unpublished working paper, 2008; and Geert Bekaert et al., "Is There a Trend in Idiosyncratic Volatility?" unpublished working paper, 2008.

10. Diego A. Comin, and Sunil Mulani, "Diverging Trends in Macro and Micro Volatility," *Review of Economics and Statistics* 88, 2 (2006): 374–83; Diego A. Comin and Thomas Philippon, "The Rise in Firm-Level Volatility: Causes and Consequences," *NBER Macroeconomics Annual* 20 (2005): 167–228; Diego A. Comin, Erica L. Groshen, and Bess Rabin, "Turbulent Firms, Turbulent Wages?" *Journal of Monetary Economics* 56, 1 (2009): 109–33.

11. Average life span of an S&P company from Richard Foster and Sarah Kaplan, *Creative Destruction: Why Companies That Are Built to Last Underperform the Market—and How to Transform Them* (New York: Currency, 2001); probability of exit data from George P. Baker and Robert E. Kennedy, "Survivorship and the Economic Grim Reaper," *Journal of Law, Economics, and Organization* 18, 2 (2002): 324–61.

12. A leading firm is defined as one in the top quintile of industry performance, and dethronement takes place when they fall from the top quintile during any five-year period for reasons including declining performance, bankruptcy, or acquisition by another firm. See William I. Huyett and S. Patrick Viguerie, "Extreme Competition," *McKinsey Quarterly* 2005, no. 1, 47–57. Their findings are supported by a more systematic study of over six thousand firms across more than forty industries and twenty-five years that also explored the persistence of superior performance. See Robert R. Wiggins and Timothy W. Ruefli, "Schumpeter's Ghost: Is Hypercompetition Making the Best of Times Shorter?" *Strategic Management Journal* 26 (2005): 887–911.

13. One recent study analyzed volatility of return on investment for an average of 5,700 business units over twenty years and found it increased from the late 1970s through the mid-1980s and decreased thereafter. See Gerry McNamara, Paul M. Vaaler, and Cynthia Devers, "Same as It Ever Was: The Search for Evidence of Increasing Hypercompetition," *Strategic Management Journal* 24 (2003): 261–78. Their findings support industry-level studies that have found that turbulence ebbs and flows within an industry over time. That said, Campbell et al., "Have Individual Stocks Become More Volatile?" found that eight of the ten largest industries they studied (ranked by average market capitalization) experienced increased volatility in returns between the early 1960 and the late 1990s. It is also important to note that volatility for the economy as a whole, as measured by fluctuations in GDP, has decreased—it was one-third less in the period between 1984 to 2002 than it had been between 1960 and 1983. This drop in volatility occurred in Japan, Germany, the United Kingdom, France, and Italy as well, although the precise timing and magnitudes

differed. Two separate analyses identified a break point in U.S. GDP variance at 1984; see Chang-Jin Kim and Charles R. Nelson, "Has the U.S. Economy Become More Stable? A Bayesian Approach Based on a Markov-Switching Model of the Business Cycle," *Review of Economics and Statistics* 81 (1999): 608–16, and Margaret M. McConnell and Gabriel Perez-Quiros, "Output Fluctuations in the United States: What Has Changed Since the Early 1980s," *American Economic Review* 90, 5 (2000): 1464–76. On volatility measured as variance of four-quarter GDP growth, see James H. Stock and Mark W. Watson, "Has the Business Cycle Changed? Evidence and Explanations," in *Monetary Policy and Uncertainty* (Kansas City, Mo.: Federal Reserve Bank of Kansas City, 2003), 9–56. This so-called "great moderation" of GDP volatility is not inconsistent with greater turbulence at the firm level, since the volatility of individual firms cancels out in the process of aggregating performance to calculate national output.

14. Summary of PricewaterhouseCoopers CEO survey 2007, PWC Web site, accessed October 3, 2008. (www.pwc.com/servlet/pwcPrintPreview?LNLoc=/extweb/insights.nsf/docid/0F319E656181B1A18525729D0073E055).

15. F. E. Emery and E. L. Trist, "The Causal Texture of Organizational Environments," *Human Relations* 18 (1965): 21–31; J. D. Thompson, *Organizations in Action* (New York: McGraw-Hill, 1967); R. B. Duncan, "Characteristics of Organizational Environments and Perceived Environmental Uncertainty," *Administrative Science Quarterly* 17 (1972): 313–27. These authors focus on *dynamism*, or the rate of change in variables that influence performance, and *complexity*, or the number of variables and interrelationships among them that must be considered in order to model a firm's performance.

16. David Miles and Andrew Scott, *Macroeconomics: Understanding the Wealth of Nations* (Chichester, U.K.: John Wiley, 2005), 555.

17. Paul Cashin and C. John McDermott, "The Long Run Behavior of Commodity Prices: Small Trends and Big Variability," *IMF Staff Papers* 49, 2 (2002): 175–99.

18. A September 2006 poll by ABC News found that 35 percent of respondents worried that they might personally be a victim of a terrorist attack. ABC News Poll, September 5–7, 2006; N=1,003 adults nationwide.

19. Ali H. Mokdad et al., "Actual Causes of Death in the United States, 2000," *Journal of the American Medical Association* 291, 10 (March 10, 2004): 1238–41.

20. David Kesmodel and Janet Adamy, "Why Price Increases Are Brewing for Craft Beers," *Wall Street Journal*, October 5, 2007, B1.

21. I am grateful to my colleague Andrew Scott for helping me to wade through the voluminous literature on globalization, and also for the summary in his excellent textbook, David Miles and Andrew Scott, *Macroeconomics: Understanding the Wealth of Nations,* 2nd ed. (Chichester, U.K.: John Wiley, 2005).

22. The study looked at the pace of diffusion globally for twenty-nine technological breakthroughs in transportation, communication, manufacturing, and medical technologies from 1750 to the present. Diffusion was measured by adoption within 80 percent of the countries for which data were available. See the International Bank for Reconstruction and Development (World Bank), *Global Economic Prospects: Technology Diffusion in the Developing World* (Washington, D.C.: World Bank, 2008). For a useful summary, see table 2.14.

23. "New Champions, Global Challenger," *Harvard Business Review*–World Economic

Forum CEO Survey, presented at "Made in India Multinationals: A Discussion," London Business School, October 2007.

24. Thomson Financial, *National Venture Capital Association Yearbook* (New York: NY: Thomson, 2007). Venture-backed IPOs represented 14 percent of all companies receiving initial funding in the period 1980–2006, while exit through M&A accounted for 15 percent.

25. Charles Emmerson, *Global Risks 2007* (Geneva: World Economic Forum, 2007).

26. The survey was conducted during September and October 2007 in twenty countries. Adam Cohen, "The Age of Fear," *Wall Street Journal Europe*, December 7–9, 2007.

27. Clark G. Gilbert, "Unbundling the Structure of Inertia: Resource Versus Routine Rigidity," *Academy of Management Journal* 48, 5 (2005): 741–63; Clark G. Gilbert, "Change in the Presence of Residual Fit: Can Competing Frames Coexist?" *Organization Science* 17, 1 (2006): 150–67.

28. J. E. Dutton and S. B. Jackson, "Categorizing Strategic Issues: Links to Organizational Action," *Academy of Management Review* 12, 1 (1987): 76–90.

29. "The Carnegie from Calcutta," *Economist*, January 8, 1998: 56.

30. Paul R. Ehrlich, *The Population Bomb*, (New York: Ballantine, 1968): xi.

31. Alberto Capatti and Massimo Montanari, *Italian Cuisine: A Cultural History* (New York: Columbia University Press, 1999), 42–43.

32. N. A. M. Rodger, *The Insatiable Earl: A Life of John Montagu, 4th Earl of Sandwich* (London: HarperCollins, 1993). Rodger notes that only one source attributes Montagu's creation of the sandwich to the gaming table, and he might have invented the meal to allow him to work rather than gamble.

33. BBC, "Obituary: Dr. Robert Atkins," April 17, 2003, http://news.bbc.co.uk/1/hi/world/americas/2957623.stm.

34. Douglas Martin, "Dr. Robert C. Atkins, Author of Controversial but Best-Selling Diet Books, Is Dead at 72," *New York Times*, April 18, 2003.

35. Howard E. Aldrich, *Organizations Evolving*, (London: Sage, 1999); and Lowell W. Busenitz and Jay B. Barney, "Differences between entrepreneurs and managers in large organizations: Biases and heuristics in strategic decision-making," *Journal of Business Venturing*, 12, 1 (1997): 9-30.

CHAPTER 2: TIME, TIMING, AND LUCK

1. Most of the information on Carnival Cruise Lines in this chapter is from Donald Sull et al., "Carnival Corporation: The P&O Acquisition," unpublished London Business School case study, interviews with cruise industry executives; and Bob Dickinson and Andy Vladimir, *Selling the Sea: An Inside Look at the Cruise Industry* (Hoboken, N.J.: John Wiley, 2008). I am particularly grateful to Stefano Turconi and Barbara Muckermann for their diligent and creative research assistance on this project.

2. Richard Tedlow, *Andy Grove* (New York: Portfolio, 2006), 178.

3. Adam Brandenburger provides the clearest definition of value. See A. M. Brandenburger and H. Stuart, "Value-Based Business Strategy," *Journal of Economics and Management Strategy* 5 (1996): 5–25. For a more accessible introduction, see A. M. Brandenburger

and B. J. Nalebuff, *Co-opetition* (New York: Doubleday, 1996). The cost here is not the out-of-pocket expense, but the opportunity cost, or the income foregone by not using the resource for its best available use, including the much-adjusted cost of capital.

4. Peter Jayaswal, "Danmarks Nationalbank's Costs of Supporting Ship Finance," *Danmarks Nationalbank Monetary Review* 43, 3 (2004): 35–46. Denmark also offered additional subsidies to support its maritime industry; see U.S. Department of Commerce Maritime Administration, *Maritime Subsidies 1978* (Washington, D.C.: Government Printing Office, 1978), 35–38.

5. U.S. Department of Transportation, *Bureau of Transportation Statistics, Air Carrier Traffic Statistics* (Washington, D.C.: U.S. Government Printing Office, 2007); Transportation Research Board, "Winds of Change, Domestic Air Transport Since Deregulation," National Research Council, Washington, D.C., 1991, 230.

6. The number of passengers embarking from the Miami port totaled 1.1 million in 1976 and had grown to 3.1 million by 1989. See Arthur Chapman, "Watch the Port of Miami," *Tequesta: the Journal of the Historical Association of Southern Florida* 53 (1993): 7–30.

7. W. Chan Kim and Renée Mauborgne, Blue Ocean Strategy Web site, www.blueocean strategy.com/qa/FullAnswer.php?qid=1, accessed September 2, 2008.

8. Constantinos C. Markides, *Game Changing Strategies* (San Francisco: Jossey-Bass, 2006).

9. The books I reviewed were *Blue Ocean Strategy*, Gary Hamel, *Leading the Revolution*, (Boston: Harvard Business School Press, 2002); Larry Bossidy, Ram Charan, and Charles Burck, *Execution*, (New York: Crown Business, 2002); Peter Senge, *The Fifth Discipline*, (New York: Doubleday, 1990); Gary Hamel and C. K. Prahalad, (Boston: Harvard Business School Press, 1994); Adrian J. Slywotzky and David J. Morrison, (New York: Crown Business, 1997); Chris Zook with James Allen, *Profit from the Core*, (Boston: Harvard Business School Press, 2001); Thomas J. Peters and Robert Waterman, *In Search of Excellence*, (New York: Harper Collins, 1982); Jim Collins, *Good to Great: Why Some Companies Make the Leap and Others Don't* (New York: HarperBusiness, 2001); James C. Collins and Jerry I. Porras, *Built to Last*, (New York: HarperBusiness, 1994). I am not arguing that these are bad books, to be clear, but only that they would benefit from qualifying their findings with the disclaimer that outcomes depended not only on managerial actions, but also on contextual forces.

10. Niccolò Machiavelli, *The Prince*, trans. Mark Musa (New York: St. Martin's Press, 1964 [1532]), ch. XXV.

11. Ibid., 209.

CHAPTER 3: THE MAP PARADOX

1. "The Communist Putsch in Vienna failed", *Die Neue Zeitung*, June 19, 1919, 1–3; "Severe blood sacrifice from the attempted putsch," *Reichspost*, June 16, 1919, 1–2 (in German, translated by author). Descriptions of the events of June 16, 1919, including estimates of the crowd size, composition, and identity of dead and injured, are from the *Reichspost*, *Die Neue Zeitung*, and *Wiener Abendpost* newspaper reports on the following day. See also Karl Popper, *Unended Quest* (London: Routledge, 2002), 34.

2. Alan Sked, *The Decline and Fall of the Hapsburg Empire: 1815–1918* (London: Longman, 1989).

3. Value of currency measured in the exchange rate of krone per U.S. dollar. Raw data from Emanuel H. Vogel, "The Currency Problem of Austria," *Annals of the American Academy of Political and Social Science* 98 (1921), supplement: "Present-Day Social and Industrial Conditions in Austria," 28–34.

4. Michael E. Porter, *Competitive Strategy* (New York: Free Press, 1980). The five forces are rivalry among existing competitors, the threat of potential substitutes, the threat of new entrants, the bargaining power of customers, and the bargaining power of suppliers.

5. Popper, *Unended Quest*, 34. Popper later published an extensive analysis of Marxist theory in the second volume of *The Open Society and Its Enemies: Hegel, Marx, and the Aftermath* (London: Routledge, 1980), a book that many Marxists viewed as the most damning critique ever written of Marxist theory.

6. See Malachi Haim Hacohen's outstanding biography, *Karl Popper: The Formative Years, 1902–1945: Politics and Philosophy in Interwar Vienna* (Cambridge: Cambridge University Press, 2000).

7. *Times* (London), November 7, 1919.

8. Popper, *Unended Quest*, 37.

9. Karl R. Popper, *The Open Universe: An Argument for Indeterminism* (London: Routledge, 1982), 42.

10. The logic of conjecture and refutation permeates Popper's writing, but a good summary exists in Karl R. Popper, *Conjectures and Refutations: The Growth of Scientific Knowledge* (New York: Basic Books, 1962). Many people think that Popper's big idea is falsifiability, the notion that there is an asymmetry between new information that confirms our beliefs and data that disconfirm our map. While we never conclusively prove a theory no matter how high we pile the supporting examples (a million white swans do not prove that all swans are white), we can conclusively disprove it with a single disconfirming example (finding a single black swan). Popper believed that falsifiability, a theory's exposure to refutation via empirical testing, provided a shining line of demarcation between true science and the deficient theories such as Marxism and psychoanalysis that falsely claimed the mantle of science. Scientists, according to Popper, should go out of their way to expose their theories to refutation and actively seek out anomalies—the black swans that reveal the limits of their theories. Critics have largely discredited falsifiability in both the philosophy and practice of science. Few tests are as clear-cut as Popper's simplified examples, for instance, and it is often the test or model specification that is flawed rather than the underlying theory. Rudolf Carnap, for example, fought for common sense and argued that confirmatory evidence must increase our confidence in a theory. See Rudolf Carnap's response to Popper in *The Philosophy of Rudolf Carnap* (LaSalle, Ill.: Open Court, 1963). I accept the critique of falsifiability but find it misplaced. Popper's true contribution lies in the iterative approach to science that alternates between periods of commitment and skepticism.

11. Popper, *Unended Quest*, 155.

12. Karl Popper, *The Logic of Scientific Discovery* (New York: Basic Books, 1959).

13. Popper, *The Open Universe*, xv.

14. Hacohen, *Karl Popper,* 148

15. Bryan Magee, *Philosophy and the Real World: An Introduction to Karl Popper* (La Salle, Ill.: Open Court, 1973).

16. Probably the most comprehensive study of start-up survival was conducted on more than two hundred thousand new establishments founded in the second quarter of 1998 across all industries and across all U.S. states. The found an average four-year mortality rate of 56 percent and a surprisingly narrow range across industries, with the lowest four-year mortality rate in education and health service (45 percent) and the highest in information technology (62 percent). See Amy E. Knaup, "Survival and Longevity in the Business Employment Dynamics Data," *Monthly Labor Review*, May 2005, 50–56. A similar study conducted of Swiss start-ups founded between 2000 and 2004 found a five-year mortality rate of 51 percent; see Bundesamt für Statistik, "Unternehmensdemografie: Überlebensraten der zwischen 2000 und 2004 gegründeten Unternehmen," *Industrie und Dienstleistungen* 2008. Canadian data found a 64 percent mortality rate across all sectors for start-ups founded between 1984 and 1994; see John Baldwin et al., *Failure Rates for New Canadian Firms: New Perspectives on Entry and Exit* (Ontario: Ministry of Industry, 2000). In two successive studies of more than three hundred thousand U.S. manufacturing firms between 1963 and 1982, Timothy Dunne and his colleagues found an average five-year exit rate for new entrants building new plants of 62 percent; see Timothy Dunne, Mark J. Roberts, and Larry Samuelson, "Patterns of Firm Entry and Exit in U.S. Manufacturing Industries," *RAND Journal of Economics* 29, 4 (1988): 495–515, esp. table 11. A study of more than three thousand Portuguese manufacturing firms found a four-year exit rate of 48 percent; see José Mata and Pedro Portugal, "Life Duration of New Firms," *Journal of Industrial Economics* 42, 3 (1994): 227–45. One study that controlled for the stage of the industry life cycle and the size of the entrant found five-year failure rates ranging from 30 percent to 43 percent; see Rajshree Agarwal and David B. Audretsch, "Does Entry Size Matter? The Impact of the Life Cycle and Technology on Firm Survival," *Journal of Industrial Economics* 49, 1 (2001): 21–43. A recent study of 788 Internet firms founded between 1999 and 2002 found a five-year failure rate of 52 percent to 60 percent (depending on whether acquisitions were coded as survival or failure); see Brent Goldfarb, David Kirsch, and David A Miller, "Was There Too Little Entry During the Dot-Com Era?" *Journal of Financial Economics* 86, 1 (2007): 100–44.

17. Michael Roberts and Nicole Tempest, *ONSET Ventures*, Case Study 9-898-154 (Boston: Harvard Business School, 1998); and author's interview with Terry Opdendyk, ONSET Ventures cofounder.

18. For a fuller discussion of entrepreneurship as an iterative sequence of experiments, see Donald N. Sull, "Disciplined Entrepreneurship." *Sloan Management Review* 46, 1 (2004): 71–77.

19. Thomas Kuhn, *The Structure of Scientific Revolutions* (Chicago: University of Chicago Press, 1962). Kuhn's influence is indisputable. *The Structure of Scientific Revolutions* has sold more than a million copies and been translated into over twenty languages. See Steve Fuller, *Kuhn vs. Popper* (Cambridge: Icon Books, 2003), 2. The book was first among all books cited in the *Arts and Humanities Citation Index* between 1976 and 1983. See Eugene Garfield, "A Different Sort of Great Books List," *Current Contents* 16 (1987): 3–7.

20. F. Scott Fitzgerald, "The Crack Up," *Esquire*, February, 1936: 19.

21. Jacques Brunschwig, "Skepticism," in Jacques Brunschwig and Geoffrey E. R. Lloyd, eds., *Greek Thought: A Guide to Classical Knowledge* (Cambridge, Mass.: Belknap, 2000), 937–55.

22. David Hume, *An Enquiry Concerning Human Understanding* (Oxford: Oxford University Press, 1951), XII: 2, 160.

23. Imre Lakatos, *Criticism and the Growth of Knowledge* (New York: Cambridge University Press, 1970), 22.

CHAPTER 4: ACTIVE INERTIA

1. For the history of Harvey Firestone, see Alfred Lief, *Harvey Firestone: Free Man of Enterprise* (New York: McGraw-Hill, 1951). The history of the early tire industry draws on Donald N. Sull, "From Community of Innovation to Community of Inertia: The Rise and Fall of the Akron Tire Cluster," Harvard Business School Working Paper 01-025, 2001; and Steve Love and David Giffels, *Wheels of Fortune: The Story of Rubber in Akron* (Akron: University of Akron Press, 1998).

2. Love and Giffels, *Wheels of Fortune.*

3. Using multiple archival sources, Stanislav Dobrev and his co-authors identified 2,197 new entrants to the automobile industry between 1885 and 1981. See Stanislav D. Dobrev, Tai-Young Kim, and Glenn R. Carroll, "Shifting Gears, Shifting Niches: Organizational Inertia and Change in the Evolution of the U.S. Automobile Industry, 1885–1981," *Organization Science* 14, 3 (2003): 264–82. Like start-ups today, many of these entrants failed to secure the funding to actually produce their design, but they nevertheless contributed to uncertainty in product and process technology.

4. Steven Klepper, "The Capabilities of New Firms and the Evolution of the U.S. Automobile Industry," *Industrial and Corporate Change* 11, 4 (2001): 645–66.

5. Zephyr Frank and Aldo Musacchio, "The International Natural Rubber Market, 1870–1930," in EH.Net Encyclopedia, 2008, http://eh.net/encyclopedia/article/frank.international.rubber.market.

6. U.S. Bureau of Labor Statistics, *Bulletin 572: Wholesale Prices* (Washington, D.C.: Government Printing Office, 1934); Lloyd G. Reynolds, "Competition in the Rubber-Tire Industry," *American Economic Review* 28, 3 (1938): 459–68.

7. See B. Stern, "Labor Productivity in the Automobile Tire Industry," *U.S. Bureau of Labor Statistics Bulletin* 585 (1933); U.S. Bureau of Labor Statistics, "Productivity of Labor in Eleven Manufacturing Industries," *Monthly Labor Review,* March (1930): 501–17.

8. More precisely, a commitment is an action taken by a person in a time period that increases the probability that she, or the organization she represents, will behave in a specified way in subsequent time periods. Commitments operate by increasing the costs of deviating from the specified behavior in the future, up to the limit of excluding the possibility of alternative courses of action altogether. This definition of commitment is closest to the construct of "precommitment" used in game theory and defined in Jon Elster, *Ulysses and the Sirens: Studies in Rationality and Irrationality* (Cambridge: Cambridge University Press, 1979), 36–103.

9. Lief, *Harvey Firestone,* 103, 105.

10. This perspective is commonly referred to as the resource-based view of the firm. See B. Wernerfelt, "A Resource-Based View of the Firm," *Strategic Management Journal* 5, 2 (1984): 171–80, and J. Barney, "Firm Resources and Sustained Competitive Advantage," *Journal of Management* 17, 1 (1991): 99–120.

11. Many scholars interpret technological innovation in terms of big breakthroughs, but the advances in tire technology were a story of many incremental improvements over decades. Improved tire construction offered the potential to enhance performance, but realizing this potential required a host of innovations in complementary technologies, especially the raw materials, including chemical additives, steel wire, and textiles. Cord tires, for example, reduced tire failure resulting from fabric friction but did not address rubber degradation. New chemical additives, however, significantly increased the durability of tread rubber, while advances in steel wire allowed the balloon tire to attach to a rim.

12. Patricia M. Zonsius, "The Centennial History of the Portage Country Club: 1894–1994," in author's possession. While the entire manuscript is a fascinating history of a social institution central to Akron's tire industry, the most valuable data are a complete list of members in 1906 that presents a snapshot of the social networks in Akron's early tire industry.

13. Sull, "From Community of Innovation to Community of Inertia," figure 4.

14. Leon Festinger, *A Theory of Cognitive Dissonance* (Evanston, Ill.: Row, Peterson, 1957). See also Gerald R. Salancik, "Commitment and the Control of Organizational Behavior and Belief," in Barry M. Staw and Gerald R. Salancik, eds., *New Directions in Organizational Behavior* (Chicago: St. Clair, 1977), 1–54.

15. Much of the research in the escalation of commitment literature has focused on the individual and is based on laboratory experiments. For a recent review of this literature, see Joel Brockner, "The Escalation of Commitment to a Failing Course of Action: Toward Theoretical Progress," *Academy of Management Review* 17, 1 (1992): 39–61. Recently, scholars in this tradition have broadened their focus to study escalation at the organizational level. See Jerry Ross and Barry M. Staw, "Organizational Escalation and Exit: Lessons from the Shoreham Nuclear Power Plant," *Academy of Management Journal* 36, 4 (1993): 701–32, and Barry M. Staw and Jerry Ross, "Behavior in Escalation Situations: Antecedents, Prototypes, and Solutions," in B. M. Staw and L. L. Cummings, eds., *Research in Organizational Behavior* (Greenwich, Conn.: JAI, 1987), 9:39–78.

16. See Lynne G. Zucker, "The Role of Institutionalization in Cultural Persistence," *American Sociological Review* 42 (1977): 726–43.

17. For an extended discussion of factors that harden commitments to a mental map, see Donald N. Sull, *Why Good Companies Go Bad and How Great Managers Remake Them* (Boston: Harvard Business School Press, 2005), ch. 3; Joseph F. Porac, Howard Thomas, and Charles Baden-Fuller, "Competitive Groups as Cognitive Communities: The Case of Scottish Knitwear Manufacturers," *Journal of Management Studies* 26, 4 (1989): 397–416.

18. D. Harkleroad, "Pneumatiques Michelin," INSEAD case study, imprint 438 (1978): 6.

19. M. French, "Structural Change and Competition in the United States Tire Industry, 1920-1937," *Business History Review*, 60 (1986): 33.

20. D. Darryl Wyckoff, *Firestone Tire and Rubber Company*, case study 9-684-044 (Boston: Harvard Business School, 1980).

21. Sull, "From Community of Innovation to Community of Inertia," table 8.

22. Wyckoff, *Firestone Tire and Rubber Company*, 3; Love and Giffels, *Wheels of Fortune*, 150–51.

23. Love and Giffels, *Wheels of Fortune*, 152.

CHAPTER 5: MIND THE GAP

1. The original incident was described by Frank Rooney, "The Cyclists' Raid," *Harper's Magazine*, January 1951.

2. Sources for Honda include "Establishing American Honda Motor Co: An Unknown Market a New Challenge," http://world.honda.com/history/challenge/1959establishingamericanhonda/index.html; Masaaki Sato, *The Honda Myth: The Genius and His Wake*, trans. Hiroko Yoda (New York: Vertical, 2006); Tetsuou Sakiya, *Honda Motor: The Men, the Management, the Machines* (New York: Kodansha, 1982).

3. The original study is publicly available because it was commissioned and paid for by the British Secretary of State for Industry. See J. V. B. Dresser, M. Goold, and B. Hedley, *Strategy Alternatives for the British Motorcycle Industry*, report prepared for the Secretary of State for Industry by the Boston Consulting Group Limited (London: Her Majesty's Stationery Office, 1975).

4. In September 1982, Richard Pascale, a professor at Stanford's Graduate School of Business Administration, assembled the six executives who had led Honda's entry into the U.S. motorcycle industry, to hear firsthand their version of Honda's move to North America. See Richard T. Pascale, "Perspectives on Strategy: The Real Story Behind Honda's Success," *California Management Review* 26, 3 (1984): 47–72. Pascale's article sparked an ongoing discussion in the strategy field. For a summary of the debate, see Henry Mintzberg, "The Design School: Reconsidering the Basic Premises of Strategic Management," *Strategic Management Journal* 11, 6 (1990): 171–95, and H. I. Ansoff, "The Design School: Reconsidering the Basic Premises of Strategic Management," *Strategic Management Journal* 12, 6 (1991): 4449–51, and "The 'Honda Effect' Revisited," *California Management Review* 38, 4 (1996): 78–117.

5. Israel Kirzner argued that surprise was the defining characteristic of entrepreneurs when discovering an opportunity. For an accessible summary of his argument, see Israel Kirzner, "Entrepreneurial Discovery and the Competitive Market Process: An Austrian Approach," *Journal of Economic Literature* 35 (1997): 60–85.

6. The sample was from one hundred founders selected randomly from the 1989 Inc. 500 list of fast-growing companies. See Amar Bhide, "How Entrepreneurs Craft Strategies That Work," *Harvard Business Review*, March/April 1994, 150–61. Karl Vesper lists deliberate search last among ways to find opportunities; see Karl H. Vesper, *New Venture Strategies* (Englewood Cliffs, N.J.: Prentice-Hall, 1992).

7. Scott Shane, "Prior Knowledge and the Discovery of Entrepreneurial Opportunities," *Organization Science* 11, 4 (2000): 448–69.

8. For a recent review on the confirmation bias, see R. S. Nickerson, "Confirmation Bias: A Ubiquitous Phenomenon in Many Guises," *Review of General Psychology* 2 (1998): 175–220; P. H. Ditto and D. F. Lopez, "Motivated Skepticism: Use of Differential Deci-

sion Criteria for Preferred and Non-Preferred Conclusions," *Journal of Personality and Social Psychology* 63 (1992): 568–84; K. Edwards and E. E. Smith, "A Disconfirmation Bias in the Evaluation of Arguments," *Journal of Personality and Social Psychology* 71 (1996): 5–24.

9. Kuhn, *The Structure of Scientific Revolutions*, 59.

10. For an excellent review of historical failures to seize unexpected success, see Peter F. Drucker, *Innovation and Entrepreneurship: Practice and Principles* (New York: HarperCollins, 1985), 51–61.

11. Sarah Thorp and Linda A. Cyr, *Kate Spade New York*, case study 9-800-002 (Boston: Harvard Business School, 2001).

12. Ibid., 2.

13. Michael J. Roberts, William Sahlman, and Jack McDonald, *ArthroCare*, case study 9-898-056 (Boston: Harvard Business School, 1998).

14. From Donald N. Sull, *Made in China: What Western Managers Can Learn from China's Trailblazing Entrepreneurs* (Boston: Harvard Business School, 2005), ch. 7.

15. Harriet Rubin, "The Perfect Vision of Dr. V.," *Fast Company*, January 2001, 146–54; Stephen Miller, "McSurgery: A Man Who Saved 2.4 Million Eyes," *Wall Street Journal*, August 5, 2006, A6.

16. Richard G. Hamermesh and Indra A. Reinbergs, *Shurgard Self-Storage: Expansion to Europe*, case study 9-804-112 (Boston: Harvard Business School, 2005).

17. Charles D. Ellis, *The Partnership: A History of Goldman Sachs* (New York: Allen Lane, 2008), 415–35.

18. Philip E. Tetlock, *Expert Political Judgment: How Good Is It? How Can We Know?* (Princeton, N.J.: Princeton University Press, 2005), ch. 2.

19. Michael J. Roberts and Alison Berkley Wagonfeld, *Joint Juice*, case study 9-803-146 (Boston: Harvard Business School, 2003), and author's discussion with Dr. Stone.

20. Mark S. Granovetter, "The Strength of Weak Ties," *American Journal of Sociology* 78, 6 (1973): 1360–80.

21. S. Kaish and B. Gilad, "Characteristics of Opportunity Search of Entrepreneurs Versus Executives: Sources, Interests, General Alertness," *Journal of Business Venturing* 3 (1991): 31–40.

22. Andrew Gowers, "Exposed: Dick Fuld, the Man Who Brought the World to Its Knees," *Sunday Times* (London), December 14, 2008.

23. Andrew S. Grove, *Only the Paranoid Survive: How to Exploit Crisis Points That Challenge Every Company and Every Career* (New York: HarperCollins Business, 1996), 159.

24. Alfred N. Whitehead, *Adventures of Ideas* (New York: Macmillan, 1931), 119.

25. In a Bain & Company survey, 46 percent of all large enterprises used Six Sigma in 2006. See Darrell Rigby and Barbara Bilodeau, *Management Trends and Tools 2007*, Bain & Company, 2007, 21.

26. Mary J. Benner and Michael Tushman, "Process Management and Technological Innovation: A Longitudinal Study of the Photography and Paint Industries," *Administrative Science Quarterly* 47 (2002): 678–708.

27. Rigby and Bilodeau, *Management Trends and Tools*. In 2006, Six Sigma was third among all tools tracked by Bain in terms of the percentage of companies abandoning the tool that year, and in terms of declining satisfaction in the preceding two years.

28. Charles C. Krulak, "The Strategic Corporal: Leadership in the Three Block War," *Marines Magazine*, January 1999.

29. U.S. Marine Corps, *Warfighting*, Fleet Marine Force Manual 1, (Washington, D.C.: Department of the Navy, 1989).

30. John C. Dencker, Marc Gruber, and Sonali Shah, "Pre-Entry Knowledge, Learning, and the Survival of New Firms," *Organization Science*, published online before print, November 25, 2008, DOI:10.1287/orsc.1080.0387.

31. B. H. Liddell Hart, "The 'Man-in-the-Dark' Theory of Infantry Tactics and the 'Expanding Torrent System of Attack,'" *Journal of the RUSI*, February 1921, 13. Quoted in William S. Lind, "The Theory and Practice of Maneuver Warfare," in Richard D. Hooker, ed., *Maneuver Warfare: An Anthology* (Novato, Calif.: Presidio, 1993), 7.

CHAPTER 6: KEEPING THE MAP FLUID

1. I recognize that some improvisational comedians will disagree, and argue that the principles of complete agreement (i.e., "yes, and . . .") or generosity in offers is the "big idea" in improvisation. This principle is important, of course, but a means to the end of discovering emerging patterns, not the end itself.

2. Claude Lévi-Strauss described *bricolage* as a process of making do with the materials on hand to respond to new opportunities or threats. Claude Lévi-Strauss, *The Savage Mind* (Chicago: University of Chicago Press, 1967).

3. Keith Johnstone, *Impro: Improvisation and the Theatre* (London: Faber and Faber, 1979), and author's interviews with Keith Johnstone.

4. Most of the data on fast fashion in this chapter are derived from Donald N. Sull and Stefano Turconi, "Fast Fashion," *Business Strategy Review*, Summer 2008; and interviews with executives, designers, and store personnel. See also Peter Doeringer and Sarah Crean, "Can Fast Fashion Save the U.S. Apparel Industry?" *Socio-Economic Review* 4, 3 (2006): 353–77.

5. J. Ginsberg et al., "Detecting influenza epidemics using search engine query data," *Nature*, 457 (19 February 2009): 1012-1015.

6. Janet Adamy, "McDonald's seeks way to keep sizzling," *Wall Street Journal*, March 10, 2009.

7. Andrew McAfee, "Do You Have Too Much IT?" *Sloan Management Review* 45, 3 (2004): 18–22.

8. Amy C. Edmondson, "Learning from Mistakes Is Easier Said than Done: Group and Organizational Influences on the Detection and Correction of Human Error," *Journal of Applied Behavioral Science* 32 (1996): 5–32; Amy C. Edmondson, "Psychological Safety and Learning Behavior in Work Teams," *Administrative Science Quarterly* 44, 2 (1999): 350–83; Amy C. Edmondson, "Speaking Up in the Operating Room: How Team Leaders Promote Learning in Interdisciplinary Action Teams," *Journal of Management Studies* 40 (2003): 1419–52.

CHAPTER 7: THE ESSENCE OF AGILITY

1. Information on the U.S. Air Force during the Korean War available from the U.S. Air Force Museum's exhibition to commemorate the fiftieth anniversary of the conflict. See www.wpafb.af.mil/museum/history/korea50/k50.html.

2. The official U.S. Air Force estimates from the National Museum of the United States Air Force, www.wpafb.af.mil/museum/ac/pg000106.html. Documents from recently opened archives from the former Soviet Union suggest a less lopsided kill ratio.

3. Any reader with even a slight interest in learning more about Boyd should read Robert Coram's outstanding biography, *Boyd: The Fighter Pilot Who Changed the Art of War* (New York: Back Bay Books, 2002). Other useful sources for this chapter include Grant T. Hammond, *The Mind of War: John Boyd and American Security* (Washington, D.C.: Smithsonian Books, 2004), and interviews with Colonel Michael Wyly, USMC (ret.).

4. Gloria Macias-Lizaso and Kiko Thiel, "Building a Nimble Organization: A McKinsey Global Survey," *McKinsey Quarterly*, June 2006.

5. Conference Board, *CEO Challenge 2007: Top 10 Challenges*, 2007. Sustained and steady top-line growth, which led the pack in 2006, slipped to second, with profit growth fourth, and finding qualified managerial talent fifth.

6. M. Baghai, S. Smit, and S. P. Viguerie, "The Granularity of Growth," *McKinsey Quarterly*, 2 (2007): 41-51.

7. Although Boyd himself never depicted the OODA loop as an iterative circle, that is how most of his interpreters have visualized the cycle. Unfortunately, Boyd never committed his expansive point of view to writing, but instead communicated it through a series of overhead transparencies entitled *Patterns of Conflict*, which he modified repeatedly over time. His thinking is summarized in the Coram and Hammond books cited above. Boyd's colleague Chet Richards has written two excellent books elaborating Boyd's thinking and extending it to modern conflict and business. See Chet Richards, *A Swift, Elusive Sword: What if Sun Tzu and John Boyd Did a National Defense Review?* (Washington, D.C.: Center for Defense Information, 2001), and Chet Richards, *Certain to Win: The Strategy of John Boyd, Applied to Business* (Philadelphia: Xlibris, 2004). Richards points out that at the end of his career, Boyd moved away from an iterative view of the OODA loop to a conceptualization that emphasized the need for constant observation.

8. Frans P. B. Osinga, *Science, Strategy and War: The Strategic Theory of John Boyd* (London: Routledge, 2006).

9. Craig Larman and Victor R. Basili, "Iterative and Incremental Development: A Brief History," *Computer*, June 2003, 47–56.

10. Department of Defense results reported in *Crosstalk*, the journal of defense software engineering, www.stsc.hill.af.mil/Crosstalk/2002/04/leishman.html.

11. A study of four hundred projects over a fifteen-year period found that less than 5 percent of code was regularly used. See D. Cohen, G. Larson, and B. Ware, "Improving Software Investment Through Requirements Validation," paper presented at the IEEE 26th Software Engineering Workshop, 2001. Alan MacCormack and colleagues have conducted extensive qualitative research comparing linear (referred to as waterfall) and agile programming approaches. See Alan MacCormack, "Product-Development Practices That Work," *Sloan Management Review* 42, 2 (2001), and Alan MacCormack et al., "Trade-offs Between Productivity and Quality in Selecting Software Development Practices." *IEEE Software* 20, 5 (September/October 2003): 78–85. A large-scale study is M. Thomas, "IT Projects Sink or Swim," *British Computer Society Review*, 2001.

12. P. Clements and D. Parnas, "A Rational Design Process: How and Why to Fake It," *IEEE Transactions on Software Engineering*, February 1986.

CHAPTER 8: THE AGILITY LOOP

1. The findings of several studies of how managers spend their time have found with remarkable consistency that formal and informal conversations are by far the primary activity. See E. Brewer and J. W. C. Tomlinson, "The Manager's Working Day," *Journal of Industrial Economics* 12, 3 (1964): 191–97; Henry Mintzberg, "Managerial Work: Analysis from Observation," *Management Science* 18, 2 (1971): 97–110; and Lance B. Kurke and Howard Aldrich, "Mintzberg Was Right! A Replication and Extension of *The Nature of Managerial Work*," *Management Science* 29, 8 (1983): 975–84.

2. See Arthur Schlesinger Jr., *A Thousand Days* (Boston: Houghton Mifflin, 1965), and Robert Kennedy, *Thirteen Days: A Memoir of the Cuban Missile Crisis* (New York: W. W. Norton, 1969). For an overview of decision making by Kennedy's team, see M. A. Roberto, *Why Great Leaders Don't Take Yes for an Answer* (Upper Saddle River, N.J.: Wharton School Publishing, 2005), ch. 2.

3. See R. E. Rubin and J. Weisberg, *In an Uncertain World* (New York: Random House, 2003), and L. Endlich, *Goldman Sachs: The Culture of Success* (New York: Alfred A. Knopf, 1999).

4. Tom Kelley with Jonathan Littman, "The 10 Faces of Innovation," *Fast Company*, October 2005.

5. This question is a slightly modified version of Professor Alexander's question described in R. E. Neustadt and E. R. May, *Thinking in Time: The Uses of History for Decision Makers* (New York: Free Press, 1988), 152–53.

6. Donald Sull, *Diageo Ireland: Building an Execution Culture*, LBS CS-07-008, -009, -010 (London: London Business School, 2007).

7. See K. M. Eisenhardt, "Making Fast Strategic Decisions in High-Velocity Environments," *Academy of Management Journal* 32 (1989): 543–76, and K. M. Eisenhardt, "Speed and Strategic Choice: How Managers Accelerate Decision Making," *California Management Review* 32 (1990): 39–54.

8. Eisenhardt, "Speed and Strategic Choice."

9. K. M. Eisenhardt and D. N. Sull, "Strategy as Simple Rules," *Harvard Business Review* 79 (January 2001): 107–16.

10. The memo was written by Brad Garlinghouse, a Yahoo senior vice president, and was published in total by the *Wall Street Journal*. For full text, see http://online.wsj.com/ public/article/SB116379821933826657-0mbjXoHnQwDMFH_PVeb_jqe3Chk_20061125 .html.

11. M. Arndt, "3M's Rising Star: Jim McNerney Is Racking Up Quite a Record at 3M. Now, Can He Rev Up Its Innovation Machine?" *Business Week*, April 12, 2004, 62–63; D. Del Re, "Pushing Past Post-Its by Allowing His Top Scientists to Peek Over the Horizon, 3M's Larry Wendling Helped Turn a Century-Old Giant into a Nanotech Pioneer," *Business 2.0*, November 2005, 54–57.

12. A survey of 125,000 respondents representing one thousand organizations in more than fifty countries found that employees in 60 percent of organizations ranked their employer as weak at translating strategic and operational decisions into action. See Gary L. Neilson et al., "The Secrets to Successful Strategy Execution," *Harvard Business Review*,

June 2008, 61–70. Another study by OnPoint Consulting of four hundred respondents found that 49 percent of managers identified a gap between their organization's ability to develop and communicate a sound strategy and their capacity to execute on that strategy, and 64 percent of respondents did not believe their company could close that gap. Seven of ten major corporate failures studied by Ram Charan and Geoffrey Colvin failed because of poor execution. See Ram Charan and Geoffrey Colvin, "Why CEOs Fail," *Fortune*, June 21, 1999, 69–78.

13. In their research, McKinsey & Company divided workers into three categories: manual laborers, workers engaged in standardized tasks (such as clerks, technicians, analysts, loan officers, programmers), and knowledge workers, who must exercise judgment in coordinating complex interactions. According to their analysis, the U.S. economy has undergone a fundamental transformation in the nature of work. In 1900, manual laborers accounted for over 80 percent of all employment, but by 2004 their share had dropped to just 15 percent. Knowledge work has increased dramatically as companies have eliminated manual labor and routine tasks by outsourcing, improving processes, and automating standardized activities. McKinsey's most recent analysis, published in 2005, studied more than eight hundred occupations in detail, and then reconciled their analysis with more comprehensive statistics published by the U.S. government, the International Labour Organization, and the World Bank. See Bradford C. Johnson, James M. Manyik, and Lareina A. Lee, "The Next Revolution in Interactions," *McKinsey Quarterly*, 2005, no. 4, 20–33.

14. For an in-depth perspective on the promise-based view of the firm, see Donald N. Sull and Charles Spinosa, "Promise-Based Management: The Essence of Execution," *Harvard Business Review* 85 (April 2007): 78–86, and Donald N. Sull and Charles Spinosa, "Using Commitments to Manage Across Units," *Sloan Management Review* 47 (Fall 2005): 73–81.

15. The Prussian army—which had a long tradition of granting autonomy to local commanders to seize the initiative when opportunities arose—originated mission-based orders, known as *Auftragtaktik*. And the Prussian approach built on the earlier *Jäger*, or hunter, tradition in the German military that stretched back centuries. *Jäger* units, composed primarily of game wardens, were accustomed to rapid movement and exercising initiative in battle. Bruce I. Gudmundsson, "Maneuver Warfare: The German Tradition," in Richard D. Hooker, ed., *Maneuver Warfare: An Anthology* (Novato, Calif.: Presidio, 1993), 273–93; Martin van Creveld, *Fighting Power: German and U.S. Performance 1939–1945* (Westport, Conn.: Greenwood Press, 1982).

16. For a thoughtful and practical guide to after-action reviews based on practices within the U.S. Army, see D. A. Garvin, *Learning in Action: A Guide to Putting the Learning Organization to Work* (Boston: Harvard Business School Press, 2003), 106–16.

CHAPTER 9: BUILDING AN AGILE ORGANIZATION

1. This chapter draws on a teaching case study of Brahma. See Donald N. Sull and Martin Escobari, *Brahma Versus Antarctica: Reversal of Fortune in Brazil's Beer Market,*

case study CS04-015-001 (London: London Business School, 2004); Donald N. Sull and Martin Escobari, *Success Against the Odds: What Brazilian Champions Teach Us About Thriving in an Unpredictable Market* (London: Elsevier Campus, 2005), as well as several interviews with Marcel Telles, his partners at Garantia Partners, and employees of AmBev.

2. GDP decline measured in real terms. Data from Laura Alfaro, *Brazil: Embracing Globalization?* case study 9-701-104 (Boston: Harvard Business School, 2002), exhibits 2, 3, and 4.

3. This and all subsequent direct quotes are from author's interviews.

4. Sull and Escobari, *Success Against the Odds*, introduction.

5. Information on Garantia from interviews with partners including Marcel Telles, Alberto Sicupira, Claudio Haddad, and Alex Behring. For an overview of Garantia, see R. Jeffrey Ellis, "Grupo Garantia: Globalization, Industry Rivalry, and Conglomerate Diversification in Brazil," *Case Research Journal* 25, 2 (2005).

6. For a comprehensive review, see Nelson Cowan, "The Magical Number 4 in Short-Term Memory: A Reconsideration of Mental Storage Capacity," *Behavioral and Brain Sciences* 24 (2001): 87–119; for an accessible summary, see Nelson Cowan, Candice C. Morey, and Zhijian Chen, "The Legend of the Magical Number Seven," in Sergio Della Sala, ed., *Tall Tales About the Brain: Separating Fact from Fiction* (Oxford: Oxford University Press, 2007), 45–59. This research builds on the seminal and better-known research by George Miller that found people can remember between five and nine items. See George Miller, "The Magical Number Seven, Plus or Minus Two: Some Limits on Our Capacity for Processing Information," *Psychological Review* 63 (1956): 81–97.

7. Donald Sull, Choelsoon Park, and Seonghoon Kim, *Samsung and Daewoo: Two Tales of One City*, case study 804-055 (Boston: Harvard Business School, 2004).

CHAPTER 10: AVOIDING A CORPORATE MIDLIFE CRISIS

1. Larry E. Greiner published the seminal piece on organizational life cycles. See L. E. Greiner, "Evolution and Revolution as Organizations Grow," *Harvard Business Review* 50 (July-August 1972): 37–76. Subsequent scholars explored the life cycle model in greater detail. See J. R. Kimberly and R. H. Miles, *The Organizational Life Cycle* (San Francisco: Jossey-Bass, 1980). For a recent review of life cycle theories, see A. H. Van de Ven and M. S. Poole, "Explaining Development and Change in Organizations," *Academy of Management Review* 20, 3 (1995): 510–40.

2. The evolution of firms in a cohort often follows the life cycle of the underlying product technology. See S. Klepper and K. L. Simons, "The Making of an Oligopoly: Firm Survival and Technological Change in the Evolution of the U.S. Tire Industry," *Journal of Political Economy* 108, 4 (2000): 728–60; S. Klepper and E. Graddy, "The Evolution of New Industries and the Determinants of Market Structure," *RAND Journal of Economics* 21 (1990): 27–44; and S. Klepper and K. L. Simons, "Technological Extinctions of Industrial Firms: An Inquiry into Their Nature and Causes," *Industrial and Corporate Change* 6, 2 (1997): 379–460.

3. M. C. Jensen, "Agency Costs of Free Cash Flow, Corporate Finance and Takeovers," *American Economic Review* 76 (1986): 323–29; R. M. Stulz, "Managerial Discretion and Optimal Financing Policies," *Journal of Financial Economics* 26 (1990): 3–27; Y. Amihund and B. Lev, "Risk Reduction as a Managerial Motive for Conglomerate Mergers," *Bell Journal of Economics* 12 (1981): 605–17; M. C. Jensen and K. J. Murphy, "Performance Pay and Top Management Incentives," *Journal of Political Economy* 98 (1990): 225–64; A. Shleifer and R. Vishny, "Managerial Entrenchment: The Case of Manager-Specific Investments," *Journal of Financial Economics* 25 (1989): 123–39.

4. H. Servaes, "The Value of Diversification Through the Conglomerate Merger Wave," *Journal of Finance* 51 (1996): 1201–25; L. H. P. Lang and R. E. Stulz, "Tobin's q, Corporate Diversification and Firm Performance," *Journal of Political Economy* 102 (1994): 1248–80.

5. Philip G. Berger and Eli Ofek, "Diversification's Effect on Firm Value," *Journal of Financial Economics* 37 (1995): 39–65.

6. J. Hagel III and M. Singer, "Unbundling the Corporation," *Harvard Business Review* 77 (1999): 133–41; C. Zook with J. Allen, *Profit from the Core: Growth Strategy in an Era of Turbulence* (Boston: Harvard Business School Press, 2000). Recently strategy scholars have argued that this logic applies not only to routine tasks such as customer service but also to innovation—the core activity in renewing a company for the future. See C. Markides and P. Geroski, *Fast Second: How Smart Companies Bypass Radical Innovation to Enter and Dominate New Markets* (San Francisco: Jossey-Bass, 2004), and H. W. Chesbrough, *Open Innovation: The New Imperative for Creating and Profiting from Technology* (Boston: Harvard Business School Press, 2003). The argument again boils down to focus. Established firms excel at commercializing innovations by reducing their cost and bringing them to a wider market. They rarely do well in developing nonincremental innovations to rejuvenate their product or service offering.

7. José Manuel Campa and Simi Kedia, "Explaining the Diversification Discount," *Journal of Finance* 57, 4 (2002): 1731–62; Belén Villalonga, "Does Diversification Cause the 'Diversification Discount'?" *Financial Management* 33, 2 (2004): 5–27; Belén Villalonga, "Diversification Discount or Premium? New Evidence from the Business Information Tracking Series," *Journal of Finance* 59, 2 (2004): 479–506.

8. See Ellis, *The Partnership*, 153–82, and Endlich, *Goldman Sachs*, 60–61.

9. Carl W. Stern and George Stalk, *Perspectives on Strategy from the Boston Consulting Group* (New York: John Wiley, 1998).

10. J. S. Armstrong and R. Brodie, "Effects of Portfolio Planning Methods on Decision Making: Experimental Results," *International Journal of Research in Marketing* 11, 1 (1994): 73–84; S. F. Slater and T. J. Zwirlein, "Shareholder Value and Investment Strategy Using the General Portfolio Model," *Journal of Management* 18, 4 (1992): 717–32.

11. Joseph L. Bower, *The Resource Allocation Process* (Boston: Harvard Business School Press, 1970). For a review of recent research, see J. L. Bower and C. G. Gilbert, eds., *From Resource Allocation to Strategy* (New York: Oxford University Press, 2006).

12. Donald N. Sull, "The Dynamics of Standing Still: Firestone Tire and Rubber and the Radial Revolution," *Business History Review* 73 (1999): 430–64.

13. Kim B. Clark and Carliss Y. Baldwin, "Capital Budgeting Systems and Capabilities Investments in U.S. Companies After World War II," *Business History Review* 68, 1 (1994): 73–109.

14. M. Baghai, S. Coley, and D. White, "The Alchemy of Growth: Practical Insights for Building the Enduring Enterprise" (New York: Perseus, 2000). For an excellent description of IBM's changes, see David Garvin and Lynn Levesque, *Emerging Business Opportunities at IBM*, case study 304-075 (Boston: Harvard Business School, 2004).

CHAPTER 11: AGILE ABSORPTION

1. Sources on Muhammad Ali and George Foreman include Thomas Hauser, *Muhammad Ali: His Life and Times* (New York: Simon and Schuster, 1991); Mark Collings, ed., *Muhammad Ali: Through the Eyes of the World* (London: Sanctuary, 1991); David Remnick, *King of the World* (New York: Vintage, 1999); Norman Mailer, *The Fight* (New York: Little, Brown, 1975). This chapter draws in part on my article, "Can Your Company Go the Distance?" *Harvard Business Review*, February 2009.

2. Ferdie Pacheco, comments in Mark Collings, ed., *Muhammad Ali: Through the Eyes of the World* (London: Sanctuary, 2001), 346.

3. In a recent study of 618 firms in the U.S. medical sector between 1978 and 1995, Janet Bercovitz and Will Mitchell found that size enhanced a firm's probability of survival, even when they controlled for profitability and diversification. See J. Bercovitz and W. Mitchell, "When Is More Better? The Impact of Business Scale and Scope on Long-Term Business Survival, While Controlling for Profitability," *Strategic Management Journal* 28, 1 (2007): 61–79.

4. James D. Thompson, *Organizations in Action* (New York: McGraw-Hill, 1967). His implicit model was clearly manufacturing operations, which led him to enumerate buffering actions such as slack inventory, preventive maintenance, smoothing demand, project scheduling, and demand forecasting. The narrowness of the original specification of buffering mechanisms helps explain why the construct has received relatively little interest among business academics in recent decades. Indeed, much of the subsequent research has focused on a single mechanism—slack resources—to buffer organizations against environmental uncertainty. See, for example, Jay Bourgeois, "On the Measurement of Organizational Slack," *Academy of Management Review* 26 (1981): 29–39. Viewed as a more general concept, however, buffering is an extremely useful lens for understanding how organizations cope with uncertainty.

5. See E. Geoffrey Love and Nitin Nohria, "Reducing Slack: The Performance Consequences of Downsizing by Large Industrial Firms, 1977–93," *Strategic Management Journal* 26, 12 (2005): 1087–108.

6. Theresa Howard, "Pepsi Beats Coke with Stock Surge," *USA Today*, December 13, 2005. PepsiCo's market capitalization was approximately 80 percent of Coca-Cola's in February 2008.

7. Antoine van Agtmael, *The Emerging Markets Century* (New York: Free Press, 2007), ch. 6; IBM research news, http://www.research.ibm.com/resources/news/20030423_edgar-passaway.shtml.

8. See Trevor N. Dupuy, *Numbers, Predictions and War* (New York: Macdonald, 1979) and Martin van Creveld, *Fighting Power: German and U.S. Performance, 1939–1945* (Westport, Conn.: Greenwood Press, 1982). These calculations analyze separate engagements and measure causalities inflicted by each force, controlling for a number of factors including weapons, terrain, air support, etc. The analyses demonstrate a remarkably robust finding that the German troops, particularly those following maneuver tactics, were more effective than the allies.

INDEX